SEX CULT NUN

SEX CULT NUN

Breaking Away from

the Children of God,

a Wild, Radical

Religious Cult

FAITH JONES

wm

WILLIAM MORROW

An Imprint of HarperCollins*Publishers*

HarperCollins books may be purchased for educational, business, or sales promotional use. For information, please email the Special Markets Department at SPsales@harpercollins.com.

FIRST EDITION

All photographs in the book's insert are courtesy of the author.

Library of Congress Cataloging-in-Publication Data has been applied for.

ISBN 978-0-06-295245-5 (hardcover)
ISBN 978-0-06-313680-9 (international edition)

21 22 23 24 25 LSC 10 9 8 7 6 5 4 3 2 1

To all of us who have fought to free ourselves from oppression,
to claim our choices and bodies, and to thrive not just survive

CONTENTS

A NOTE FROM THE AUTHOR

Free love and sex, communes, withdrawal from society, living off donations instead of having jobs, staying vigilant for the rise of the Antichrist and the return of Jesus, spiritual revolutionaries against the system: these are some of the beliefs I grew up with.

I was born into the Family, a religious movement founded in Huntington Beach, California, in 1968 by my grandfather David Brandt Berg, with help from his four children, Deborah, Aaron, Faithy, and my father, Hosea. It was known as the Children of God in its early days and often referred to as a cult by outsiders.

With its aggressive proselytizing tactics and its demand that all its members serve as full-time missionaries, its live-in disciples quickly grew to over ten thousand, an average it maintained for over four decades and spread worldwide to 170 countries. With people leaving and joining, I'd estimate over sixty thousand people passed through the group as full-time members during its fifty years in existence. But its missionary activities reached millions more, with hundreds of thousands of converts.

The group's more radical practices led to police raids and negative press in many countries, with accusations of kidnapping, prostitution, and child abuse; my grandfather was on Interpol's wanted list for decades.

In 2010, it disbanded its communes, releasing into mainstream society thousands of people who'd never held a job or finished school. According to its official website at the time of this writing, it continues as "an online Christian community of 1,450 committed to sharing the message of God's love with people around the globe." I left the Family in 2000 and do not have firsthand knowledge of its official practices or beliefs since that time.

This book is based on my recollections, interviews with family members, and written records. I have made my best efforts to ensure accuracy of detail and emotion in this recounting. I changed the names and identifying personal details of certain people who appear in the book to preserve their anonymity. As memory is sometimes fallible, there are places in the text where some dialogue is approximated, combined, or moved in time. I omitted specific people and events, but only when those omissions had no impact on the substance of the story. The Family had thousands of members, and I cannot speak for all of them. Depending on when and where those thousands were born, we had different experiences. I can only tell my story.

Through all of this I never doubted that my parents loved me. They acted based on their sincerely held beliefs at the time, which have since changed dramatically. We have a good relationship today, and they understand my purpose in writing this.

There are two ways to read this book: as a story about a cult or a young woman's personal story. If you are interested in the latter, feel free to skip the history section and jump straight into my story, beginning with Chapter 1. You can always go back to the history later if questions come up about the cult.

I write about my experiences from my perspective at each age, so you can peek into my mind and see how I saw the world and my family through the lens of the cult's beliefs. My understanding of my experiences shifts with each realization I gain. Thank you for coming with me on this wild and crazy journey to its final destination—freedom. True liberation is in the mind.

Faith Jones
March 2021

SEX CULT NUN

A (NOT SO) BRIEF HISTORY
OF MY FAMILY AND THE CHILDREN OF GOD

FOUR GENERATIONS OF EVANGELISTS

My father is a fourth-generation evangelist. His great-grandfather John Lincoln Brandt of Muskogee, Oklahoma, was a Baptist minister who moved between churches in Denver, Toledo, Valparaiso, and St. Louis. Later, he became a leader in the Campbellite movement (now known as the Disciples of Christ), building and pastoring churches across the United States and around the world. His travels took him to Canada, Mexico, Europe, Asia, Africa, Australia, and the Pacific Islands. He was also the author of over twenty books and a lecturer.

His daughter, Virginia, my father's grandmother, was also a famous preacher. She was the nation's first female radio evangelist with her program *Meditation Moments*, which started in Miami, Florida, in the 1930s. She was a prominent evangelist and revivalist who drew crowds of thousands at her evangelistic tabernacle events across America.

But her dedication to Jesus came later in life. Although she had been raised a Christian, her faith was shaken with the loss of her mother when she was in her early twenties, and for a time, she declared herself agnostic. It took a miracle to bring her back into the fold. After giving birth to her first child, Hjalmar Jr., she fell and broke her back in two places, leaving her in terrible pain and often bedridden. Several surgeries failed to correct the problem, and doctors ultimately diagnosed her condition as untreatable.

But her husband, Hjalmar Berg, an evangelical minister, kept praying over her.

MY GREAT-GRANDMOTHER'S MIRACLE HEALING

One afternoon, in pain and at the end of her strength, Virginia called out to God for help. A scripture came to her—"Whatever you desire, when you pray, believe you will receive them, and you will have them" (Mark 11:24). She said, "I believe." At that moment, as the story goes, she was miraculously healed and rose from her bed.

Hjalmar ministered to a small congregation in Northern California, and she shared her testimony there the following morning. Soon, speaking invitations started pouring in, and Virginia's reputation and following began to grow. Preaching about miraculous healing was against her church's doctrine, but Virginia and Hjalmar refused to keep quiet and were ultimately expelled from the Disciples of Christ.

Subsequently, they joined the Christian and Missionary Alliance, an evangelical Protestant denomination with a heavy emphasis on missionary work. By then, Virginia and Hjalmar had added their second and third children to the family: a daughter, also named Virginia, and my grandfather, David, who was born in Oakland, California, on February 18, 1919.

The family of five spent the next several years on the road, holding revivals at churches across the United States. Virginia's story of her miraculous healing always drew crowds, usually between four thousand to ten thousand strong. Turnout was so great, and her words were so moving, that she was invited to stay as a full-time preacher at a church in Miami, Florida.

After fifteen years in Miami, Virginia missed her time on the road, and by the late 1930s, she returned to her role as a traveling evangelist. David, my grandfather, was the only one of her three children interested in pursuing a life in the ministry, so she took him on the road as her driver and assistant, staging massive events and tent revivals at venues all over the country.

GRANDPA'S REBELLION AND REDEDICATION

In 1941, at age twenty-two, David was drafted into the army. He could have gotten out of it; ministers and divinity students were exempt from service. But he was tired of being under his mother's thumb and wanted some adventure. In boot camp, he contracted double pneumonia, and, the way he told it, the doctors didn't have much hope he'd live, so he promised God that if he was healed, he'd devote his life to God's service. And just like his mother, David claims he was immediately and miraculously healed, to the amazement of all the doctors and nurses.

David was given a medical discharge due to a heart condition and rejoined Virginia. He enjoyed being on the road but was frustrated with his modest role as his mother's assistant. He, too, wanted to preach. Yet God told him to be patient and that his time would eventually come.

The two were visiting California when Grandpa met my grandmother Jane Miller, at the Little Church of Sherman Oaks, where she was working as a secretary. A petite brunette and a devout Christian, Jane was born in Kentucky and raised in a Baptist home. The two eloped in July 1944, and two years later they had their first daughter, Deborah, followed by a son, Aaron, in 1948. That same year, David was ordained as a minister of the Christian and Missionary Alliance and was sent to Valley Farms, Arizona, a sandy desert town about sixty miles south of Phoenix.

The congregants were a mix of southern whites, Native Americans, and Mexicans, all of whom were struggling to get along. He further exacerbated the tension with his preaching by urging integration and advocated that those of means share more of their material wealth with those less fortunate. David's inclinations would become more apparent later, but he was just beginning to formulate his ideas of Christian communism based on Acts 2:44. His message infuriated the white members more closely associated with the church's leadership, and he was eventually expelled. The experience permanently soured him on organized religion. Disappointed but undeterred, David took his family of six back on the road—including my father, Jonathan "Hosea" Emmanuel, who was born in 1949, and his younger sister, Faithy, after whom I would later be named. They eventually ended up in Huntington Beach, California, where David's parents had now settled in retirement. David found odd jobs to support the family, including a stint as a teacher and bus driver at a local Christian school. But he was profoundly unhappy, and in 1951, he turned to the Lord for direction and received a revelation that set him on a completely new and different path. He became convinced that God wanted him to drop out of the "system"—basically, the established church—and take to the road to save souls for Christ. So, he abruptly quit his job and enrolled in a three-month course at the Soul Clinic in Los Angeles, a missionary training school founded by the Reverend Fred Jordan.

GRANDPA JOINS FRED JORDAN'S MISSIONARY SCHOOL

Jordan was one of the nation's first television evangelists, and he opened the Fred Jordan Mission in 1949, where he ministered to the poor and homeless, and ran his missionary training school. Jordan's message resonated with my grandfather, particularly his belief that God was everywhere, and parishioners did not need to assemble in a church building to communicate with the Lord.

The Reverend Jordan had a huge impact on David, and the two would work together in various capacities over the next fifteen years, which dictated where and how he and his family lived. Part of David's missionary training included a period at Jordan's Texas Soul Clinic, or the Ranch, located in Thurber, Texas, where his converts were subjected to a military-style boot camp to prepare them for the hardships they would face as missionaries.

My father was three years old when my grandfather moved the family to the Ranch the first time. They stayed there for two years before heading to Florida, where David and Jane opened a branch of Fred Jordan's missionary training school in Miami.

In Miami, they lived communally, sharing a big house with other people who were also training to be missionaries, and spent summers traveling around the US, evangelizing with their parents.

Witnessing on the road was a family affair throughout my father's childhood. While my grandmother Jane had initially worried that having four small children meant her days assisting in the ministry were over, she soon realized that even as a mom, there was a role for her. She noticed that people were more receptive to her husband's message when he was accompanied by his cute kids, so she fashioned their children into a singing group to perform along with his sermons. They performed in churches, on the street, and on Fred Jordan's radio and TV programs.

Everything was going fine for a while, but David's fiery sermons, calls for disciples to "forsake all" to become Christian missionaries, and aggressive "marketing" tactics landed him in hot water with the area's church leaders. Every Sunday, he sent his children and a few of his missionary students to the local churches to distribute religious literature, instructing them to blanket the buildings and all the cars in the parking lots. These antics infuriated church leaders, who sent local law enforcement after him. He needed to get out of town, so just after my father had completed the eighth grade, David announced they were leaving Miami to hit the road again, thereby marking the end of my father's formal education.

WARNING MESSAGE OF THE END TIME
The family loaded into their twenty-eight-foot Dodge motor home, which David lovingly named the Ark, and returned to the Ranch. Virginia visited the Ranch twice to deliver urgent prophecies to

her youngest child. First, "The Warning Message" said the Coming of the Antichrist and the End Time were imminent. Second, "The End-Time Prophecy" claimed that David would have "the understanding of Daniel" and ability to forecast the Coming of Christ.

They stayed at the Ranch until the fall of 1967, when Virginia asked David to bring his children to California to witness to the hippies. Only his eldest daughter, Deborah, stayed behind. She had married her childhood boyfriend, Jethro, with her father's blessing when she was sixteen, and the two remained in Texas, where they started a family of their own.

Despite being in her eighties, Virginia had been spending her days passing out peanut butter sandwiches and talking about Jesus to the hippies, surfers, and homeless who gathered at Huntington Beach Pier, the Haight-Ashbury of Southern California at that time. Passionate in her belief that these young people needed to be saved, she urged my father and his two siblings, Aaron and Faithy, just teenagers themselves, to try to reach them.

HIPPIES AND JESUS FREAKS

At the Light Club, a coffeehouse near the pier, my father and his siblings began drawing crowds of young hippies with their musical performances and free sandwiches. It was here that David finally found his flock. These idealistic young people had already turned their backs on the system. They didn't need to be convinced to leave their old lives. They needed a mission, a direction, and a place to belong. David started showing up at the Light Club in the evenings to preach his progressively more radical sentiments. He grew his hair and beard long, wore a beret, and took on the look of a radically hip evangelist; everyone called him "Dad."

His words resonated with these young people, and they embraced his unorthodox message of "dropping out of an evil system"—by forsaking everything, including money, education, jobs, and families, and devoting all their time to serving God as missionaries, God's highest calling. He also emphasized living communally, like disciples of the early church (first-century Christians); Christian communism; and the End Time and the Warning Prophecies about the coming punishment of America, which was popular during the Vietnam War era. They took him at his word, showing up with their backpacks, ready to dedicate their lives to God as disciples. They emptied their pockets, turned over bank accounts and trust funds, swore off drugs and alcohol, and instead got high on Jesus as their Savior.

GRANDPA FINDS HIS PEOPLE

Virginia Berg's death in the late spring of 1968, just four years after the passing of her husband, Hjalmar, proved a turning point for David. It was as if he became unfettered from any remaining need to abide by traditional norms and doctrines. He began railing against the church system, organized religion, institutionalized education, the federal government, capitalism, and even parental authority, all very popular sentiments for his audience of young people. He was out to start a religious revolution, and his new disciples were ready and willing to follow him anywhere. The End Time was imminent, and he needed to save as many souls as he could before the Tribulation, the Second Coming of Jesus and the Wrath of God.

With hundreds of hippies showing up at the Light Club, the group began to garner local media attention, which was at first positive. Here was a group of Christians who were motivating hippies to clean up their act and get off drugs! Soon the family began receiving invitations from preachers who wanted to start youth ministries, including one from an old missionary friend in Tucson, Arizona. David happily dispatched my father and Esther, one of the group's first recruits. She was a nineteen-year-old who had just completed her freshman year at Kansas Wesleyan University and had been searching for a group that would allow her to serve God as a missionary.

THE OTHER WOMAN

Among the new recruits at the Tucson church was Karen Zerby, a shy, bucktoothed Nazarene minister's daughter in her early twenties who had recently graduated from college and was a trained stenographer. Zerby was so enthusiastic that my father recommended she travel to Huntington Beach for training at the Light Club. She did, and almost immediately, she became David's secretary. In the months to come, the two would begin a secret affair and start living together in the Ark, which he now shared with his wife. Though Jane appeared to accept her husband's new intimate partner, my aunt Deborah recalls her crying often and doing her best to avoid being in the trailer with Karen.

David was stepping up his recruitment efforts in California, sending disciples to local universities to witness to students and distribute literature. But university administrators were not happy with the group's presence on their campuses and called in police to have them removed. With law enforcement now involved, journalists began highlighting the conflict and the group's more radical teachings. To avoid further negative publicity, David, Jane, and some of their disciples fled to Tucson, where they joined up with my father and Esther. Deborah rejoined her father here, bringing her husband and three children.

THE JESUS PEOPLE MOVEMENT GROWS

Once in Arizona, David decided to send teams of disciples on the road to witness, but he wanted the leaders of each team to be a married couple. So, he asked my father and another male disciple if one of them would marry Esther. In working with her for the past year, my father had been impressed with her dedication to the Lord, and he felt God's call to marry Esther. As both men said yes, the decision was left to Esther, who chose my father.

My twenty-year-old father and nineteen-year-old Esther headed a team of disciples to New Mexico to witness at a university there, and then on to El Paso, where they were married on May 16, 1969, with my grandfather, an ordained minister, presiding over the ceremony.

BECOMING MOSES DAVID AND THE CHILDREN OF GOD

From there, they fanned out across the United States and Canada. At one point, there were 120 people on the road, traveling in more than ten vehicles. A local journalist who caught up with them in St. Louis dubbed them "The Children of God," a name they kept. The reporter likened David, leading his ragtag group through the wilderness, to Moses, prompting David to adopt the prophet-leader name of Moses David (later shortened to Mo) because, like biblical Moses, who led the Israelites out of Egypt, he was leading his disciples out of the "System."

Moses David instructed his followers to take a new biblical name to demonstrate they were being reborn as Children of God and leaving their old life behind. Jane took the name Eve and became known as Mother Eve, and Karen Zerby took the name Maria. From then on, all new disciples, or "Babes," as they were called, from the biblical reference to "babes in Christ," were required to change their names when they joined.

During a stop in Louisiana, the police raided the group's campsite. They found a few people who had arrest warrants out on them from different places, mostly on drug charges from before they joined the Children of God. Some of the disciples were arrested, and the rest of the group was warned to get out of town, so they left and set up camp in various parks around Houston.

Needing a safe place for his growing caravan, Moses David reached out to Fred Jordan to ask permission to bring his disciples to the Ranch in Thurber. Jordan agreed, on the condition that he and his disciples would care for the property and make improvements to the existing buildings, which had fallen into disrepair. So, in January of 1970, all the teams gathered at the Ranch, including my father and Esther, who was now eight months pregnant with my half brother Nehi.

THE RANCH

The group settled in at the Ranch and enthusiastically set about making the run-down buildings livable. Hippies, flower children, high school and college dropouts, Jesus People, former drug addicts, and homeless people viewed this as an opportunity to live communally and create their own family to serve God and save the world. Moses David ran the place in the same militaristic style Fred Jordan had employed to operate his missionary training school. It was a challenge to train young people from vastly different backgrounds to live and work together harmoniously. Everyone was on a strict schedule, early to bed, early to rise. The days were filled with construction, cooking, cleaning, and prayer, as well as reading and memorizing the Bible; disciples were expected to memorize up to three hundred verses within the first three months.

Shortly after settling, Moses David began sending teams across America to gather more disciples, expanding the number of people at the Ranch from 160 to 250 in a year. The new disciples psychologically severed all personal family and social ties to devote themselves fully to their new family in Christ, citing Luke 14:26: "If any man comes to Me, and does not hate his own father, and mother, and wife, and children, and brethren, and sisters, yea, and his own life also, he cannot be My disciple." Still, David encouraged his followers to write home and allowed friendly parents to visit the Ranch to keep them from turning into enemies.

MY MOTHER IS A HIPPIE DROPOUT

My father and Esther had been together for two years when they first met my mother, Ruthie, who joined the Children of God in the summer of 1971. Whereas Esther had grown up a soft-spoken church girl, my mother was a bohemian, outspoken, uninhibited ex-hippie. She was born on Long Island, New York, the middle daughter to Evelyn and Gene Jones. As a crack pilot in the air force, Gene moved his family around a lot to various military bases. Hawaii was Ruthie's favorite of all the places she'd lived. With her dark frizzy hair and deep surf-girl tan, she was often mistaken as a Hawaiian during the three years they lived there.

After Hawaii, the family moved to Atlanta, Georgia, in 1964, right in the middle of the civil rights movement. As a teen, my mother sat in the back of the bus, where only Black people were supposed to be, and often got kicked off for her protest. While her idealism and rebellion could get her into trouble, she focused her energy into her passion, dance. At seventeen, she was accepted into the Atlanta Ballet company, but she had her sights on adventure and Broadway, and a few months later, she ran away from home.

Her father hired a detective, who located her in New York City, sleeping on the couch of an actor who at least respected the fact that she was underage. Her father agreed to let her stay in the city if she would move to a women's hotel. Eventually, she got her own apartment, found a job waitressing, and was hired to dance in the off-Broadway show *Kismet*, and later in a summer season of musicals in the Pocono Mountains.

Around the time she was finally booking real work, she started getting into marijuana and psychedelic drugs. She dropped out of the shows and moved to a cabin in upstate New York with other hippies, searching for a spiritual path. She bounced around for a while, attended the Woodstock festival, and then hitchhiked across the country, landing in San Francisco, where she experienced a horrific trip after dropping LSD poisoned with strychnine. She phoned her father, Gene, who sent her a ticket to come stay with him and his new wife in Atlanta. That was the last time she ever took psychedelic drugs. Soon after arriving in Atlanta, she called her best friend to announce her plan to join an ashram in India, but her friend instead invited her to meet the Jesus People group she'd joined in Atlanta called the House of Judah. Ruthie agreed, and during the visit, she realized she'd found the way to fulfill her childhood dream of serving God.

MY MOTHER JOINS THE JESUS PEOPLE MOVEMENT

Six months into my mother's time with the House of Judah, my aunt Faithy, my father, and Esther came to meet with the group in Atlanta. My mother was captivated by their passion and joy. She and thirty others hopped on the prophet bus heading to the Ranch to join the Children of God. My mother had been looking for something to give her life meaning. She also craved a close family, affection, and praise that she didn't have growing up with two kind but emotionally repressed parents, common in people who suffered the horrors of World War II. She found all this and more as a disciple of Jesus with the radical Children of God.

My mother did her Babes training at the Ranch during the summer of 1971. From the beginning, Moses David pushed God's "Drop Out" message, but now his forsake-all requirements and the militaristic lifestyle started bringing unwanted attention. Parents of some new followers accused him of running a cult and brainwashing their children. My mother's very worried dad, Gene, visited the Ranch to try to get her to leave, but at nineteen she was legally an adult, and she convinced him that it was her choice to stay with the group. But some concerned families went so far as to alert the authorities and hire professional deprogrammers to try to get their kids back. Media coverage turned negative, with parents and former members alleging brainwashing, censorship of mail and phone calls, and cult-like subservience to Moses David's family, as well as (unfounded) allegations of drugs, hypnotism, and kidnapping.

Then, Moses David got a call from God to send missionaries overseas to pioneer more fruitful fields. "America has had its chance," he told his followers. As he prepared to send four- and six-person teams overseas, far away from oversight, he needed to deal with the issue of sex, which was currently permitted for only those who were married. He called an offsite meeting at a motel in Dallas with his four children, their spouses, and a few other couples who were considered top leadership.

THE "LAW OF LOVE" MEANS SEXUAL FREEDOM

There, in a two-room suite he had rented, Moses David laid out the doctrine of "The Law of Love." He explained that the Old Testament rules were superseded and covered by only two commandments from Matthew 22:36–40. "'Teacher, which commandment is the greatest in the Law?' Jesus declared, 'Love the Lord your God with all your heart and with all your soul and with all your mind.' This is the first and greatest commandment. And the second is like it: 'Love your neighbor as yourself.' All the Law and the Prophets hang on these two commandments."

According to Moses David, *all* things were lawful under love, including sex outside of marriage. He declared it a new revelation of the Bible for a new generation that was ready for more freedom. As always, he backed it up with his interpretation of the scripture.

This doctrine, which had been in the works as theory for some time, helped to justify and legitimize his relationship with Maria, who was "chosen by God" to help him in his new ministry and to further experiment with it. And it gave singles and young couples separated by long distance for work the possibility to have sex outside of marriage. Incorporating the sexual freedom of the hippie generation marked a huge departure from the traditional, celibate-until-marriage doctrine that my father's family had grown up with in the church. This revelation was only for top leaders and would not filter down to the disciples for a few more years.

Aunt Faithy, my father, and Esther were chosen to lead the pioneering efforts in Europe in the late summer of 1971, leaving Nehi and Hobo, my father and Esther's second son, born only a few months before, in a colony in Washington.

MY MOTHER IS ASSIGNED A HUSBAND

In the fall, Ruthie was picked to go to Europe with the next wave of disciples. She was first sent from the Ranch to a Home in New York, where a young man with dark Italian good looks approached her. He introduced himself as Giddel, then told her that it was God's will for them to get married. My mother was completely flabbergasted. She'd never even talked to this man before and didn't know how to react when he told her that the leader of the Home where they were staying had suggested they marry immediately so they could lead a team in Europe; only married couples could open new Homes, he said.

My mother wanted to be yielded to God's will, so she prayed about it and reluctantly agreed. Two weeks later, she and Giddel and five other baffled and excited couples were married in a communal ceremony. The following week, Ruthie and her new husband were on their way to England to join the overseas evangelistic efforts. But after three months together, the marriage wasn't working, so it was a relief when Giddel traveled with a team to Italy, and Faithy, after receiving many letters from Ruthie, took my mother on as her personal secretary. At just twenty-six, Faithy was a top leader of "The Revolution," a true firebrand who was passionate in her missionary zeal and already known for her drinking and her temper.

PIONEERING EUROPE AND DAMNING AMERICA

My mother traveled with Faithy to London and Paris, where the two would now be headquartered. My father, who was also tasked with overseeing the pioneering work in France, split his time between Paris and London as well. In Paris, he and my mother became reacquainted, although their relationship remained strictly platonic. Nehi and Hobo were finally brought to London to rejoin Esther six months after she had arrived, and in the three years that followed, Esther gave birth to four more children in quick succession: the twins Josh and Caleb, then Aaron and Mary.

In the spring of 1972, Moses David, who was now also living in London, wrote a letter to his disciples titled *I Gotta Split*, warning that all escape routes out of America would be closed as soon as "the Storm of God's judgments begins to break upon the wickedness of the Lowlands of America!" Moses David informed his followers that due to the ongoing persecution, he, like Jesus, had to go away in body (physically) to be with them in spirit. Instead of teaching his flock in person, as he had at the Ranch, he would now be communicating with them strictly via the written word—communications that came to be known as the Mo Letters. None of his followers were aware that he had already left the country, but Grandpa knew that with the law already on his tail in the US, he had a better chance to lead his flock through his writings while staying mobile. New York's charity-fraud bureau was investigating the group based on activities at its Staten Island commune, with accusations of fiscal chicanery, obstruction of justice, and alleged physical and mental coercion of followers.

Grandpa immediately followed up this first written pronouncement with a second dire warning that he outlined in an emergency Mo Letter, *Flee as a Bird to Your Mountain*, in which he urged his followers to run for their lives from the coming doom of America, which was going to be punished for its sins. His forewarning sparked a mass exodus, and by 1973, there were more than 130 colonies, with some 2,400 disciples in fifty countries, including Australia, New Zealand, and parts of Europe, Asia, and Latin America. Not many of the original three hundred disciples remained in America, but new disciples would steadily join over the years and Homes continued to thrive there, with small communes in every state of the union.

GRANDPA TAKES A SECOND WIFE

With Moses David and Maria now living "underground," his personal family members and their spouses, whom Grandpa referred to as the "Royal Family," carried out his edicts and set to work printing and distributing his writings in hundreds of thousands of leaflets distributed by hand for donations around the world.

In one of the first Mo Letters, *One Wife*, Moses David introduced to his disciples the idea of sharing mates, proclaiming the wife of one man was also the wife of God, and of all other men. He pointed to biblical examples of polygamy as justification to take up the practice, deeming traditional marriage "selfish" and against God's will. Then, in the Mo Letter *Old Church, New Church*, he compared Mother Eve (Jane) to the Old Church, the traditional church, critical, rebellious, stuck in her ways, and unwilling to follow the new revelations. Moses David said that one evening in the Ark, when Eve was criticizing him for always demanding sex, saying that he was too carnal to be a true man of God, the spirit of God rose in him, and he slapped Eve for her rebellion. He had prayed for God to send him a woman who believed in him. Maria, he explained, "like the sexy New Church, or the Family, eager for Jesus's and King David's seeds, and willing to do anything he asks," had been the answer to his prayers.

Having paved the way for plural wives, he publicly took his young disciple Maria (Karen Zerby) as a second wife. But she soon became his only wife, as Eve took up with another, somewhat younger male disciple. With Maria now at David's side, urging him on, the Children of God would forge a path far outside the bounds of societal norms and even laws.

Meanwhile, Aunt Faithy, eager to harness the group's musical appeal, launched Les Enfants de Dieu, a musical performing group, complete with a troupe of dancers that included my mother. Ruthie had not fully realized her dream of dancing on Broadway, but the recognition she was receiving as a member of this traveling troupe delighted her. The band's popularity was instantaneous, with their hit single "My Love Is Love" topping the French charts in 1974. Soon, there were record contracts, regular television appearances, bookings at live-stage venues, and a month-long Europe 1 tour of France.

FLIRTY FISHING BEGINS IN SECRET

Back in London, Moses David and Maria started secretly experimenting with a new form of witnessing in the local nightclubs. Maria would seduce men on the dance floor under his direction, bring them home for sex, and later introduce the men to Moses David to witness to.

At first, he told only the top leadership about this exciting new ministry of "Flirty Fishing," where the female disciples, the "bait," would flirt with and often have sex with preferably well-to-do men called "Fish," as a witnessing technique to gain followers and monetary donations. The Fish were Systemite men in need of God's love and salvation. Moses David wrote that "sex is a bodily need as great as hunger or shelter. Jesus fed the multitudes with loaves and fishes, so they would not be so hungry and could hear his teachings. In the same way, the women have to satisfy a man's sexual desire before they are ready to hear about Jesus."

Moses David wanted to bring more women into his inner circle to expand his experiment, but he was concerned about how this technique would be received by English society, which tended to be uptight when it came to sex. So, in 1974, Moses David, Maria, and a group of carefully selected female disciples moved to the Canary Island of Tenerife, a tourist destination with a more relaxed attitude. The women were expected to "go fishing" two to five nights a week. "Just as Jesus laid down His life, so must you lay down your life (or wife), for these men," Moses David preached.

THE NEW PRINCE IS BORN
Early the next year, on the twenty-fifth of January, Maria gave birth to a baby boy named Davidito. Moses David was thrilled, and "Little David" was immediately heralded as the young prince, the new heir to the throne. With Maria's new role of mother, Moses David began calling her "Mama Maria," and eventually Queen Maria to his King David; he would later declare that Davidito and Mama Maria would be the Two Witnesses cited in Revelation 11 who would lead the true Church through the End Time.

MAKING FRIENDS WITH GADDAFI
Several months after Davidito was born, Grandpa paused his activities in the Canaries to visit Muammar Gaddafi, Libya's head of state. My father and Faithy had met him at a press conference in Paris, after which Gaddafi issued a formal invitation for Moses David and the Children of God to visit him in Tripoli. Moses David had been courting a relationship with the enigmatic, revolutionary young colonel from a distance, so he saw this as an opportunity for his Flirty Fishing ministry. He traveled with several members of the Royal Family, including my parents, and brought his girls from Tenerife to win over the Libyan leaders. My mother was excited to be included, but she was more thrilled that the End-Time Prophet himself had extended an invitation to her and that she was going to finally meet him in person. What a rare and incredible honor! Other than the few months of her marriage, my mother hadn't had

sex for nearly five years while evangelizing in Europe, since the sexual freedom of the Royal Family leadership was still forbidden to the disciples.

MY PARENTS BECOME POLYGAMISTS

In Libya, Moses David took a liking to my mother; he admired her dedication and her willingness to do anything for the cause. He advised my father to take her as his second wife and secretary to help with the fledging publishing work of the Mo Letters. My mother was flattered but told Moses David that she'd prefer to stay on as Aunt Faithy's secretary. But he told her to be with my father and to love his son as she loved him, Moses David. Her faith was such that she yielded to his will as to God's. Aunt Faithy was not pleased at losing her secretary and faithful servant, but no one dared oppose the Prophet's direction.

After two months in Libya, it became clear that Gaddafi was not going to convert from Islam; he was more interested in using the Children of God's thousands of followers to distribute positive literature about himself across the globe. Disappointed but recognizing a dead end, Grandpa returned to Tenerife to continue "FFing" with his team of women.

But he had a new mission. Up until then, the Mo Letters were distributed to the disciples as tracts, and now there were many hundreds of Letters. He and my father decided they should be compiled and printed into books with an index of topics to enable members to study the many thousands of written pages. Grandpa gave that job to my father, with assistance from Ruthie, as she was a fast typist.

Upon their return from Libya, my parents spent a couple of weeks with Esther, who was now in Italy, to bond as a threesome marriage. Then my mother and father took recordings and transcripts of Moses David's writings to a hotel room in Malta, where they worked tirelessly for a month putting together the first volume of the Mo Letter books.

I'M BORN IN HONG KONG

A few months later, my parents were sent to Hong Kong to set up the printing, binding, and shipping contacts. It was there, while on a trip to a deserted beach, that I was conceived, according to my mother. She was thrilled to learn she was pregnant, though flabbergasted. At twenty-seven, after years of unprotected hippie sex in her teens, she didn't think she was able to get pregnant.

When the books were finally ready, my father left my six-months-pregnant mother behind in Hong Kong to travel to Tenerife to bring the printed copies to his father.

Around this time, Moses David decided to introduce FFing to the rank-and-file disciples, now that he had tested the model on a small scale for a few years. To prepare his disciples for this new revelation, over the previous year, Grandpa had been incorporating more and more explicit sexual material into his Letters. In 1976, Grandpa published a twenty-three-letter series titled *King Arthur's Knights*, about Mama Maria's escapades in London. The FFing Mo Letters came in quick succession, describing and justifying this new ministry and touting its success. Not everyone was immediately on board; some of the leaders and disciples, especially those who were already happily married, were reluctant to participate. But for the most part, followers were eager to follow Grandpa's edict, convinced he was speaking God's message for a new day.

AUTHORITIES MAKE PROSTITUTION ARRESTS

However, not long after he went public to the Family with his revelation, a photographer who had gone undercover sold a photograph of the End-Time Prophet posing with some of his Flirty Fishers to the West German magazine *Stern*, and they opted to feature it on their cover. *Time* magazine followed suit, publishing the photo alongside a feature article entitled "Tracking the Children of God" in its August 22, 1977, edition.

Authorities in Tenerife acted swiftly, arresting a handful of the women from Moses David's home and charging them with prostitution. Everyone not arrested in the sweep, including my father and Esther, who had just arrived for their visit, hightailed it out of the country. The police were looking for Moses David to arrest him as a pimp, but he and Maria escaped the island with Davidito and eventually formed their new Home in Barcelona.

After nearly six months in Europe, my father finally returned to Hong Kong, where I, at three months old, was living with my mother and a small team of disciples in a high-rise apartment building. My father insisted Esther and the kids join him and my mother in Hong Kong. Fearing she might lose her children and place if she disobeyed, Esther joined us there a few months later, and not long after my first birthday, my six siblings arrived with their nanny. For the first time, my father and his two wives and all his children were living together under one roof.

THE RNR BOMB—GRANDPA FIRES ALL THE LEADERS

To house his ten-person family (plus helpers) on a small income, my father moved us to the nearby Portuguese colony of Macau in 1978. Just as everyone was settling in, Moses David sent out a shocking order for the "Re-Organisation, [sic] Nationalisation [sic] Revolution," or RNR. In a Mo Letter, *REBIRTHDAY!*, published on his birthday, February 18, 1978, Moses David fired three hundred of the top leaders, including the Royal Family, his children and Mother Eve. He declared that the Children of God's leadership, or "government," as he called it, had "become so complicated with such a tangled web of officers and so top-heavy with bureaucracy that it could hardly move and get the job done."

He was tired of the leaders dragging their feet in implementing his decrees. *"MANY A DEMOCRACY HAS FAILED and ended in wrangling confusion, corruption and economic collapse, necessitating a military or political coup by a strong man fed up with it all!"* he wrote.

The Children of God had started with the very strict, even abusive militaristic "training" period at the Ranch in 1970, designed to make all but the most die-hard disciples leave, and that same dictatorial leadership and culture had continued during the pioneering of Europe and other countries. But the disciples were ready to implode, prompting the Prophet to loosen the reins of strict control and unquestioning obedience for a time with his reorganization decree. He told the Homes they could hold elections for the new local leaders.

He used this opportunity to officially disband the Children of God and create distance from the ongoing allegations of sexual and financial illegality. He told everyone to call themselves the Family of Love, which would eventually be shortened to the Family.

Although my father was no longer considered a top leader, he continued to work on publishing the Mo Letters in Hong Kong, an important, if narrower, sphere of influence. But many of the old leadership who had lost their privileged positions, including Mother Eve, left the Family. For years, Mother Eve had been focusing on her own team of disciples based in southern France, so she, her helper Steven, and a few other disciples went to Houston, Texas, and started a more traditional church ministry. She continued to receive money from Moses David for years and never publicly condemned him.

For the next several years, there was no real leadership. Moses David continued to direct his followers through the *Family News,* a monthly compilation of members' testimonies and tips, and Mo Letters, but disciples could pioneer and do what they wanted and go where they had the faith for without asking for permission. Some even started taking System jobs to earn money, which was easier than the constant fundraising on the streets and knocking on doors for donations. The freedom was a welcome relief for the disciples, who, without birth control, had been forming large families.

Despite my father submitting to the demotions and eagerly jumping on board with FFing and Moses David's new revelations, the storm was not over.

MY PARENTS' DISMISSAL AND HUMILIATION

At Christmas in 1980, without warning, Esther was rebuked in a public Mo Letter. She had been accused by members of a Home she visited in the Philippines of stating that Grandpa and my father approved of pornographic movies. To this day, she claims she still has never seen a porno film and never said anything of the sort. But under public threat of excommunication and losing her children, she could not defend herself; her only hope was to subjugate herself completely.

This began a series of a dozen Mo Letters called the Prodigal Prodigies, which rebuked my father for not keeping Esther under control and for his own independence and disobedience. Hosea was running a printing business out of Hong Kong, where he printed books for System clients, against his father's instructions, as well as the Family Mo Books. My father, like Esther, had to write a public confession of his wrongdoing and apology, which was printed with Moses David's and Maria's commentary.

This public disgrace of my father seemed to justify Moses David's decision to remove him from top leadership in the RNR, despite his continued loyalty, and to set up a new Royal Family with Davidito and Maria.

Within a month of the Prodigal Prodigy series, a wave of bad publicity about the Family—and our personal family—hit the newsstands in Hong Kong. Unlike the positive press we'd gotten previously, these articles, written by reporters from England and the US, accused the Family of promoting prostitution and agitated the Hong Kong government into banning Family members from the country.

My parents, unsure what the fallout would be, decided to head to

Hac Sa, a remote beach at the farthest end of Macau. Battered from within and without by the Mo Letters and the media, they felt that the isolated village of Hac Sa seemed like a haven to try to rebuild their lives with minimal interference. Little did they know our lives would be anything but quiet.

1

THE GREAT ESCAPE!

"Faithy," my father's Texas drawl barks in my ear. "Get up. Don't say one word. Not one word, you understand?"

It's pitch-black outside the window. I nod, half-asleep.

Mommy Ruthie's long, brown-black hair forms a frizzy cloud around her head as she runs around the tiny room, stuffing things into the type of cheap, colorful, striped canvas bag the Chinese market hawkers use to carry their goods. My father gathers me in his arms and throws me over his shoulder, and my world turns upside down. My bare foot scrapes his cowboy belt buckle. Through half-closed eyes, I see the orange linoleum tile floor, the threadbare living room carpet. I strain my neck up to see Mommy Esther, my father's other wife, standing by the door with her six blond children, my half siblings. She brushes her straight pale hair from her lovely face, which is now pinched with concern. They all have small bags in their hands.

"We're all going to walk down the stairs and get into the van," my father says. "Make no noise."

Struggling to hold up my head against gravity, I spy eighteen feet and four paws racing down five flights of dirty white-tiled steps, the slap of my older brothers' flip-flops loud in the dark stairwell. We wait as my father unlatches the heavy steel door entrance to our small apartment building before stepping out onto the worn, rounded cobblestones that were brought as ballast by Portuguese trading ships several hundred years before. As we pile into our old Dodge Ram van, Daddy passes me to the back. I'm pulled onto my mother's lap while he wrestles with a sliding door that refuses to stay shut. His wiry frame is surprisingly strong, and the door eventually closes with a hushed clunk. We're off. Questions bubble to my lips, but as soon as I open my mouth, I feel the pressure of Mommy's finger.

"Just keep quiet," she whispers.

The narrow, colonial-style streets are empty as my three parents, six siblings, and beloved Doberman escape into the darkness.

It's July 1981, a couple of months after my fourth birthday, when my parents decide to flee our home in the city of Macau, a province of China and, until 1999, its own country and a Portuguese colony.

I curl up on my mother's lap and settle into the vehicle's soft rocking motions. From my position, I can't see much, just shadows and momentary glimpses of empty cobblestone streets. It looks so different from Macau during the day, when the thriving city is a hive of activity and people shoving and shopping.

This city I've called home since before I can remember is built on a peninsula jutting out from the south China coastline and connected to two trailing islands by bridges. In the 1600s, the peninsula was only one square mile. But by 1981, the inhabitants added another five square miles to the city by dumping all their garbage in the sea and gradually claiming land as the refuse built up. Even with the added land, Macau is listed in the *Guinness World Records* as the most densely populated country on Earth. Its 250,000 citizens (95 percent Chinese and 5 percent Macanese, an Asian-Portuguese blend, and a far smaller population of Portuguese government officials sent over to govern this neglected colony) occupy a considerable amount of cubed space by standing on each other's heads in their six-hundred-square-foot apartments. My family rents one of these on Rua Central, right off the main shopping area, hardly big enough for our family of ten and various other helpers who live with us.

In ten minutes, we're on the mile-long bridge that links the peninsula city of Macau to Taipa, the first island. A three-foot-tall white statue of the Virgin Mary sits at the bridge intersection—the Catholic protector for bad drivers. We continue around Taipa and over the causeway to the next island of Coloane, traveling over pitch-black water until the bridge releases us into the dark countryside. The only sounds I hear are the thrum of the old V8 engine and our overnight bags rattling around in the rear cargo area.

Finally, my father breaks the silence. "We're moving to a new home," he announces.

"Isn't it exciting?" Mommy Ruthie adds, squeezing me reassuringly.

She is answered with a soft snore; my siblings have passed out on top of each other in a tangle of small arms and legs. I don't know what to say, so I say nothing.

Even with my eyes closed, I hear the crunch of dirt under our tires as we leave the paved road. When we finally stop, my mother grabs my hand, and we march into the darkness to a chorus of chirping crickets. I feel my way through a doorway but trip on the raised stone lintel, hurtling into emptiness until I'm lifted off my feet and hustled onto a hard mattress.

The next time I open my eyes, the morning sun is leaking in through a dirt-streaked skylight. I am in a big room with newly plastered white walls and a cold concrete floor hastily covered with beige linoleum.

I roll off my mattress to find myself sandwiched between two very tall beds of unpainted pine, three and four bunks high, where my siblings are sleeping. Mary, three years older than I and closest to me in age, is on the other bottom bunk. Our older brothers are like stair steps, all one year apart. Aaron (or Bones, because he's so skinny) is sleeping above me, the goofy clown still for once. Standing on my toes, I try to make out Josh and Caleb, identical twins, curled up on the two bunks above Mary. Everyone has trouble telling them apart, but Caleb has crossed eyes, wears glasses, and rarely brushes his hair, so that helps distinguish him from Josh, who always has a comb in his pocket. Mary, Caleb, and Josh all have white-blond angelic hair that belies their naughtiness. For the rest of us, our hair has darkened from a reddish-gold when we were toddlers to a nondescript brown. I can't see Hobo until he pops his messy head over the bunk rail. I'm the youngest, and at four, I'm still too short to see the tops of things.

Nehi is still fast asleep. He's in the highest bunk because at eleven he's the oldest. I like him well enough, but he'd rather clean his Nikon or play guitar than pay attention to the rest of us. "Head in the clouds," my parents say. "Nose in the air," counters Josh.

Hobo is the second eldest and my favorite because he watches out for me and stops the twins from picking on me. He thinks he's cool, and Josh, unable to pass up a taunt, calls him a Goody-Two-Shoes. Josh is the instigator and Caleb his loyal shadow. The twins fight with all of us, like it's them against the world.

Mary is the only other girl and my nemesis, and we bicker like breathing. She's just jealous that she's no longer the youngest and only girl anymore. Mommy Esther told us she chose the name Mary Blessing because after five boys, it was such a blessing to have a girl. We don't buy it. Mary's a tattle and a pain in the neck, so we call her Burden. This, of course, sends her running to the grown-ups and gets us red bottoms, so now we just say, "Mary B," and look at her *meaningfully*. She still cries to the adults, but we can honestly and righteously defend ourselves: there's nothing wrong with calling her by her initial. The adults know what we're up to, but they haven't figured out how to punish us, so they just tell her to be quiet.

My siblings came from Mommy Esther, and I came from

Mommy Ruthie, but they always tell us it doesn't matter, that they are both our mommies.

I've had two mommies since I can remember. They are almost opposites in looks—Mommy Esther's face is angular with a straight, aquiline nose, blue eyes, and straight hair, while Mommy Ruthie has a rounded face, slightly olive skin, dark brown eyes, and frizzy hair. My coloring is closer to Mommy Esther's than to my blood mother's because I also take after my father, with his white Swedish German skin and light brown hair that we see less of each day. He claims his fast-growing bald patch is from an excess of manly energy.

When my siblings and I talk together, we often interrupt each other to ask, "Which mommy, Ruthie or Esther?" The confusion is normal to us. But when other kids taunt, "She's just your half sister," we are all very fierce in our defense of each other. "She's my *sister!*" my brothers shout.

A couple of my friends in Macau have two mommies as well, but most have only one. I'm glad my mommies don't fight like the mommies in those other families do. Mommy Esther says she and Ruthie are friends, and she is grateful to have help with all the kids.

I know that Systemite men are not allowed to have more than one wife, but we live by God's rules, not the World's. Many of the biblical patriarchs had more than one wife—Abraham, Isaac, King David, and King Solomon—though I think King Solomon had way too many: three hundred wives and seven hundred concubines. He wouldn't be able to sleep with them all in a year! My father has only two, and he can alternate whose bed he sleeps in each night to keep it fair. I feel sorry for Solomon's wives.

I find my mother and tell her I need to go to the bathroom. She leads me outside, where the sun is shining bright. We walk along a dirt path to a small, rough wood-plank shack about ten feet from the house. Our Doberman Sheba is there, getting acquainted with her new home, sniffing some garbage near the outhouse. The door whines on its rusted hinges as my mother pulls it open, and the droning buzz of flies get louder just before the smell smacks me in the face. Inside it's just big enough for a hole in the ground with two concrete blocks on the sides for your feet—a traditional Chinese squat toilet. No seat, no flusher. Just a long, dark drop. "Always check for spiders and snakes," my mother tells me. "And make sure to look up. They can fall from the ceiling." I squirm at the idea of snakes or spiders dropping on me from above.

My stomach clenches into a fist as I tiptoe over the shadows, my eyes darting to the walls, the corners, my feet. I glance fearfully at the spiderwebs covering the corrugated metal roof while trying to keep my flip-flops from slipping on the concrete blocks. There is no light bulb. I'm in almost complete darkness when the door shuts. The sharp stench of years of other people's poop burns my nose as I squat. I finish as quickly as possible and dash back into the bright sunlight. As I gulp down fresh air, tears leak from my stinging eyes. *Will I have to risk my life every time I go to the bathroom?* I want to go home, back to a real toilet, back to our apartment with a balcony and tiled floors and street noise.

The red dirt gets between my toes, and I try to shake the pebbles out of my flip-flops as I trail my mother back inside. She is chatting brightly.

Although Coloane Island is part of the tiny country of Macau, twenty minutes outside the city, it feels like another world. Our new home is a traditional Chinese farmhouse, a hundred-year-old granite-block and adobe structure with pine tree trunks as roof beams and a white-and-black clay tile roof. The front door is two pieces of roughhewn wood on hinges that open inward and lock with a handmade sliding iron bolt. The house is shaped like a C, made up of two rectangular forty-by-ten rooms connected by a ten-foot-square living room/entryway with a large round metal folding table and stools for dining. Only one of the long rooms is habitable, our bedroom with a small wooden loft in the back.

A small three-by-five-foot lean-to on the outside of the house is the "kitchen," with a built-in concrete countertop and a portable camping stove connected to a big tank of gas. There is no electricity or plumbing, so any washing will have to be done in the red plastic dish basin filled with water from the hose outside. The rest of the house is in disrepair, with dirt floors, crumbling adobe brick walls, and countless roof leaks, as we discover during the first rainstorm. My father says the place has stood empty for seven years, ever since its owner abandoned it to move to the two-story-house he built just behind this one. It's no wonder he's renting it to us for cheap—500 patacas a month, the equivalent of about $80.

As Mommy Ruthie brings me back inside, she points to the loft at the back of the bedroom. "I'm sleeping up there, but I don't want you climbing the ladder; it's not safe," she tells me. A tall bamboo ladder leans shakily against the edge of an open loft platform. There is no railing.

"Mommy Esther's bed is behind that curtain," she explains, pointing to a makeshift privacy screen my father has created by tacking a king-size flowered sheet to the edge of my mother's loft platform, so it hangs down, curtaining the area just beneath it.

"Breakfast is ready!" I hear Mommy Esther call from the other room, and I run to join the others. She is carrying in a large steaming pot of plain oats from the outside kitchen as we all jostle for stools around the folding table. Josh elbows Nehi in the ribs, and I'm about to "accidentally" stamp on Caleb's foot when my father walks in from outside.

My father's bounding energy and booming preacher's voice make a far more imposing man than his wiry one-hundred-nineteen-pound frame suggests. At five-four, he fits right in with the smaller Chinese population. His blue eyes are deep-set, and when he smiles, his lips pull back until every tooth in his mouth is visible, top and bottom. With no fat on his face, he resembles a grinning skeleton— which makes people nervous even when he's smiling.

But now his brow wrinkles into a stern frown.

"Boys," he says, "it's time for a serious talk." His serious voice is a deep growl, three octaves below his peppy "praise the Lord" voice.

Mary and I are assumed in the word "boys" most of the time, unless it's something fun. He's always mixing up our names, calling me Mary and my sister Faithy, but he doesn't like it if we correct him, so we've learned to just go along with it.

Elbows drop into place, and we sit on our stools, silent as the boiled oats.

"We're hiding from bad people," he begins. "They want to stop us from doing the Lord's work. We can't let them find us, so it's very important that nobody, including your friends in the city, know where we are. It's absolutely *Selah*."

The silence makes my nose itch, but as I wiggle around to scratch it, my father rumbles, "Faithy?"

I freeze.

"Do you know what *'Selah'* means?"

My gaze flicks to Hobo for salvation, but he's staring in his bowl. My head gives a faint shake no. *Is that the wrong answer?*

"It means completely secret. Your lips are sealed. You cannot tell anyone where we live. Do you understand?"

Ah. I nod, solemn as a soldier. I want to ask, *Who are these bad people? What will they do to us if they find us?* But I keep my lips pressed together. I know what happens when Christians are captured. It usually involves torture, death, or lions in the Bible stories read to us before bed each night.

After my father's speech is over, we say grace and eat in silence, glancing at each other over our oatmeal. With him at the table, we are afraid of talking noisily over each other as we usually do when we are just eating with Mommy Ruthie or Mommy Esther, or our caregivers. *Where is Uncle Michael?* I wonder. He usually watches us after breakfast.

It's strange having just our personal family around the breakfast table. My siblings and I are normally taken care of by other Family members, like Uncle Michael, since our parents spend much of their days doing leadership work. My father and mother have the very important job of working on the Word of God by helping to edit and print the Mo Letters Grandpa sends to his disciples around the world. These paper booklets, formatted like a newsletter, arrive by mail every two weeks. They're filled with Grandpa's latest prophecies, testimonies, and dreams. Everything that Grandpa says is captured on tape by a person who follows him around with a recorder to transcribe his thoughts for the Mo Letters and other Family publications so not one gem that drops from his lips will fall to the ground.

I feel very close to Grandpa, even though I've never actually seen him. He's been in hiding since before I was born, and all photos of him have been burned to protect his identity. The black-and-white pictures sprinkled through the Mo Letters are either cartoons or, if it's a real photo, there is always a drawing of a lion head (he started referring to himself as Papa Lion after having a dream of being a powerful lion) or a white-bearded man who looks like Moses from *The Ten Commandments* movie pasted over where Grandpa's real head should be.

After we stack our orange plastic camping bowls for washing, Mommy Esther holds up what looks like a large bamboo bowl with a pointed top. It's a Chinese farmer's hat. "Every time you leave the house, you need to wear one of these," she says. "No white people have ever lived in this village. If anyone sees your blond hair, it will cause suspicion. We don't want the bad people who are trying to persecute us to find us, so you must promise me you won't leave the house without your hat." Seven little heads bob up and down.

How will this help? I wonder. *Surely, everyone will be able to spot we are not Chinese, hat or no.*

My mother hands them out, and we put them on. I look at Caleb and giggle at the bulky, awkward shape on his head that almost covers his nose; he shoves me, and when my hat slides off, the wide brim bumps into Bones, who theatrically falls to the ground.

"Kids!" My father's voice cracks like a whip, and we sit up straight as broomsticks. "This is very serious. The forces of Satan are out to harm the Family and Grandpa," he barks out, followed by a punishing grip of the tendons in the back of Bones's neck as he drags him to his feet.

I wince in sympathy. We've all been on the receiving end of that painful pinch.

"Why do we have to hide now?" Hobo bravely asks my father.

For years we've been Christian singing stars on local radio and TV in Hong Kong and Macau, despite being Grandpa's grandchildren. We stare at my father in confusion.

My father's voice dips to his deep growl. "We have been betrayed. By Lynne Watson."

A gasp goes around the table.

Lynne Watson's image pops into my mind. She is a British woman with wavy blondish hair who looks to be about my mom's age; nothing about her stands out as evil. I'd seen her a few times, when my parents brought her by the apartment to study the Mo Letters.

My parents are always so happy when people want to learn about Jesus. It's hard to imagine someone like Lynne Watson could betray us when all we are trying to do is help more people get closer to God.

"She was only pretending to be our friend to get close enough to confirm my identity," Dad continues. "She's written terrible things about us and published our *real* names in the newspaper."

"Ho?" I whisper. Everyone calls my father Ho, short for Hosea, but also a common Chinese surname. Systemites call him Mr. Ho, and Family members call him Uncle Ho.

"No," Mommy Ruthie explains. "Ho is fine. It's his *other* name, his legal name, which we can never say."

"What is it?" I ask. I had no idea he had another name.

"We don't use our last name *ever*," my father emphasizes, staring at the older boys, who had seen their last name on their passports, which are normally kept in his safe. "You don't even tell other Family members. If someone lets it slip, enemies of God could find Grandpa."

At all costs, Grandpa must be protected.

"I can't believe she deceived us like that!" Mommy Esther's pale blue eyes are blazing. She is normally meek and quiet, hanging in the background even when she is supporting us onstage with her guitar, but this morning she is fuming. "She lied about wanting to get to know Jesus and study His Word, just to get close to us and learn our *secrets!*"

The adults' sense of betrayal and mistrust seeps into me.

"We thought she was a sheep," Mommy Esther continues. "But she wasn't even a goat! She was a wolf in sheep's clothing, a snake in the grass."

People who are receptive to our message about Jesus are Sheep, from Matthew 25:31–46: "But when the Son of Man comes in his glory, and all the holy angels with him, then he will sit on the throne of his glory. Before him all the nations will be gathered, and he will separate them one from another, as a shepherd separates the sheep from the goats." People who reject us are Goats.

"We will pray against her!" Mommy Esther declares, gazing at us children with unusual fierceness. How dare they threaten her children!

My father soothes, "The Devil always sends persecution. That lets us know we are doing God's work. We are God's Family. His End-Time warriors, the true disciples who have dropped out of the evil System. Praise the Lord!" he finishes in a singsongy voice.

Fear of "persecution" is a constant companion.

Since before I can remember, my parents and caregivers have read me stories of persecution against God's children. Daniel in the lions' den, the first Christians killed in the gladiator rings by the Roman emperor Nero, missionaries being eaten by cannibals in Fiji, the slaughter of Christians in the Chinese Boxer Rebellion, or Christians who refused to denounce their faith drowned in ice water by Stalin's soldiers. Sometimes God delivers you with a miracle, and sometimes you die and go to Heaven. With the Antichrist and the Tribulation spoken of in Revelation due to start any day now, anything is possible.

As part of God's End-Time elite army and Grandpa's grandchildren, I'm told the Devil's forces will target us especially. This persecution targeting my personal family rather than the Family at large seems to confirm this. But I secretly hope I'll also have greater powers to perform miracles, like calling down fire from God to burn up the Antichrist soldiers.

When Mommy Esther finishes praying, the air is still and heavy, and none of us dare say a word. Our entire Family is at risk. No one is safe.

Grandpa is in hiding—and now we are, too.

With our big hats in hand, my father takes us around for a tour of our new home.

I didn't know that my father and mother had been coming out here secretly for the last few months as a work hideaway to escape our cramped apartment. Back in the city, we'd first rented three six-hundred-square-foot apartments in the same building for us, our caregivers, and other Family members who would pass through. We were one of several families who moved to Macau in the last few years to pioneer the Portuguese colony as a new mission field. At least three families with kids my age, as well as numerous single adults, all lived with or near us in the same neighborhood. As rents in the city kept going up, our family had to cram into two apartments, then one. So, we were desperate for more space on our tiny income.

"We'll all live in this one room where we slept last night until the rest of the house is fixed up," he says. "But don't worry, with our new Chinese worker, it shouldn't take long. Maybe a month or two, praise the Lord," he says with optimism.

"Thank God we sprayed and managed to get rid of most of the fleas!" Mommy Ruthie says with relief. "When we first walked in here, fleas swarmed my legs."

"Ew," I squeal, moving my feet more quickly and checking to see if any of the almost-invisible black biting creatures have jumped on my naked legs.

As we continue our tour, my father's spirits are high. "Praise the Lord!" he says. "I've been looking for a way to get our family out into the countryside so you boys can have farm animals like I did growing up on the ranch in Texas. I want you all to learn the value of hard work and responsibility! And keep you out of trouble." My father is always regaling us with stories of ranch life in the dusty desert town of Thurber, where he tended cows, goats, and chickens as a kid.

"We just had to speed up the timing of our move to the village with the persecution from the newspapers, but God works in mysterious ways. Praise the Looord." His voice swings up a couple of octaves on the last word in a singsong. Unless he's angry, his voice ends on a high note.

We follow him through the short door to the connecting room where we just ate breakfast, which is about half as long as the side rooms. "This will be our living room once we finish cleaning it up," he explains. He points to a rough wood-plank whitewashed dividing wall separating the back third from the rest of the living room—it's a space full of dried-out paint cans that I'd missed earlier. "We can turn that small back room into a bedroom for you two girls."

We cross through the next doorway into a long room like the first.

"This will be the boys' room."

There is dirt and chunks of plaster all over the floor.

"You boys can work with me to chip off the rest of this old plaster from the adobe bricks, then we will replaster it." There is no glass in the windows, just rusted iron bars. "We will put in some mosquito screens and fix the hinges on the shutters that are falling off. And we'll cement the floor in here and lay down linoleum just like in the other room. It will be great! You'll see!"

All of us kids gaze in dismay at the mess around us, recognizing a big cleanup job when we see one. I feel an itch on my ankle and slap myself hard. I hope it's not a flea.

At the end of the house tour, my father says, "Come on, kids. Let's look at the village. Put on your hats."

I follow my siblings out the front door, trying to balance the big bamboo hat on my head while being careful not to trip over the stone lintel as I step out into the blinding tropical sun. The thick adobe block walls and small windows keep the house dark and cooler. Now the full blast of the sun's rays hits us. I'm glad for my big hat.

Macau has a subtropical climate with mainly two seasons, summer and winter. The almost daily spring rains of April are followed by a steaming summer, hot and muggy even at night, with occasional summer showers, thunderstorms, and days-long typhoons. October is the official start of autumn, but the summer heat and thunderstorms often linger until November. Though it never freezes in winter, the wet cold seeps into your bones. In late July, the red dirt sizzles in the humid heat, burning the bottom of my foot as my flip-flop slips off.

The first thing I see is that our small village is nestled against dark green hills. Mommy Esther points up to a road hugging the hills' curves above us.

"That is the road to the beach from Macau," she explains. "We are safe here. Almost no one from the city even knows this tiny village is tucked back here. But if some nosy reporter driving to the beach spots our blond heads from the road above, our enemies will find us."

Now I understand why we are wearing these uncomfortable hats. But what would these enemies do to us if they found us here? I know better than to ask. Usually, my father shuts us down when we ask a question like that. "Because I said so!" or "Revolutionaries don't ask questions!" are a couple of favorite responses.

With a skip, I follow my brothers and sister down the dirt driveway and see small, squat one-room houses with walls made of mud bricks and tile roofs. *Where are the paved streets? Where are all the people?*

I learn that the "village" is just a hodgepodge of twenty-five or so buildings, a couple of two-story "modern" tiled houses where the more well-off villagers live, a few ancient fishermen's houses like ours, and a row of one-room mud shacks with tar-paper roofs. There are no roads, so each house sits where the owner chose to put it generations ago and is connected to other village houses by dirt paths formed by foot traffic over the years.

There is no zoning, street planning, building codes, or even title deeds. More than a hundred years ago (there are no records), the Chinese fishermen or pirates (depending on your point of view) built their huts on this patch of neglected land with narrow three-foot-wide paths to and between the houses. Their late-twentieth-century descendants live much the same way, happy to be ignored by the outside world. The village doesn't have city water, electricity, sewage, or garbage collection. Most villagers scavenge electricity by running illegal wires through the jungle to power lines on the main road to Coloane Village, the only town on Coloane Island. Our nearest small shop is at Hac Sa beach, a ten-minute walk down the dirt road.

Unlike our village, Coloane Village, which is a fifteen-minute bus ride from Hac Sa beach, is a real town with streets, a small government doctor's office, and a market with stalls and tiny shops on a lane too narrow for cars. A Portuguese Catholic church holding a finger bone relic of Saint Xavier sits on a cobblestone square lined by Chinese restaurants. A large primary and high school and Macau's prison are only a few blocks away.

We trail my father like ducklings around our new neighborhood. I see a few gnarled, elderly villagers staring at us suspiciously and hear men and women alike scream at each other between their houses in true fishwife tradition. Cantonese doesn't have the smooth melody of Mandarin, which is considered the language of the emperors. It is the harsh language of Southern China—high, low, sharp, guttural, squeaky. Every other word is a swear word, which my brothers are gobbling up with glee.

Some of the larger houses have three generations residing together, so there are some Chinese kids for us to wave shyly at, but unlike us, they attend school in Coloane during the day. There are few young adults. Any young person with a lick of ambition or love of creature comforts moves to Macau.

I spot leafy bok choy in rows and bean vines tied to sticks in small, scattered vegetable patches behind the houses. Weeds grow wild—big elephant ears, long stalks of dandelions and others I don't recognize line the dirt paths.

But among all the vibrant, lush flora, there is trash everywhere. No matter where I look: Coke cans, candy wrappers, shreds of plastic bags, Styrofoam lunch boxes, decomposing cardboard boxes, rusted nails, twisted wires. A mountain of this garbage sits in an open space in front of the houses where the dirt path enters the village.

"There is no garbage collection here," I hear my father saying. "The people just throw their garbage out the windows or onto that big dump in the field. Praise the Lord, we will clean it up and show them a good sample of cleanliness." Grandpa teaches that we must always be good examples of Bible virtues even as we preach them.

My father seems excited to have such a challenging place to prove himself.

I overhear Mommy Esther nervously whisper to him, "There aren't really pirates still here in these outer villages, are there?"

"Of course not. I'm sure that's just a rumor. But Centurion did once tell me that the police won't come out here for fear their cars will be smashed by the villagers, who don't want any outsiders interfering."

Centurion is our code name for our friend Alfonso, who is the chief of the Portuguese police force in Macau. He is nicknamed after the centurion in the Bible, a Roman official who was friendly to Jesus. Family members are encouraged to befriend local authorities and powerful people who can provide protection when persecution inevitably comes, and evil people lie about us to stop God's work. My parents have made many friends in the few years we have been here, several high up in the government. We often give them code names for security reasons, so they cannot be identified by an eavesdropper listening to a casual conversation. We want to protect those who protect us.

My father lowers his voice so we kids won't hear. I lean closer to Mommy Ruthie, pretending to ignore them but listening intently. "Apparently, there was a bloody fight a few years back between the police and some villagers, and some people were killed. So the government, in typical laid-back Portuguese style, just ignores them. Of course, that means they have no municipal services like water or garbage collection. Hac Sa is the most isolated village on Coloane," my father crows, very pleased with himself for discovering it. "No outsiders ever come here, not even Chinese. It's a perfect place for us to lay low. Praise the Lord!"

Our extreme secrecy, it turns out, is less about my father's fear of bad publicity and more about not wanting reporters or people from the Catholic Church making our acceptance harder by spreading lies about weird sexual practices or drugs, like they usually do.

My father's legs bounce like bedsprings as he pulls me down the red dirt path by my hand, my short legs running to keep up. "Praise the Lord! God has provided, and He will protect us. We just need to be a good sample of God's love!" he repeats, then casts a look over his shoulder to Esther and the boys. His attention is drawn like a missile to trouble, his eyes narrowing on Josh and Bones, who are squabbling. "Boys!" The sharp bark freezes them mid-sentence. Then the threatening grimace splits into a grin as one of our new neighbors passes. Offering a cheery wave, he calls out, *"Jo san!"* in Cantonese. "Faithy, smile and wave!" He pinches my shoulder, and I reflexively obey.

The man pauses in his slow shamble to stare. Thin legs and arms stick out from his graying shorts and singlet. Sun-browned skin grips his bones like the wizened bark of a manzanita tree. After a long stare, he gives an imperceptible nod and moves on.

Ever positive, my parents are buoyed by this slight sign of recognition, but the road to acceptance is long and bumpier than a bike on cobblestones.

WATCH OUT FOR SNAKES

Life in Hac Sa lacks even the basic comforts we had in the city.

Here, like it does for our neighbors, our electricity arrives through a few exposed wires connected to other wires illegally connected to one of the city's fuse boxes on electric poles lining the main road a few miles away. Without grounding or electric-current regulation, it is a touchy affair. At night, when everyone in the village is using the trickle of electricity, the orange glow of our single 20-watt bulb flickers so dimly my parents can barely see to read the Bible or Mo Letters to us, but in the morning, the electricity surges and explodes the bulb. With daily blackouts, a refrigerator is pointless, as is anything else that needs electricity other than a few lights and a fan.

We eat simply: meat, vegetables, and rice twice a day, with oatmeal and sometimes eggs for breakfast. Since we don't have refrigeration, we buy our fresh food every day as part of our daily walk. A mile up the road just over the hill from the beach is our fresh meat supplier. He raises Dobermans, and we bought our dogs, Sheba and Rex, from him a year earlier. He goes early every morning into the big wet market in Macau to buy meat and vegetables, and some of the other villagers, like ourselves, buy from him. Everything else we buy in bulk from the market in Coloane—rice, oats, and powdered milk come in forty-pound sacks.

Air conditioning is out of the question. The trickle of electricity is so low, we use a broom handle to turn the ceiling fan just to get it going, then hope it will spin long enough for us to fall asleep. The stuffy summer heat inside the house is so oppressive we do almost everything we can outside, where we can get a breeze, including cooking, studying, and bathing. The shower is a metal pipe fastened inside the roof of the dark outhouse that drips on our heads as we go to the bathroom. When we want to take a shower, we lay a wooden board over the smelly toilet hole and stand on it. I'm afraid the board will slip or break and I'll fall into all the disgusting poop below.

In the tropical summer, each day is hotter than the last, so we cool off as best we can. Our parents let us wear our bathing suits all day, so they can spray us off with the outside hose to stay cool.

At the end of our first week, our father excitedly calls my siblings and me to the living room. Still sweaty from our morning of chores, we stare in delight as he rolls in a big wooden barrel that he has found washed up at the beach. It's wide enough for all seven of us if we squash in. He uses our green rubber hose to fill it up, adds a bit of soap, then shouts, "Jump in!" All of us fight to be the first to leap into the cool water of our makeshift bathtub. Relief! Splashing and making soap bubbles, we forget the unforgiving tropical sun.

We have a big job to do, and now that we have a lay of the land, we are ready to begin. Our father hands out tall rubber boots. "For the snakes," he tells us. "There are lots of snakes out here, black snakes, pythons, but the ones you need to really watch out for are the king cobras, because their bite is deadly. If you disturb a snake in the grass or the garbage pile, it will curl up and strike. Usually only as high as your ankle or leg. The boots should stop its teeth."

"What if it bites above the boot?" I ask with a nervous glance at my feet. My legs and boots are shorter than everyone else's.

"Just be careful."

We are each handed a large black plastic garbage bag and a two-foot-long sharp metal stick with a wooden handle. I stare at it, confused.

"This is a barbecue skewer." Our father marches us down to the big pile of rubbish at the edge of the village and explains to us, "We can't just tell people about Jesus. We must be examples of good Christians. Remember, cleanliness is Godliness. We are going to clean up this garbage dump."

I'm grateful for my stick when, as I stab an old piece of cardboard, I see maggots and worms wriggling in the dirt under it. "Gross!" I jump back in horror. I never had to deal with these slimy worms in the city.

I fall in line behind my brothers as my father leads us into the village to do what becomes our daily afternoon cleanup. For at least two hours a day, we pick up garbage around the village. I help my father and brothers fill truck after truck with trash; then I sweep, rake, shovel, and pull weeds until my hands blister. The villagers look at us with suspicion and curiosity, not sure what to make of the crazy family of *gweilos*, Cantonese for "foreigner" or "white devil," in wide-brimmed hats stomping around their houses and the vacant field at the edge of the village. I see them staring at us as they walk slowly past where we are picking up garbage. "Wave, kids!" our father instructs. "Smile and say hi." Obediently, we shout, *"Jo san!"* A couple smile and wave back.

While I'm nervous to talk to our neighbors, who smell like pungent herbs and sweat, my father bounces around the village, happily chattering away to the locals and our Chinese worker in simple Cantonese. According to my parents, he was shot when he swam to Macau to escape communist China. An old, childless lady in the village took care of him until he got better. We have gotten to know her through him and have adopted her as our Chinese grandmother. We bring her food and blankets. Like the Good Samaritan, we are here to help.

Seeing our interactions with a Chinese grandma helps some of the villagers feel more comfortable. A few approach us to say a few words. The braver ones reach out to touch the strands of our hair that poke out from beneath our hats. Most of them take a "wait and see" approach. However, there are a couple who are angry about the intrusion, like the one who takes to throwing rocks. We never catch the assailant, but instead of feeling angry, my father only doubles down on his efforts to win over the attacker (if he could just find him). My father is convinced that we will be accepted by our suspicious neighbors into this closed community, and his optimism never falters.

A few weeks after our arrival in Hac Sa, our village garbage cleanup is finished, and I get a big surprise. We are all sitting around the table for our lunch of stir-fried meat and carrots with rice when I hear our white Dodge van crunching over the gravel. We run outside to see who has arrived. My father gets out of the driver's seat as the van's sliding door opens and out jumps my best friend, Patrick, followed by his parents, Daniel and Grace, who is holding baby Colum.

As soon as I see Patrick's fat short legs stretching to reach the ground, I run forward. "Patchy!" I shout. His family arrived in Macau from England a few months before we moved to the village, and we had become fast friends. Back in the city, we spent much of our time together building LEGO houses, racing Matchbox cars, or playing hide-and-seek with the rest of my siblings; now he's here with me, and I couldn't be happier.

With money only to buy food and necessities, we have very few toys, so a playmate is essential. Grandpa says playing cards and board games are the "Devil's time wasters," so we make our own fun. My brothers make slingshots out of sticks and rubber bands.

I collect things around the village: interesting rocks, feathers, broken toy pieces. I have one small baby doll that's supposed to pee when you feed her water, but one of the boys glued her mouth shut and she doesn't work now. I don't care. My brothers won't play dolls with me, saying, "Dolls are boring," and I agree, though secretly I dream of having a life-size realistic baby doll. I know better than to ask my parents for any expensive toy, though. "We don't have money for that" is the standard reply.

But Patrick will play anything I ask.

Patrick and his family will be moving into the smaller house just outside our front door. We've nicknamed it the Cottage and started calling our house the Main House. The Cottage has three rooms laid out railroad style, and like our place, it, too, needs a lot of fixing up.

Mommy warmly hugs the slight brunette woman we call Auntie Grace. "Praise the Lord, welcome to Hac Sa!" she chirps.

"Thank you! We are so grateful to be here," Grace and her husband, Daniel, chorus in their Irish brogue. Uncle Daniel has the black hair of the Northern Irish, a skinny, meek man. Auntie Grace has freckles on her pale skin and light brown, untrimmed hair past her shoulders, like all the aunties.

In the Family, all adults are called "auntie" and "uncle" to emphasize that we are all a family and everything is shared. Since we are all "family," any adult can spank any kid. The aunts and uncles can slap you, knuckle your head, swat you, or put you in the corner. Parents are not supposed to show favoritism to their own children. Grandpa says, "OUR CHILDREN BELONG TO THE FAMILY and *all* of us, and we are *all* their parents and they are *all* our children."

The adults encourage all the children in the Family to call our prophet "Grandpa." Sometimes, if I'm feeling petty, I want to tell the kids from other families, "He's not your real grandpa! He's mine." But that would get me a smack and a lecture on how he is all our grandpa in spirit.

Here, in our little village at the end of the world, we live communally, like nuns and monks, each person fulfilling their small role of work and chores.

From the moment we wake up until the moment we fall asleep, we are immersed in prayer, songs about Jesus, and hours of religious reading. Prayer comes before everything: eating, driving, getting out of bed, going to sleep, exercising, witnessing, having sex, and doing chores. There is no activity too small to pray over, often just a few sentences asking for protection, for blessing, and for God's will to be done. Grandpa says to apply the Bible verse "Pray without ceasing" literally, praying before and during an activity. I admit, I forget a lot.

Our life is scheduled from early morning to bedtime. Every morning after breakfast, we have Devotions—two hours of prayer, singing praise songs, and reading the Word of God, which is the Bible and the Mo Letters.

As directed in Acts 2:44–45: "All that believed lived together and had all things common and sold their possessions and goods and divided them up to each person as they had a need"—each new member donates their belongings to the Family. We own no property, not even our own bodies, according to the Bible, so it's only right that we give up our own will and desires to submit to the will of God by obeying our leaders.

After Devotions are morning chores, called Joyful Job Time, or JJT, sometimes classes, followed by lunch, an hour nap, afternoon work, one hour of exercise, and a shower. We eat all meals together and have an hour of family time or united evening activity before we retire to our rooms to pray and read God's Word, then it's lights out. That schedule is the underlying rhythm of our lives no matter which Family Home we travel to in any country, with slight changes depending on a person's main role: cooking, cleaning, fundraising, teaching. We must humbly do any task that is asked of us, without complaint or shirking, as unto God.

Conversations about sports, cars, movies, clothes, makeup, or other worldly things are frowned on. Our daily outdoor playtime, Get Out, is for exercise, not goofing around. When we kids start laughing too loud, we are stopped short with a slap or a sharp word: "Stop being foolish! If you have time to do that, you have time to memorize scripture. Idleness is the Devil's workshop!" We memorize Bible verses and Mo Quotes daily to flood our mind with the Word of God, so that there is no room for the Devil's doubts.

Our main job is witnessing. We always carry Gospel tracts in our pockets to give to people we pass on walks in the park. We call it "Litnessing," because it's witnessing by passing out Gospel litera-ture. If a person looks *Sheepy*, interested, we ask them if they want to receive Jesus as their Savior and give a donation.

We befriend Systemites to show them God's love. We invite them over for food and go to their houses when invited, but we always know the purpose is to witness. We must vigilantly guard against being sucked into Systemite thinking or worldliness from spending too much time with them or talking about things other than the Bible. "Love not the world, neither the things [that are] in the world. If any man loves the world, the love of the Father is not in him," says 1 John 2:15.

We are separated from the outside world—in it, but not of it: "Come out from among them and be ye separate, says the Lord, and touch not the unclean thing; and I will receive you" (2 Cor-inthians 6:17). Our friendships are one-sided because we are not equals, for as the Bible says, "Be not unequally yoked together with unbelievers" (2 Corinthians 6:14). Our true friends and family can only be those in our tribe.

We do not have reminders of the outside world in our homes—

nothing to taint us. Outside influence is strictly controlled—no secular music or novels, and just one approved movie per week. The Family produces its own books, music, and education to make sure they align with our beliefs, and we add to it outside religious music and books that Grandpa has approved. The images on our walls are posters of Jesus and Heaven.

All vices are given up—smoking, drugs, excessive drinking, porn. Adults may consume one alcoholic beverage at the weekly movie night. Our young women are supposed to be natural; they can wear makeup but shouldn't be overly concerned with their appearance or trendy clothes. According to Grandpa, "a woman's hair is her crowning glory," so we must grow it long to be attractive for the men.

But unlike most Christian denominations, sex pervades our lives. It is glorified, Godly. Cartoon images of naked women fill our religious literature. The Holy Spirit of the Trinity is a buxom, hot, horny goddess wearing only a heart-shaped bikini held on with pearl strings. Photos of bare-breasted women adorn our monthly newsletters. Instead of covering up, women can show as much skin as is allowed in the countries we live in, and they often wear nothing more than a sarong around the house. Our sex is our service to God. Refusing sex is being hard and selfish, unyielded to God's will. And our absolute obedience is expected.

We have been in our new house for several months when I wake up from a nightmare. I'm a big girl at four—my mother tells me how serious and mature I am for my age, but I still want her when I'm frightened. Searching around in the dark, I see a little flickering light and hear some noise coming from my mother's loft. Trembling, I quietly climb the shaky bamboo ladder. I'm not supposed to be climbing it, and I hope she will forgive me for disobeying and cuddle me instead of swatting me.

As my head peeks over the platform, I see her and my father naked on the mattress. More scared of my father than the bad dream, I hesitate. I'm stuck—afraid to climb back down and afraid to be seen. My mother spots me, and before my father can bark at me to go away, she says, "What's wrong, honey? Are you okay?"

"I had a bad dream," I say, quaking.

"Oh, sweetheart, come here." She plucks me off the unsteady ladder and pulls me over to her mattress on the floorboards of the loft.

My father looks very annoyed at the interruption.

"Would you like to watch a magic trick?" she asks, as if the idea for a great game has just struck her.

I nod, relieved to be allowed to stay.

My mother sits me next to her and kneels beside my father, who is laying on his back, unusually quiet. She begins to stroke his penis up and down.

I watch in surprise as it starts to grow and stand up!

"If you keep doing this, eventually the man will come," she says in her teaching voice.

I watch, fascinated and confused about what it means to "come."

My father grits his teeth with a grunt, and white stuff sprays out of the top of his penis onto his tummy.

"Did you see that!" my mother exclaims. "Like a magic trick."

I stare quietly. *That's gross*, I think, as she uses tissues to wipe it up. But I say nothing.

"Only big boys like your father have semen come out. Little boys like your brothers don't have semen yet."

I nod, taking in the instruction.

"Daddy wants to sleep," she says, glancing at him. "Are you ready to go back to bed?"

"Yes," I say, eager to leave. No one disturbs my father's sleep without painful consequences. She helps me down the ladder and tucks me into my bunk, and we pray together, "Protect and keep us safe, give me a good sleep and good dreams. Send Your angels to guard me." I've forgotten about my nightmare. Somehow, I know that my playmates don't have this knowledge that I've just learned.

I feel odd. And strangely older.

Of course, even though I'd never seen sex that up close before, I already *knew* all about it.

The Mo Letters the adults read at Devotions often have cartoons of nearly nude people, with titles like *Child Brides*, *The Devil Hates Sex*, *God's Whores*, and *God's Witches!—Beware!* "We want our kids to have a healthy, natural attitude about sex and not think it is something to be ashamed of or feel guilty about," Grandpa says. "Sex is Godly and natural. If we introduce it to the kids at a young age, they won't have hang-ups about it like we grew up with."

One of my first coloring books was about sex. It had realistic drawings of a naked, fully aroused man having sex with a woman with a flower crown on her long hair. It had a full-frontal diagram of an open vagina with arrows pointing to the clitoris and urethra, and an equally detailed diagram of a penis and scrotum. "You need to know where babies come from," my mother said as she placed it in my little three-year-old hands.

It was boring to color because most of the comic had to be done in skin tone. A quick once-over with a beige colored pencil that was closest to my own skin color and I could move on to the naked, chubby cherubs floating on hearts that surrounded the couple having sex. One of the coloring pages showed a baby growing inside a naked hippie woman's tummy, and another showed her giving birth. I snickered with pity when I heard that some Systemite kids thought babies were brought by storks or grew in cabbages. *How could they be so stupid? Babies come from sex.*

In his Mo Letters, Grandpa attacks the unhealthy and restrictive American attitudes toward sex. He fondly describes his own early sexual encounters with his nanny as an example of good parenting, telling about how, when he was just a few years old, his South

American nanny used to put him down for his nap by sucking on his *penie*. He proclaimed how he loved it, but one day his mother caught the nanny and fired her. His mother took a bowl and knife and warned him that if she ever caught him playing with his penis, she'd cut it off. Her threats freaked him out, but it didn't stop him from having sex once he figured out how to do it with his cousin at seven years of age.

Since the year before we've been receiving advance chapters from *The Story of Davidito*, the new child training book Davidito's nanny, Auntie Sara, is writing. It describes Grandpa and Mama Maria's ideas for how to raise healthy, Godly kids, with stories from Grandpa's home about how they are educating their young son, Davidito, who is a couple of years older than I.

This handbook provides a detailed description of Davidito's sexual development. Chapter 36, "Learning Fun at 20 Months, Sex!" explains how Auntie Sara puts toddler Davidito to sleep by playing with his penis, just like Grandpa's nanny had done with him when he was a boy.

"He gets quite excited when I wash his bottom and his penie gets real big and hard," she writes. "I kiss it all over till he gets so excited he bursts into laughter and spreads his legs open for more. . . . He got to where he liked it so much, he'd pull people by the hand down onto the floor and would spread his legs apart for 'the treatment.'"

I like to look at the photos of Davidito in the book, curious to know what he is like. In one picture, he is in bed with Auntie Sara, naked with her hand on his thigh next to his penis. There are also bare-breasted pictures of Sue, another of Davidito's nannies, with my young uncle.

Grandpa teaches that sex is pure and Godly and that it has been corrupted as something dirty and shameful by the Devil, who is deceiving God's people. He says that if sex is pure and Godly, then why shouldn't children engage in sex play with each other or with adults? "It's all perfectly innocent after all if it is done with love," he says. While fondling is fine, adult men should wait to have full sex until a girl has entered puberty, at least twelve, because an adult penis might physically damage a young girl if they are too small. It's not loving to act in a way that can cause lasting or severe physical damage. But a boy can engage in sex earlier if he wishes.

It's not a big deal to walk in on my parents having sex, though normally my father will growl, "Get out!" and I run, giggling. I never hear my father talk about sex, but my mother has no problem openly discussing it with any of us.

As a former free-love hippie, my mother readily accepts Grandpa's teachings. When she was growing up in the early 1960s, wife-swapping and nudism were becoming popular. Though no one laid a hand on her as a child, she remembers how, at thirteen, when she was living in Hawaii, her friend's parents walked around their house naked, following a Swedish trend gaining traction in the US. "It was perfectly natural," she recalls. At fifteen, she had a secretarial job at Goodyear and was routinely pushed into closets by men trying to have sex with her. "No one thought anything of it," she tells me.

With sex so casual and open, Patrick and I make up silly sex games when we're supposed to be napping in the middle of the day. ("Only mad dogs and Englishmen go out in the midday sun!" my father says with a laugh when we ask to go outside to play instead of staying in during the hottest hours.) We do Rock, Paper, Scissors to see who will go first. When I win, as I usually do, I lie on my back and stare intently at the diamond shape I make with my fingers in front of my face. It is very important not to look at the other person during this game or it will be too embarrassing to play. Given how open my family is about sex, I don't understand why I still feel embarrassed, like sex should be a secret. If the adults caught us, they'd just chuckle about "how cute that is!" and make fun of us until we are even more embarrassed.

Patrick pulls down my panties and his pants and puts his "pee pee" against my "pum pum" (which are what Mama Maria calls a penis and vagina in the Mo Letters) and bounces up and down like we've seen the adults do. Then we switch places to keep it fair.

I can't see what all the excitement is about for the adults, but it is something to do at naptime and makes us giggle. Us kids are encouraged to experiment with sex as normal behavior. We are told all the time in the Mo Letters and their illustrated version for children, *Kidz True Komics*, that sex is good, normal, and healthy, and that Godly people have lots of it.

In a Mo Letter called *Hooker for Jesus*, there is a picture of a fisherman, who looks a bit like my father, holding a fishing rod with a long line and a large fishhook at the end. A naked woman is stabbed through the chest with his fishing hook. It's her job to wiggle seductively and lure the Fish to bite the hook.

This is Flirty Fishing, which the Family women have been practicing for nearly ten years now. Grandpa says having sex with the Fish demonstrates your ultimate commitment to God and to Jesus: *"HOOK THEM THROUGH HER FLESH! Crucify her flesh, Lord, on the Barb of Thy Spirit! O God, even if it penetrates, and crucify her flesh, impale her on the point of Thy Spirit that she may die, that those that feed of her flesh may be caught to live!"*

The only trick is that the Fisherman must keep a good hold on his pole, or a big Fish might grab the female bait and swim away with her. That can happen if a woman who is FFing falls in love with her Fish and leaves the Family for him rather than the other way around.

Sometimes a Fish might join the Family, but they don't have to; they are fulfilling God's will by providing support and protection that they may not be able to do as effectively if they joined full-time. If we need a piece of equipment or something we can't afford or get donated to us, the women will ask one of their Fish to buy it or give us the money.

On the weekends, my father takes the Family women, including my mothers, to the bar at the Mandarin Hotel in Macau, where Portuguese government officials and wealthy men hang out. They talk to the Systemite men to see if there are any Sheep willing to listen to God's Word and dance with these sexy women. The women are very popular and get approached a lot. If the woman thinks a man is "Sheepy" and would listen about Jesus, she might invite him to have sex. She always tells him that she is spending time with him to save his soul, and the men are usually willing to be saved.

Men can Flirty Fish as well, but Grandpa says it doesn't work as well. While male Fish are usually happy with just sex, female Fish often fall in love and want marriage. Some Family men FF their wives into the Family, but in general, men FFing doesn't fulfill the Family's goals of generating Kings, or wealthy supporters. In his Letters, Grandpa sympathizes with men struggling with jealousy because their wives are FFing, but he is harsh with women who don't want to FF.

While women can't refuse to FF, they can usually choose who they want to FF, unless leadership tells a woman to FF a particular Fish they think is important for the cause. If a leader asks, you don't dare refuse, or you might get publicly rebuked in a Mo Letter.

Before we moved to Hac Sa, I didn't like when my mother went out FFing in the evenings and left me behind at home. When I protested, she would read me the *Kidz True Komics* on FFing to explain why she had to go away and why I needed to be a good soldier and not cry, so she could do her job of winning souls for Jesus. But now I'm old enough to sit quietly when she is with her Fish, so sometimes she takes me with her. We ride in a fancy car with leather seats and all kinds of buttons for the windows and eat at a nice restaurant, where everything is clean and yummy. Then we go back to the man's apartment, and I amuse myself in the living room while they go in the bedroom. I have to be very good on these trips or my mother won't take me with her again.

A lot of the men come and go, but Uncle Ashok is my mother's longtime Fish. He is my favorite and always sneaks me little treats and never spanks me. He's a gentle man, short, but strong and stocky. His family from way back is Indian from Kenya, but he's British through and through, from his tea to his accent. I feel safe and loved in his strong, hairy arms. I'm not afraid of him losing his temper like my father.

He has only one bed, so at night, we all climb in together. I pretend to go to sleep right away so they can get started with sex. My mother doesn't care if I'm awake, but Uncle Ashok does. He is a Sheep, and Systemites can be uncomfortable with having sex in front of a child. It's easy enough to turn to the wall and pretend that I'm asleep while the bed shakes and he grunts on top of my mother.

My mother enjoys going FFing—dressing up in a pretty dress and putting on makeup and perfume and flirting like Grandpa instructs. She doesn't mind sleeping with some of her Fish, but she doesn't like to sleep with Uncle Ashok. When she thinks I'm not listening, I've heard her tell my father she's just not attracted to Uncle Ashok; it's a trial for her. Still, it's her duty.

My mother tells me that this is about the love of God. That sometimes women must sacrifice their own personal likes or desires to show God's love to a man who needs it even if she finds him unattractive. I shudder. A few times I have seen her crying before she needs to sleep with a man and I know she is upset about it, but she knows that God is happy with her when she does it.

I obediently repeat my memory verse, 1 Corinthians 1:19–20, to my mother: "For ye are not your own; ye are bought with a price, therefore glorify God in your body and in your spirit, which are God's."

"Do you know what that means?" she asks. I shake my head. "It means that you belong to God. Each of us does. We can't do what we want. We must do what God wants. God owns our bodies. So, if he asks us to wash the dishes, or go witnessing, or even have sex with a Fish, then we must obey God, even if we don't feel like it." I nod. I'm not sure I understand, but I know I'm supposed to.

There is no difference between men and women in God's eyes—we are all equal, Grandpa teaches. In the Family, unlike many of the System churches, women can even be top leaders. But women are still the helpmeet for the man—there to "help his meat," Grandpa says, laughing—and must always show their yieldedness and submission to God by being willing to sacrifice their bodies to God and submit to the men in the community, giving them sex when they need it. So, a woman should not refuse to sleep with any man who asks her, even if she finds him unattractive. This is particularly true with Flirty Fishing.

I'm not sure I understand it all, but I try to be a brave soldier for Jesus and not cry when my mother goes out at night and leaves me behind.

3

IT TAKES A VILLAGE

As Mary and I lay side by side on our bed, her cold toes touch my left leg. I kick her and whisper-yell, "Your foot is on my side of the bed!"

A few minutes later, I turn over sleepily and feel a painful pinch on my arm. "Ow!" I sit up, angry.

"Your arm was on my side," Mary snaps.

"It was not!" I hotly deny.

"Was to."

"Was not!"

I don't like sharing a bed; my bed is the only space I have that's my own. Mary and I agreed that if either of us goes on the other person's half of the bed, we're allowed to punish them, only we can't agree on exactly where the halfway line is in our sleep. In a brush of genius, we take a broom and, after carefully measuring for the exact middle of the bed, lay the pole between us. Satisfied, we can fall sleep. Now, we know if we hit the hard broom handle, our limb has strayed too far.

Mary and I have been moved into the small room behind the living room. Our double bed touches the wall on three sides. There is only enough room for a dresser, which has four drawers, two for each of us to hold all our belongings. They are half-empty.

My father wants to annex the small house next to ours on the opposite side from the Cottage—the Pink House. But first he plans to finish the renovations on the Main House, which are moving along thanks to help from Uncle Daniel and my father's two Chinese workers, who we've given the biblical English names John and Peter. Even though they are not in the Family, they take new names since they're easier for us to remember. Already, they have fixed the roof and plastered the second, long room of our house for my brothers to sleep. Next, they will enclose our front yard to create a large indoor patio that can be a dining room and a larger kitchen.

My father and Uncle Daniel mark out the border of our new patio with tent stakes in the dirt in front of our house. A truck dumps a load of small red bricks out front, and the guys go to work. I watch as my father and Uncle Daniel use shovels to mix water into a gray powder that becomes a thick gravelly paste—cement.

Sherck layer of cement, brick, *Sherck* layer of cement, brick—on and on all through the hot, sticky day. I watch the wall rise in front of our house.

Very satisfied with the progress on the wall, we go to bed. The next morning, I see my father outside in the early light scratching his head. The wall has fallen, and bricks are scattered around. *Maybe it's the wind?* He and Uncle Daniel go to work again and build it back up. But the next morning, the same. The scattered bricks have cement footprints through them that follow the footpath through what is supposed to become our dining room. It seems a person, not the wind, has destroyed our hard work. But who? And why? The villagers have been relatively friendly to us.

My father asks Cap San, the village elder. Cap San has a big chicken farm on the other side of the village and lives in the only other modern two-story house in the village aside from our landlord, Lok Keen. But he just shrugs. No one will fess up. My father suspects the culprit is a neighbor we call Tiger. Tiger is a gruff middle-aged man who we've spotted nearby in the wake of a few of the stone-throwing incidents.

After the third time the wall is knocked down, my father ponders the situation. It doesn't matter that where we are trying to build is part of our property and we have permission from our landlord. There are no building codes or rhyme to the patchwork of mud houses here anyway. They just don't like change in a village that has not had outsiders in a hundred years. The villagers are used to walking through this yard and don't want to change their normal route.

My father tries a new tactic. He lays one layer of brick around the perimeter. The next morning it's undisturbed, so he leaves it for a few days. Then he and Daniel lay a second layer of brick. Still nothing happens—the cement hardens.

A few days later, he puts a third layer of brick around the wall, which is now barely a foot tall. It is still low enough for the villagers to easily step over, but it is slowly inching higher. After six months, he eventually finishes the tall brick walls that now enclose our front yard, and it stands strong. Once the metal corrugated roof and plastic mosquito screens are added, the large space becomes our dining and activity room.

"It just took some time for our neighbors to get used to the idea of change and learn to walk around the wall, instead of through it," my father explains with a big smile.

Most of the villagers appreciate the work we've done to clean up the neighborhood, and we are slowly forming friendships. Lok Keen's kids, Ah Gong and Amy, are about my brothers' age, and we have started having them over to our house to learn English and play.

Each time we see our neighbors, they greet us with "*Sik fan*," which means "Eat rice" or "Did you eat yet?" But I prefer to say, "*Jo san!*" for good morning, instead of answering truthfully (usually "no"), because then they will immediately invite me into their yard for a bite of food. This can be dangerous, as I can never be sure what they might stuff in my mouth with their chopsticks!

I learned this the hard way. Lok Keen had a new black puppy

that was a big fluff ball we called Fluffy. All of us kids would sneak over to his yard any chance we got to play with roly-poly Fluffy. One day, Lok Keen's wife saw me walking by and called out, *"Sik fan le mei ou?"* Have you eaten? I shook my head no, so she fed me some chunks of meat and rice from her bowl. It was a bit chewy but tasted okay. When I was done eating, I looked around for my playmate and asked, "Where is Fluffy?"

She laughed and pointed to her bowl.

"No!!!"

For weeks after, I wouldn't walk by Lok Keen's house and felt tears prick my eyes when I thought of the quiet, empty yard.

The summer heat is cooling into fall when one afternoon Caleb spots someone wandering up the driveway. Six feet tall and stocky, the brown-haired, pale-skinned, shirtless British man dripping in sweat stands out like a lighthouse. The man spots us and waves his arms over his head.

"Hey," Hobo shouts. "Look, it's Uncle Michael!"

We run to him, excited to see one of our Family caregivers from Macau. My father waits at the door, his mouth a flat line.

"I was doing a bit o' exploring, and who should I happen on but a group of blond kiddies in the middle of a Chinese village." He winks at us, tousling the boys' sweaty hair, passing it off as a chance discovery. But my father is not fooled. We are living a secret adventure, and Michael wants in. While my parents no longer hold top leadership roles, Family people still want to be around Grandpa's flesh and blood.

Since arriving in Hac Sa, we've been trying to prevent those left behind in Macau from learning our location and tipping off reporters. "Loose lips sink ships" is one of my father's favorite sayings, and other Family members can be the worst security leaks. My father is concerned that if the other Family members know where we are, he won't be able to keep them from visiting and perhaps being followed by reporters on the hunt for a good story.

But his annoyance with Michael's unannounced visit is pushed aside by Mommy Esther's relief. As the main caregiver, she is exhausted. My brothers are perpetual-motion machines, running, fighting, and arguing, getting into dirt and scrapes, and she's at her wit's end. This is the first time she hasn't had full-time helpers to care for them.

Our father will watch the boys only when he feels like it, taking them outside to burn off energy for a few hours. Unlike other Family men, he doesn't cook, do cleanup, or take care of kids, unless he chooses to. Gender roles aren't distinct, and no one says you can't do a particular thing because you are a woman. After all, the Bible says, "There is no male or female in Jesus Christ" (Galatians 3:28). Men are supposed to be willing to do any work around the home, same as the women, although I never see a woman drive, do construction work, or handle the home finances. Male guitarists lead our inspirations, as well as witnessing and provisioning teams (because they drive), so women must do more housework and childcare.

As far as my father is concerned, the tough stuff, like making the kids sit still for meals, school, or cleanup, falls to the other adults in the household. Mommy Ruthie helps, but she also has the responsibility of editing the Mo Letters. Grace is busy with baby Colum, though she helps with cleaning and cooking when she can, and Daniel lends a hand when he's not working with my father on a building project. That leaves the lion's share to Mommy Esther, who is not shy about her need for help.

Uncle Michael is a calm, patient presence, she insists, convincing my father to allow him to stay. So, Uncle Michael joins our hideout band as our new caregiver, "You can call me 'governor,'" he says with a jolly smile. "That's what we call a male nanny in England, where I come from, governors and governesses."

With Uncle Michael here and the weather finally cooling off, Mommy Esther declares we must organize some sort of schooling again. The Family is proud of its early-education focus, using Montessori and Glenn Doman methods to teach children to read starting at one year old. At four and a half, I'm a late learner. Mommy Ruthie has tried to teach me a few times, but it's ended in tears of frustration for both of us, as it does when she tries to teach me almost anything. So, I color quietly with Patrick while my older siblings sit with Uncle Michael for two hours of homeschool a few times a week.

Back in the city, my siblings attended the Catholic Santa Rosa Elementary School, which was the only school in the city that taught in English. My parents decided to send them there after Grandpa had released the Mo Letter *Becoming One*, which encouraged missionaries to become one with the locals by participating in local Christian schools. But after two years, my parents were not pleased with the education. "We thought it would be a chance for you kids to pick up the local language from your Chinese classmates, but instead the only thing you seemed to learn was to lie and swear in Cantonese," Mommy Esther often laments.

I never attended the school, but as far as I can tell, Chinese kids are very tame compared to my brothers. Tales from their school days in Macau are already family legend—like the time Josh came home with only one eyebrow. "I was minding my own business when one of the boys ran past me in the hallway with a razor and shaved it off!" he told our father, not wanting to confess that he'd shaved it off himself on a dare. But the tale that beat them all was when the boys came home with Josh's backpack full of "onions" for dinner, only to find out after our father got a very angry call from the school that the boys had dug up all the newly planted flower bulbs. They all got a serious walloping for that stunt.

"You don't need a System school education anyway," my father says. "They only teach a bunch of lies, like evolution. Learn to read so you can read the Mo Letters and basic math to add, subtract, divide, and multiply, in case you need to do the Home finances one day. Science you can learn from seeing it happen in real life with the farm and garden. Everything else you need to learn is practical: witnessing, cleaning, cooking, and taking care of babies. Your grandpa pulled me out of school when I was twelve to become a full-time missionary and start the Revolution! It didn't hurt me one bit."

Despite our father's dismissal, our mothers agree that we need at least a basic sixth-grade education. The question is how? Hac Sa feels like the end of the world; there are no English bookstores to pop into and buy grammar books. Mommy Esther decides to mail-order the English Calvert and Super Workbook textbooks that American homeschoolers use. At least Uncle Michael follows a curriculum of the three R's: Reading, 'Riting and 'Rithmetic.

As the first kids born into the Family, we are the guinea pigs for everything. The adults try to figure out how to give us a basic education in line with the Family's changing beliefs. Esther makes sure to send updates to the *Family News* about what we are doing in education so other new parents can follow. Family Care, a division that produces our child educational materials, sends us Family readers, comics, flannelgraphs, and story tapes for us children to learn the Bible and Mo Letters, the main focus of our education.

My father, always on the lookout for more space, gets permission for us to use an abandoned wooden shack behind the village temple. Our parents set up a makeshift classroom with some plywood tables and benches. When it's too hot, we move our benches outside to sit under the huge fiscus tree, but in winter we all huddle around a single kerosene heater. My rambunctious brothers dread the hours they're forced to sit at their desks, copying sentences or math problems from the chalkboard. So, when our father stops by for volunteers to paint the shed, the boys are off like a shot and Uncle Michael is forced to let out lessons for the day. My father says the most important lessons are the practical ones.

The comforts of city life seem like a distant memory, and I find that I like being outside, even if I am doing chores most of the time. And with all the space we have, I am mostly able to stay out of my father's way and avoid punishment, which is fortunate since he has a terrifying temper.

He has two speeds, happy and mad, and that switch can flip without warning. One moment he'll be laughing and playing, taking us on fun adventures to the beach; the next second, one of my brothers is dangling on his toes as our father grips him painfully by the back of the neck. Anything less than instant obedience, even forgetting to say, "Yes, sir," can set him off.

We are all scared of him when he gets mad; usually just the threat is enough to get us to behave properly. He has a paddle that he uses for spankings that he carved from a wooden two-by-four with the words "Rod of God" burned into the handle, just like the one the principal at his elementary school in Texas used when he was a boy. The spankings hurt, but at least he never punches us or breaks a bone.

As Grandpa taught him, he spanks us on the soft tissue of our bottoms where we might get welts but not permanent injury. Similar with pinching our arms, squeezing pressure points on the backs of our necks, an open palm smack in the face, or a knuckle to the head. All designed to cause maximum pain without leaving a permanent injury. This is "Godly child-rearing."

Sometimes one of my mothers' Fish or government official friends will invite our whole family to dinner. If we are eating at a restaurant, something we might do once or twice a month, and one of the boys starts getting too rowdy, our father can't haul off and smack him in public like he would at home. Instead, he thickly spreads Tabasco sauce on a piece of bread and hands it to the culprit, saying through clenched teeth, "Eat it all."

We watch expectantly as the boy's face gets redder and redder and silent tears and snot run down his face as he unwillingly gulps down the punishing chunks. We feel a little sorry for him but admire him for the feat of strength. We know it is harder than taking a smack because your mouth will burn for a *looong* time, no matter how much water you drink.

My mother and Mommy Esther occasionally discipline us with a few swats with a hairbrush or a time-out, but for anything serious, we are sent to my father. Once it's in his hands, they stand by helplessly with an "it's up to your father now" attitude.

Only a few times has my mother stepped in and stood up to my father when she thinks he has gone too far, like throwing one of the boys against a wall. Mommy Esther never speaks up to defend them, though, and I can tell Josh resents her for it.

I don't get spanked very often, especially in comparison to Josh. He thinks it's because Mommy Ruthie protects me. He gives me extra elbow jabs and cutting comments to make up for it. But the truth is I've watched so many spankings, I've learned to avoid the worst of them. And my mother tells me that I learned fast.

"When you were six months old, you used to throw temper tantrums. I was a new mom and didn't know how to handle you. Esther instructed me to spank you really, really hard. You were so shocked. I felt guilty, but after that you never threw another tantrum. Now you just pout."

Yes, I do. Whenever I feel so angry and hurt I want to scream, I go completely silent, arms crossed tight over my chest, refusing to speak to anyone. My parents call it sulking. No smiles or teasing can jolly me out of it. My silence screams in a house full of noisy kids.

Of course, sometimes you just have to cry.

"It itches!" I wail.

It's at 3:00 a.m., and I am running to my mother, frantically scratching my bottom.

Mommy Ruthie sighs groggily and says, "Turn over and pull down your panties. Let me look." She finds tiny, white wriggly worms in my anus and confirms it's pinworms.

"I'm not surprised," responds Mommy Esther, woken by the commotion. "The kids have their grubby little paws in the dirt all day, picking up trash or playing with the dogs."

"This is why we keep telling you kids not to bite your nails or pick your nose! The worm eggs in the dirt get into your mouth and hatch in your tummy," Mommy Ruthie lectures.

It's not the first time we've heard this lecture. If one of us has worms, we all have them. When we got them in Macau one time, Mommy Ruthie bought a small, nasty-tasting pill that we all had to swallow. The itching went away, and a few weeks after that we took the second dose to kill any eggs that may have hatched.

But upon this diagnosis, Mommy Esther exclaims, "I read in the *Family News* that if you eat only coconut for three days, it will cure you! This way we don't need the System medicine!"

The adults are always pulling natural healing remedies from the testimonies that arrive in the Mo Letters and *Family News*.

When we all came down with the measles and were stuck in bed, covered in red, itchy spots with a high fever, our parents didn't take us to the hospital. "There is nothing the doctors can do. Just drink your onion-garlic broth and I'll pray over you again," Mommy Esther said as she dipped her finger in canola cooking oil and drew an oily cross on my forehead. "Now don't wipe it off."

According to Grandpa, doctors and medicine are as likely to kill you as help you. He won't even go to the hospital for his bad heart. He does admit, though, that there are a few mechanical fixes that doctors are useful for, like setting broken bones, stitches, and some surgeries. For other things, we need to just trust Jesus. So, when someone gets sick, we follow the biblical prescription to gather the elders of the church (in our case, our parents) and lay hands on the afflicted person, anointing them with oil and praying over them, "Dear Lord, You are the greatest doctor in the universe. Please touch and heal Faithy and take away the measles. We command healing in Your name. Amen. Praise God!" In a week, we were better.

So, when we get pinworms, the adults are eager to prove they have no need to rely on System doctors when God has provided a natural remedy. For the next three days, seven kids are force-fed chunks of dry coconut for breakfast, lunch, and dinner.

"I can't eat any more coconut!" I wail, real tears coming now. My jaw aches from trying to chew the dry husks that make my stomach hurt. *No wonder this is supposed to cure pinworms. Is it supposed to starve them out, so they leave to find food?*

After seventy-two hours of starving, crying, hungry kids who can't face another square of coconut, natural medicine is forced to give in. We all still have pinworms.

Our parents finally admit defeat and pick up the medicine at the pharmacy in Coloane Village. Never have I been so eager to swallow a nasty-tasting pill and get back to real food. But the adults are disappointed. They think that needing to go to the doctor shows that their faith is not strong enough for the miracle of God's healing. But there are some things they haven't found a natural remedy for, and pinworms, it seems, is one of them.

During the spring monsoons and the summer typhoons, the whole village struggles with flooding. The water rushes from the sky as if the house is sitting under a waterfall, and sometimes I swing my legs groggily out of bed to land ankle-deep in ice water. My father, brothers, Uncle Michael, and Uncle Jeff, a tall American who has come to stay with us, are working with Cap San, the local village elder, and his laborers to dig ditches and drains around all the village houses to protect us from the worst of it.

Our friends in the Portuguese government agree to supply us with culverts, pipes, and materials if we will do the installation. So, our father decides to fix our water problem at the same time. We dig ditches along the side of the dirt lane and lay the water pipes from the village to the main road, so the municipal government can finally hook up the village to a clean consistent water supply from the reservoir.

Our joy at getting connected to public utilities is temporarily dampened when everyone's water pipes explode. The city water pressure is too strong for the ancient pipes compared to the village catchment that we've been using to collect rainwater from the mountain. We pitch in with Cap San's workers to get plumbing pieces and water pipes to replace the broken ones in the villagers' houses.

Despite our cheery waves, Cap San has been rather cool toward us, but after months of sweaty labor installing new pipes for half the village, even Cap San reluctantly thaws and now greets us with *"Sik fan"* when we pass. Our parents praise Jesus for softening his heart. I'm just glad that when I try to wash my hands after a rainstorm the water doesn't spurt red with mud anymore.

We know we've made good headway with our new neighbors when on my fifth birthday the villagers invite us to their annual village dinner for Communist Labor Day, which the villagers stubbornly celebrate despite Macau's status as a Portuguese colony. The event is held in a makeshift square surrounded by red light strings and colorful banners painted with Chinese characters. Eight or nine huge round tables are set out in a square, with ten to twelve people per table. Our family, Patrick's family, and Uncle Jeff and Uncle Michael, who did much of the construction work, have been invited. We all sit at different tables, mixing with the village families and stuffing ourselves on the delicious fourteen-course meal, until even my brothers' bottomless-pit stomachs can't hold another bite.

My father's laugh booms louder. Mommy Esther's face is less pinched. Our goal has been accomplished. Now we don't have to worry about nosy reporters following us home; we can drop our pointy hats and secrecy. Once the closed villagers accept you, they are fierce defenders of their own. The village is our home, their children our playmates. When I see white tourists climb off the bus at Hac Sa beach, I point with the villagers and laugh at the strange *gweilos*.

4

DON'T WORK FOR MONEY, HONEY

Before the persecution that sent us into hiding, we performed regularly in Hong Kong and Macau—restaurants, holiday festivals, prisons, the refugee camp for Vietnamese boat people escaping the Communist regime, schools, orphanages, anywhere we can share Jesus's love—to witness and raise money.

While my father receives a small stipend of $1,000 per month to pay for the property rents and some basic food, it's not enough to cover all our expenses for two families and renovations, and no one in the Family would ever work at a System job for filthy lucre. I can hear my father's preacher's voice saying, "You cannot serve God and Mammon." That would be selling out to the World. We raise money by passing out literature and asking for donations. God provides what we need if we pray and stay in His Will by being obedient to His Prophet, Grandpa, and witnessing.

The public has a short attention span, and my father feels the bad publicity has died down enough for us to return to some of our regular weekend busking spots to earn some needed money.

At breakfast today he tells us that we are going into Macau to sing.

"Do you think it's okay?" Mommy Esther questions, concern creasing her forehead.

"We will just be very careful that no one follows us home, no different than what we've been doing whenever we go into town for shopping," he asserts.

Of course, this is different than a quiet trip into town to pick up supplies. When we go out as a family, we draw a lot of attention. Everyone in Macau recognizes us. We are seven blond singing kids, like the von Trapp family in *The Sound of Music*, but for China.

I'm excited to return to Macau to sing. I have been onstage with my brothers and sister as long as I can remember. My mother says the first time, I was not even two years old. My brothers and Mary were singing up on the stage and I started dancing in the aisle, my fat diaper bouncing. I was stealing the show, so she lifted me onstage and that was it. Back then we often performed on the main Hong Kong and Macau TV channel, TVB Pearl, as well as on radio shows and huge live-televised performances.

We sang at the Hong Kong governor's Christmas tree lighting and all the Chinese New Year events just a year before we moved here, but that was before the first big persecution. The very next week, after we went home to Macau, we were quietly banned from Hong Kong. My parents heard a rumor that officials from America agitated the Hong Kong government to put all known Family members on the immigration blacklist, even babies. They heard the local Baptist and Catholic churches strongly supported the move. My parents called it a witch hunt. *How can a baby deserve to be on a blacklist?*

I didn't understand. They hadn't charged us with any crime, but it seems our beliefs had earned us a spot on the country's unofficial blacklist. We are permitted to enter Hong Kong for only twenty-four hours at a time, and we must convince the immigration officer that doing so is for necessary business, like renewing our passports or accessing the airport, as there are no airports or embassies in Macau.

We used to sing so often we didn't need to practice unless we were learning a new song or skit. But it has been a while since we've been onstage, so Mommy Esther organizes a practice session. After Devotions, she gets out her acoustic guitar to accompany us. We all line up, from oldest to youngest, in our T-shirts, shorts, and flip-flops. Our everyday clothes are hand-me-downs by Family members or donations; only the clothes we wear for performances and singing appearances are purchased new with our busking money. I will get to change into my special clothes later, but for now I'm wearing my favorite dress, a simple gingham, blue-and-white-checked dress that came in a donation box. The dress is old and stained, but I love how the skirt spins out flat around me when I twirl. My mother keeps trying to throw it away, and I keep fishing it out of the garbage when she turns her back.

Mommy Esther plays the guitar and coaches our voices as we run through our repertoire. Mommy Ruthie stands in front of us, demonstrating the hand motions that act out the words of the songs and helping us with some simple choreography.

Before setting off for the city that evening, we pray, "Keep us safe on the roads, and protect us from any accidents or bad drivers." Everyone is wary of persecutors and journalists.

Our white Dodge van pulls up in front of the Hotel Lisboa and Casino, Stanley Ho's opulent twelve-story hotel on Lisboa Avenue, and all ten of us clamber out.

Stanley Ho, Macau's most powerful man, is a respectable mobster who owns all the casinos and famously has multiple wives and more than a dozen children. Polygamy was part of Chinese culture until Mao banned it, and child brides, in 1950. Even the straitlaced British only banned polygamy in Hong Kong in 1971. The Portuguese have a "live and let live" attitude, as well as a long history of mistresses. My father is openly envied by our male Systemite friends, who can't figure out how he got two beautiful women to agree to marry him. Since his name is also Mr. Ho, he gets a knowing smirk from the local officials, who compare him to the other Mr. Ho with many wives.

The Jade Garden, a fancy Chinese restaurant inside the Lisboa Hotel, is just one of the places where we used to perform regularly.

Today, Mary and I wear dark green velvet dresses shaped like a bell, and the boys are wearing button-down shirts and dark blue pants. I look up curiously at the familiar flashing neon lights. It's good to be back in the city. *Will people remember us? Will they let us sing?* I worry.

As we walk through the lobby of the Hotel Lisboa in our matching singing outfits, a Chinese man calls out our family name in Cantonese. I turn and smile and wave like I've been taught. A young Chinese woman rushes over with her camera and grabs me off the floor, shoving her camera into her friend's hands. I smile politely, posing for the photo while my parents wait with indulgent looks.

I learned long ago to never get upset or show displeasure when people grab us for photos on the street, no matter what mood I'm in. "You need to be a good sample of God's love!" my father scolded angrily after I grumpily refused to smile in a photo for border guards in China one time.

The crease of concern on Mommy Esther's face melts away as she asks for the manager of the Jade Garden and he gives us an enthusiastic greeting.

The waitresses in their long green Chinese *chi pau* (traditional dress with little buttons trailing up the side to the high collar and a slit all the way up the thigh) crowd around, laughing, touching our hair, and trying to pick me up. The manager finally shoos them back to work, and we follow him, weaving through the food-covered tables to the center of the round room. My Mary Janes race to keep up, struggling to turn away from the temptation of so much yummy food at eye level.

Fifty large round tables create concentric circles widening out from where we stand on a slightly raised circular platform in the center. The green carpet muffles our stomping feet but does nothing to dampen the din of hundreds of Cantonese voices and clashing cutlery. The china bowls clatter louder than the slap of mah-jongg tiles in a gambling den. Singing without a microphone is a shouting match—us against them. But we know if they like it, they will quiet down.

We line up in the cramped space between the tables, with Mommy Esther and her guitar behind us. She strums her guitar once to alert us, saying under her breath, "One, two, one, two, three . . ."

"Sai zhong shu shan ga liang tai!" we belt out in unison, and we're off, twisting, singing and smiling with all our might. This song is one of my favorites. It is not a witnessing song. It is a funny Cantonese song about a guy who gets dressed up in a new shirt and tie and goes out and all the girls go crazy for him. Then he goes and changes into a new outfit and does it again.

Hundreds of faces stare at us in surprise, but the audience soon starts clapping and laughing with us. Bones, our family clown, is twisting out in front and hamming it up with facial expressions, pretending he has all the girls fawning over him.

For most of the songs we just do hand motions—pointing to Heaven, hand over the heart, arms spread toward the audience to welcome them to Jesus—but there are a couple like this one where we rock out.

I spot my father in between the tables, facing us. He has his camera raised and is giving us the gimlet eye, with his mouth stretched into a grin so wide he looks like a grimacing skeleton. That is how he reminds us to smile bigger, bigger, wider, more! Otherwise, we know what will happen when we get home. I stretch my smile until my cheeks hurt and twist lower and more forcefully until I'm out of breath.

After "Sai Zhong Liang Tai" ("Cool Suit, Beautiful Tie"), we roll straight into "Do, Re, Mi." We are lined up in order of our ages. I'm the youngest, at the end of the line. For the chorus, we each sing a line. Nehi starts low with "Doe, a deer, a female deer." Until it gets to me at the end with "Tea, a drink with jam and bread!" It is my only solo line, and it's super high. My voice sounds like a mouse squeak in my ears.

We sing popular songs like "Twist" and "Yellow Submarine" in English and "It's a Small World" in Cantonese, mixed with some religious songs. But we always end every performance by inviting the audience to be Saved by singing with us, "Come into my heart, come into my heart, come into my heart, Lord Jeeeesus. Come in today, come in to stay, come into my heart, Lord Jeeesus." We repeat the song over and over in Cantonese and English, sometimes in Portuguese, depending on the audience, until we can get the crowd singing with us.

I look meaningfully into the eyes of individuals in the audience, so they know I am singing directly to them and that Jesus wants to be in their heart. From the stage, we try to count how many people are singing it with us, so the adults can put in their witnessing report the number of souls we saved for Jesus. After our final song, we join hands, swing them, and take a bow, then file offstage very proud of ourselves.

After we finish our repertoire, we walk around to the tables in teams of two, shaking the diners' hands and collecting the money they give us. I am the youngest and the cutest, so people always want to shake my hand and give me money. I always remember to say, *"Doh geh"* ("Thank you") and *"Yesu oi lei"* ("Jesus loves you"). We also have our own album, *The Ho Family Singers*, as a cassette tape we sell at the tables for 30 patacas, or $5.

My velvet dress has big pockets, so I can usually make it around the restaurant without having to take the cash from my pockets and give it to Daddy. If we do have to empty our pockets midway, that is a very good night. Mary and I try to sneak to the bathroom after our rounds so we can count how much money we made before the adults take it. Then we compare our take. I usually win. I would never keep even a single coin, though. I would be dead scared. All money belongs to God . . . but only the adults can use it. The adults check our pockets before we go home, and if any of us are caught with money, we get spanked.

When it comes to money, we are to rely on God for His provision, not on man. "If we do God's work, He will provide for us," Grandpa says. We cannot have jobs or anything that might take priority over our service for God or draw our loyalty away from the Family. Performing is a way God can provide through donations.

Without financial security or consistency, the ability to feel safe or plan for the future, we have to stay completely dependent on God for everything. Any doubts or mistakes that might keep us from God also threaten our livelihood and ability to survive. We must follow the Word of the prophet closely so that God will continue to provide for us physically. Any thought of relying on ourselves or income we control is rebellion against God.

Ten percent of any money we receive we must send to Grandpa to help support his Home and all the people who work on the Mo Letters, since they must stay *Selah* and can't go out witnessing. All Family Homes are required to send their tithe with a mandatory monthly report called the Tither's Report Form (or TRF) to the head office. These offices are called World Services (WS), the administrative homes of the Family where finances, publications, and special projects are handled.

Each country or region has a WS Home, but the locations are a closely guarded secret. When people go to WS, they can disappear for years. They cannot leave or even call their own children to protect the secret. Macau is too small for a WS Home (it would be nearly impossible to operate one without detection), so we send our TRFs to the WS Home in Japan. TRFs must include detailed accounting of all income, expenses, members' personal information, and outreach statistics. A Home that fails to submit a TRF will be excommunicated, cut off from the source of God's Word and fellowship. No one wants to be labeled a "Backslider," a person who has turned their back on God and slid back into the cesspit of the System.

After our regular singing spots, we try to get into a few other restaurants around town. Sometimes they let us sing, but often as not we are turned away by a brusque manager. The adults always perkily say, "Oh well, let's try the next place. They have missed God's blessing." But I look down at the floor, embarrassed, as we are ushered out. I know that we are here to give them a special blessing from God, but when we are turned away, I feel like a beggar.

No matter how upset I feel, I forget about it when I am singing. Then there is only the audience and bringing them into the songs.

Tonight has been a good one, and after four hours of singing, my father gets us each an ice-cream bar as a reward. "Ice cream! Ice cream!" Our tired voices revive for one last push.

"I scream, you scream, we all scream for ice cream," Hobo says, and soon we are all chanting it.

"Quiet!" my father yells. "The next person who talks won't get any!" We all get quiet waiting as he gives us each a chocolate-covered vanilla-ice-cream bar on a stick.

As we clamber over each other back into the van, we are silent and exhausted, our voices dry from shouting out the songs in noisy restaurants. "You kids did great tonight. Praise the Lord. He really provided," our father's deep voice intones, as he executes a series of sharp turns down dark alleys to ensure no one is following us before heading home.

"Yes, and I counted at least a hundred people who received Jesus by singing along with you!" Mommy Esther cheers us on. "I know it was a long night. You kids were real soldiers. Even little Faithy. It was good we came tonight."

When the media remains quiet after our busking foray into Macau, we relax slightly, glad we can return to witnessing, although we know the threat of negative publicity is never truly gone.

5

TRAIN UP A CHILD

It's no secret that my father has grand plans to re-create the farm experience he had as a kid at the Ranch. And now with the village in working order, he is ready to put his plan into action.

"Kids, I have a surprise for you," my father calls out as the spring warmth chases away the winter. He opens a cardboard box as we gather around. There are tiny chirping sounds. He pulls out a small, dirty white fluff ball and places it in my cupped palms. Its tiny, sharp talons poke my six-year-old hands, but I'm mesmerized. "Daddy, what is it?"

"These are baby geese," he says as he hands one to nine-year-old Mary and the last one to Aaron, who is now ten. "They are cute now, but they will grow up to be good guard animals."

I want to put my face to the fluffy fur, but I'm hesitant of its pointy beak. I hold it very still, trying to calm it. "Don't worry," I say as it wiggles, trying to escape. "You're safe here." I smile with pride as the little chick settles in my arms. I can't wait to show Patrick!

"It's you kids' responsibility to feed and take care of these goslings. Can you do that?"

"Yes, Daddy," we chorus.

Mary and I sprinkle feed in their box every day. We let them out to run around and get some exercise, but we always put them back in their box, then eventually their cage, so the wild dogs in the neighborhood don't eat them.

After five months, my father praises our results: "You girls are doing very good taking care of your geese. You don't need to worry about a dog getting them now." He laughs, seeing the huge gray-and-white geese flapping their wings and honking menacingly at one of the neighbor's dogs who wanders close to our farmyard.

The older boys are annoyed at the extra work hosing down the goose poop that drops all over the yard. But Mary and I ignore their complaints. For once we each have our own pets that we raised from babies, even if they are too big to pet now, unlike our Dobermans, who belong to everyone.

One evening a few weeks later, as we all gather around the dinner table, Josh and Caleb are nudging each other. I notice Aaron is staring miserably into his bowl.

"What smells so good?" I ask.

"It's goose!" Josh crows evilly.

"My goose? You killed my goose!" I scream.

"Quiet!" my father shouts. Then more softly, "It was time, girls. Animals are for food when you live on a farm. They are not pets. Don't get attached to them. You need to learn this young."

The three geese had become a nuisance in the village, so it was time to let them go, and our father saw it as an opportunity to teach us a good lesson about life on a farm.

Mary and I gaze at each other helpless in horror as our geese are served up. We shake our heads when offered a piece of meat, thankful the adults don't force us to eat like they normally would. Staring down at our empty plates, tears streaming down our faces, neither of us can imagine eating our pets.

The twins chow down on their drumsticks, smacking their lips extra loudly while staring at Mary and me.

"Cannibals," I mouth at them. Mary and I are for once united in hatred. The retaliation I might normally execute—dumping a basket of leaves on their head, putting frogs in their bed—seems paltry against the magnitude of their crime and my broken heart. But I learn his lesson.

When my father unloads a truck of goats from China, which are later joined by a crate of chicks; a coup of pigeons, myna birds, and parakeets; and a baby calf, I tamp down my excitement. I can enjoy them but not love them. Death is always around the corner.

Hoping to distract me from the loss of my pet, my mother takes my hand. "Want to come see what Uncle Ashok is working on?"

Uncle Ashok has been working for weeks now in one of the old sheds in the area that used to be the garbage dump.

I hear a roar and chugging sounds that get louder as we approach the shed at the top of the farmyard. By the time we enter, the roaring is so loud, I could not be heard shouting over it.

Uncle Ashok's sweaty back is facing us as he tinkers with a monster machine that is bigger than he is. I cower a little, covering my ears with my hands. His strong hands, covered in pink burns and black grease, lay down the metal wrench to lift me over his head. He hits a button and the noise sputters out.

"What do you think?" he asks, smiling into my face.

"What is it?" I ask, still shocked and confused.

"This is your new generator. I made it from a diesel taxi engine," he says proudly, in his posh British accent.

Uncle Ashok, one of the best engineers in the city, builds Formula One race cars for the Grand Prix. Of course he would know you could make a generator out of an old car engine.

"That's amazing!" My mother leans in to give him a kiss on the mouth.

It is going to be very noisy, but the steady source of electricity will allow us to finally, after over a year with almost no electricity, have a refrigerator again, so we don't have to buy our fresh food daily and can run lights and fans during the night. Before long, Uncle Ashok's taxi engine generator is powering half the village.

Ah Gong and Amy, Lok Keen's kids, come over to our house to enjoy the perks of our new electricity. Most days, they play hide-and-seek with us, but sometimes they learn English seated around the green, water-warped ping-pong table that doubles as our school and dining table. My brothers chat easily with them in Cantonese, but I'm struggling to remember the words. At six, I am still shooed away by my brothers when I try to tag along with them as they roam the village, so I console myself playing Matchbox cars and Playmobil with Patrick.

Of course, there are some problems with having neighbor kids as playmates. On their way home from public school, they stop off at the snack cart outside the school gates to buy candy. Our parents warn us repeatedly about the evils of white sugar, and that if it's offered, we should accept politely and throw the candy away later. But if Mommy Esther doesn't see Lok Keen's wife slip me a Sunburst, I'll hide it in my pocket until I can eat it by myself in the bathroom.

Today, though, something is really wrong. The adults are whispering. My father is angry, and even Mommy Esther is angry. And she rarely *ever* gets angry. My siblings and I don't know why, but even we are speaking in whispers, catching each other's eyes with questions, waiting for the lash to fall.

"Where is Mary?" I whisper to Aaron.

He shrugs his skinny shoulders, to say, "I don't know."

"Boys! Come to the living room," our father's voice booms out.

I reluctantly trail in behind them, knowing I am included in this.

"Line up against the wall," our father directs. We are trembling. "We need to talk to you about a very serious matter. You are here to witness the punishment. Esther, do you want to explain what happened?"

"Well, I discovered some money was missing from my purse. I didn't know who had taken it, until the candy kiosk owner outside the school said that Mary had bought some candy from him. I asked Mary about it, and she denied it." Mommy Esther is wringing her hands. "So, I looked in her room and found the candy wrappers under her mattress." She winds up with a sad and angry expression.

"So," my father booms, "Mary not only *stole money*"—we gasp in shock—"She bought *candy*"—the forbidden white sugar we are not allowed to touch—"And then to make matters far worse, she *lied* about it! Repeatedly."

I am shocked to my bones. This is an extensive litany of crimes. *How could she do such things? Or think she could get away with it all?* Of course, she must be punished.

My father has read us Grandpa's instructions on spanking many times, and he follows them to the letter:

> *Disciplining a child is hard work. Spanking & lecturing & punish-ing & keeping up with a child & catching him in everything he's done wrong is hard work.*
>
> *You can't let them get away with a thing; otherwise, you'll end up with a spoiled child who thinks he can get away with murder!*
>
> *The Bible says spare not the child for his crying. Remember when child-training the Chastening. A child not only has to love you, but he's also got to be controlled through fear, he has to fear you & not be allowed to get away with anything.*

"Mary, come here," our father bellows.

Mary walks out from my parents' room, where she had been awaiting punishment. My siblings and I are practically holding our breath. No one has done something this bad before.

Mary steps into the room, shaking.

"Come here, Mary," our father repeats solemnly. I can see she wants to run away with all her might, but she walks slowly forward to the center of the room, where he is waiting next to a stool. In his right hand is the dreaded Rod of God.

"Pull your pants down and lean over the stool."

Mary starts to cry. "I'm so, so sorry," she pleads. "I'll never do it again, I promise, I promise, I promise."

The adults' faces are impassive. She has broken the law; she will be punished. "No, you won't, because you will never forget this spanking. Bend over."

With shaking hands, she drops her shorts and panties. She can't escape. She leans over the stool and grips the legs with knuckles gone white.

"I'm going to give you one hundred swats, and you are going to count them."

We gasp in horror. No one has ever gotten one hundred swats from our father. Ten or twenty for horrible crimes like lying or breaking something. But Mary's crimes are compounded: disobedience, stealing money, buying candy, lying, and lying about lying. He calculates twenty swats for each crime and adds them up to one hundred matter-of-factly.

Thwack! I jerk at the first swat.

Mary yells.

"Count!" my father commands.

"One," her teary voice escapes.

Thwack.

"Two."

Thwack.

Mary screams, and her hands automatically reach behind to cover her bottom.

"Move your hands," our father barks. "If they get in the way, I might accidently break them."

Mary whimpers as she grips the stool again.

"Three."

Thwack.

Mary's cries are getting louder and louder.

"Be quiet!" he thunders. "Screaming just shows your rebellion has not been chastised out of you! If you keep screaming, you get more."

Mary gulps, trying to hold back the screams. *How can she not scream?* I watch, wide-eyed with terror, as the paddle comes down again and again, and we methodically count. Even more frightening is my inability to control my emotions. I'm horrified to realize I want to laugh hysterically. I cover my mouth, trying desperately to hold in this laugh that is trying to tear its way out of me.

This is not funny. I'm not happy. I'm desperately scared. If anyone sees me, I'll be on the chopping block next. *So, you think that's funny, do you?* I can hear my father's scream in my head.

This is wrong. Something is wrong. Mommy Esther, who is usually passive, starts squirming. At fifty swats, Mommy Ruthie tries to speak. "Maybe that's enough. I'm sure she's learned her lesson."

"No. I said one hundred, and she will get one hundred," he says, his lips pulled back in a parody of a grin as he continues relentlessly.

I look down at the stool legs, which shake with every blow. I dare not look away. There is the faintest veiled threat; one wrong look or sound, even a leg scratch, and I could be next. The air vibrates with anger. "This is for all of you to learn from Mary's mistakes."

My father is exhausted after the hundred swats. Mary hangs limp, whimpering, snot and drool dripping from her face, stretching to the red-tiled floor.

He gives her a hug. "This is for your own good. 'Whom the Lord loves, He rebukes and chastens.' Hebrews 12:6."

Mommy Esther grabs Mary and hurries her into the bedroom to take care of her and put her to bed. We all stand still, frozen.

"I want you kids to remember that. Now, go to bed."

For the first time in my memory, we go to bed in absolute silence. No one daring to speak. But we all are a little nicer to Mary for the next few weeks. We are also a little in awe of her surviving that spanking. It can hurt to sit down for a few days after even ten swats. Our father might be slight, but he is a strong man.

We've learned our lesson for now. Money is not for us. It belongs to God, and woe be to any kid who takes some.

6

HEAVENLY HOURIS

Family members from the entire Asia Pacific area—Macau, Hong Kong, even a few from the Philippines and Japan—are gathering in Hac Sa for a General Area Fellowship, or GAF. It's a week of prayer, fellowship, and sharing. Three years after the RNR, Grandpa began the Fellowship Revolution, having decided the disciples' independence had gone far enough. He created more Home Rules, fellowship requirements for local and regional Home gatherings, and a stratified leadership structure.

Local Area Fellowships (LAF) are monthly gatherings of just the Homes in your local area; in our case that's about thirty Family members living in Macau, but we might have a GAF only once or twice a year. It's a special occasion! Our Fellowships are getting bigger as more members arrive to help pioneer the region and new Chinese disciples join.

There is not enough room for all the visiting Family members to stay at the Farm, so my father decides to host everyone at the beach as a camping trip. He loves camping, and I'm dancing with excitement to have little Family girls to play with. Everyone is laughing and hugging. I've hardly seen my friends Ching-Ching and Sophia, whose families stayed in Macau when we went into hiding. I grab their hands, and we wander a few feet away to whisper our news. I'm glad we don't need to be *Selah* anymore.

Our out-of-town visitors love the isolated breezy beach where we pitch our tents under the pine trees near the barbecue pits. We all sit on blankets under the trees to read Mo Letters and sing songs. Then the adults have meetings about policies, witnessing statistics, relocation requests, and leadership responsibilities, so we kids are free to run around the beach and play.

The Family has grown to more than ten thousand members in over one hundred countries. Many of the new disciples have been joining in Latin America and Asia, but much of the increase is homegrown with families having lots of kids. Grandpa doesn't believe in using birth control: "Children are a blessing from God, and we should have as many of them as we can." He said that if teens had babies, the teens' parents would help raise their grandkids as good, youthful grandparents, and babies would keep the teens too busy to get into trouble. While my family got an early start to reach seven kids already, some of the other families are looking to catch up with us soon.

It is a rare occasion for families from the other countries to come together, as travel is expensive, but we feel connected even with the distance since everyone receives the monthly *Family News* that Mama Maria has been compiling since the RNR five years ago. They have become the social media channel of the Family. Arriving once or twice a month in the Mo Letter packets, they contain private letters written to Grandpa, FFing stories, words of gratitude for the Mo Letters, love letters to Grandpa accompanied by pictures of bare-breasted Revolutionary women, testimonies of salvation and joining the Family, miracles of healing and God's supply and protection, confessions and lessons learned, announcements of marriages and babies born, news about persecution, media, and court battles. They are an encyclopedia of how-to tips for everything that a Family member needs to be able to do in the "Family way," from home medical remedies and school activities to how to apply makeup and sew your own sexy dress for FFing.

Grandpa and all the leaders publicly praise obedience to the

Family policies and rebuke any dissent. "Sin before all, rebuke before all, that others may beware" is Grandpa's motto. The *Family News* even contains critiques of Family leaders, accompanied by letters of apology from those leaders singled out for reprimand. This public discipline of leaders and their published apologies not only keeps the leaders in line, it allows Grandpa to show his rank-and-file disciples that *he* is on their side and not simply aligned with the local shepherds who carry out his orders. Not knowing if you will be praised or rebuked at any moment keeps people off balance and on their toes—eager to prove their dedication.

Like the communists' self-criticism technique, we are expected to confess our sins, reporting on ourselves voluntarily—sometimes in prayer sessions or Home meetings or on a written report. This atmosphere of self-confession and vulnerability creates strong group unity. But we also know that if we don't report on ourselves first, someone else will tell on us. It is ground into us children that if we see a sin and don't report it, we are as guilty as the sinner and will also be punished when it eventually all comes to light—as many a sore bottom proves.

Grandpa's public exposure extends to himself. His unfiltered openness about sex, toilet habits, even his struggles with alcohol and his health, is a huge departure from leaders of his day; it demonstrates to his disciples his vulnerability and honesty, allowing even those who have never met him to feel like they know him intimately.

But with the GAF this week, instead of just reading about news and testimonies of all the miracles God is doing for us, we can share our testimonies in person. When they are not correcting us, the adults are eager to share their stories and praise God, quote verses, sing, and hug. It's a love fest, except for the occasional tense moment between some of the men who think everyone should listen to them. But the Farm is my father's domain; he and my mother are the Home Shepherds, even though all the adults living here attend the weekly Home Council meetings to discuss decisions.

Since the RNR, Homes are supposed to elect their Home Shepherds, but everyone knows that this is "Ho's Farm," and my parents decide how to run things. I can't remember there ever being an election. The other adults who join the farm form the Home Council, and they have regular Home Council meetings where they can give input on policies and receive instructions. But my parents, with consultation with Mommy Esther, administer the rules based on Grandpa's revelations in the monthly Mo Letters, from what movies to watch, how much to drink, how many times we should poop, what to wear, how to have sex, how to spank, and how to repent, to how to pray, how to wash clothes, and how to clean.

Home Shepherds report to Area Shepherds, who report to the Country and Regional Shepherds up the chain of command. The higher-level Shepherds are appointed by Grandpa and Mama Maria and live in secret WS Homes. The Shepherds answer requests for help, counsel, correct and mete out punishment for transgressions, and occasionally visit the Homes under their supervision.

My father is running around taking pictures and making short videos of everyone with his Nikon. For years, he has made us film the Children of Love shows for other Family kids. We sing, quote Bible verses and Mo quotes, and do skits to teach other children important biblical and Family lessons. These videos are copied onto videotapes and circulated for families far and wide as Godly, Family entertainment. But today we are making a different type of video.

Grandpa always talks about his love for women: *"I'm convinced that God made the most beautiful of His creations last—His crowning creation, the woman! I always admire & wonder at the beauty of the lines, the curves, the forms of His Hands. . . . As far as I'm concerned, the body of a woman is a work of art. . . . And since we've been here in this nice warm clime, we've been running around naked & getting into bed so often, I hope it doesn't wear me out!"*

In a recent Mo Letter, Grandpa spoke of a dream about heavenly, sexy naked women, Heavenly Houris, appearing to him and dancing for him with see-through scarves. These goddesses also appear to him when he is having sex, and they speak through him in tongues, begging for him to send missionaries to their countries to save their people.

Grandpa has suggested that he would really enjoy seeing videos of Family women and girls dancing sexy like the goddesses of his dreams. "Glorifying God in the dance," he says, should be done very tastefully and beautifully, like the naked art of old masters and artists, not pornography. Of course, my mother and the other women enthusiastically agree, eager to prove how yielded they are to God. The men like the idea, too, as they'll get to watch the videos as well.

My mother knows she is a good dancer and loves to show it off. She is not just doing a simple dance and rubbing a see-through scarf against her body. She wants real choreography and begins picking out different-colored scarves to create costumes for our production of *The Asian Angels Volume Two*. I appeared in my first *Asian Angels* video when I was three, a video compilation of Family women living in Asia doing sexy dances.

Most of the women seem excited, but I hear some complaining that they don't know how to dance like that, and they will feel silly. They are told, "Do it for the Lord and for our prophet, Moses David. Remember you are not your own; you belong to God. Any embarrassment is just your pride. Pray against it."

Mary and I and a few other little girls, daughters of some of the other families visiting for the GAF, are told to pick out scarves, too. I love scarves and dressing up. Sometimes I wear my long Christmas singing dress and my mother's purple feather boa and a see-through scarf over my head and pretend to be a princess.

To give it an artistic setting, my father wants to record us dancing under the pine trees by the beach near where we are hosting the GAF.

"We are going to do a dance of forest fairies," my mother explains. "I'll be fairy queen in the middle, and you girls dance around me."

I jump up and down. I want to be a fairy dancing in the woods. It's like a princess.

My father is there with his camera, ready to film us.

When we are instructed to remove all our clothes, I'm embarrassed to take off my panties, but my mother helps me and ties the see-through white scarf around my waist. She has us practice dancing a few times to get it right. "Hold hands and dance around me in a circle, first one way then change direction," she says. "Now raise your hands up to Heaven like you're praising Jesus."

Finally, someone hits play on the boom box, cued to a popular Family song, "Mountain Children," and my father starts filming. Five of us little girls, naked under our see-through scarfs, hold hands and circle my mother while she dances in the middle, rubbing her scarf on her naked body. One of the adults off to the side motions to us to change direction and poses.

I try to copy my mother with my scarf, but I feel clumsy and unsure. The sharp twigs poking through the pine needles hurt my bare feet; this isn't as fun as I was told it would be. After a few more takes, us little girls are finished; the adult women will take turns making videos dancing by themselves. I dress and run back to where Patrick and the boys are playing tag. *Why don't they have to dance?*

Whenever we have a GAF or a LAF, one of the adults puts all of us kids to bed while the other adults have dance and "sharing" nights. My sister, Mary, and I are still too young to go to these adult "dance" nights, but my brothers are old enough, according to Grandpa in the *Child Brides* Mo Letter, and are invited to join this time. *"Boys get semen and girls get their periods. If God didn't intend them to start having sex then, they wouldn't be able to procreate at that age."* He then expanded this in *The Devil Hates Sex—But God Loves*

It!, saying, "*There is nothing in the world at all wrong with sex as long as it's practiced in love, whatever it is or whoever it's with, no matter who or what age or what relative or what manner. . . . When Paul said 'All things are lawful unto me, but all things are not expedient' (1 COR 6:12), he was as good as saying, 'I can indulge in any kind of sex I want to, but I've got to watch out for the System because it's against the law!' (Mama Maria: At least not let 'em find out if you do it!). . . . We are free in privacy, and that's about all, and we mightn't be free if they discovered what we do in private! . . . There are no relationship restrictions or age limitations in his law of love.*"

Grandpa said that for hundreds of years, when a boy reached puberty, it was common for his father to take him to a prostitute to give him some experience, even in Victorian England. I never hear a word of complaint from my brothers; quite the opposite.

When Hobo was ten, he went to Australia for a few months with the top Family leaders over all of the Pacific area who were trained at Grandpa's house. He came back telling his brothers about how he was having sex with adult women there. This activity was obviously blessed by the top leadership and the Homes would follow suit. My brothers were invited to join the adults on the next sharing night. The boys were asked which auntie they wanted to have sexy time with, and then they went into different rooms and did what the boy wanted—full sex or just cuddling.

The next night, back at the Farm, we gather for our regular guitar-led Inspiration, singing rousing, emotional Family songs of dedication to get us in the Spirit. I am sitting on Uncle Jeff's lap; it feels solid and secure. On my father's lap, I try to sit perfectly still, afraid to get a slap or a pinch. He can lash out at any minute, and I am never quite sure what will set him off. But Uncle Jeff never spanks us, so I'm not afraid to wiggle.

After Inspiration, I see Uncle Jeff speaking with my mother. She smiles and asks if I want to go spend some time with Uncle Jeff. I nod happily. I feel warm and comfortable in his arms.

Uncle Jeff takes me to his room and lays me on the bed beside him. He takes my hand and puts it over his crotch, showing me how to stroke it up and down. When it bulges, he unzips his pants, and his penis pops up. I remember how my father's penis popped up that time when my mother invited me to the loft. I sit up, surprised.

"Don't worry. Do you want to touch it?" He takes my hand and places it on his bare penis, directing me to grip it. My hand is too small to reach all the way around it.

My mind is in shock. This isn't anything like the little-boy penises I am used to seeing on Patrick and my brothers. Uncle Jeff shows me how to grip it more firmly and stroke up and down to an even rhythm, then puts his hand over mine to stroke faster and faster until his body gets all tight. He makes a strange grunting sound, and white stuff spurts out all over my hand and his tummy.

Gross, I think, but say nothing, staring at my hands, which are covered in that white sticky stuff. It smells strange and metallic.

He takes me to the tiny bathroom and holds me up at the sink so I can wash my hands. The single neon bulb reflects the sickly light green of the walls, as I scrub and scrub my hands. I wash them three times before he sets me down, but they still feel dirty.

"I want to go back to my room," I whisper.

I am confused. I have heard my parents and caregivers talk about our bodies as good and natural, and how babies are made. *So why do I feel yucky?* I am so embarrassed and ashamed that I never speak about it to anyone. When my mother asks me smilingly the next morning, "Did you have fun with Uncle Jeff?" I just duck my head and hurry away. *If she doesn't know, I don't want to tell her. It's my fault. I agreed to go with him to his room. They just let me do what they thought I agreed to.* I avoid Uncle Jeff now instead of running up for a big hug. He doesn't invite me to his room again. To the adults, it's like it never happened. I pretend it didn't, too.

Except I am changed. From this point forward, I don't like to be around adult men. I hide in a group of kids to avoid being alone with one.

It doesn't always work.

It's already been a couple of years since Lynne Watson published her article that sent us to the Farm, and while things have been quiet, it seems we are never safe.

Gathering all of us in our enclosed patio living room, Mommy Esther solemnly tells us, "You kids are not to go anywhere on the Farm without an adult with you. Nowhere! Not even to walk the short pathways between our houses. We've had a very serious threat."

We hold our breath, our eyes wide. She explains that she's received a letter from her relatives in Kansas. Her parents are upset by the accusations of abuse they are seeing in the media and have offered a reward to anyone who will kidnap us kids and bring us to America.

Shocked gasps escape our mouths.

Reports of prostitution and child abuse have sparked police raids, arrests, and harassment of the Homes of Family members, with authorities locking up and blacklisting members, even trying to take children away from their parents.

The *Family News* we receive each month with stories of Family members being kidnapped and imprisoned only confirm our fears. Ted Patrick, an American cult deprogrammer also known as Black Lightning, has masterminded numerous kidnappings for parents who hire him to "rescue" their sons or daughters. But those happened in the US and Europe—far away from our little village. We often have desperate prayer sessions for the deliverance of Family members around the world who are being persecuted.

I've never heard anything about Mommy Esther's parents. I don't even know their names. But Mommy Esther's high and shallow voice and jerky movements tell me to be afraid. We're finally no longer in danger of getting thrown out of the village or kicked out of the country, but now we have to worry about being kidnapped!

"Don't worry," our father says, "God will protect us, but until we tell you otherwise, *no one* goes anywhere without a buddy and big stick." He holds up a heavy wooden tree branch that's taller than me and two inches thick. "I'm putting these near the doors. Any time you go outside, you take one with you. If you see someone you don't know, run. If someone grabs you, scream and bite and kick, and do whatever you can to get away. Do you understand?"

Now I am scared. I've never heard them talk like this before. But it doesn't make sense.

How silly, of course we are not being abused. Abuse was starving kids, burning them with cigarettes, punching them in the face until they broke their nose or had to go to the hospital, like Systemite parents did. It's those silly Systemites trying to ban corporeal punishment in places like the UK, saying it's child abuse, who are the problem. "I got spanked plenty and see how I turned out," the adults always say. Grandpa says Dr. Spock is inspired by Satan to teach parents not to spank their kids, so they can raise spoiled criminals and drug addicts.

And our sexual freedom is not abuse; the Systemites just don't know the difference, because they don't accept God's Word.

Of course, everyone agrees. *How ridiculous! We would never abuse our children. That's just the Devil's excuse to persecute us.*

For the next two months, we are on high alert. On the Farm and moving between village houses, we kids are accompanied by adults armed with a huge stick. If there is no adult available to walk us to the other house for school or naptime, Patrick and I peek out the front door at the twenty meters separating the Main House from the Cottage. I check carefully for strangers lurking behind the short stone wall surrounding the Cottage yard before clenching the heavy stick in one hand and Patrick's sweaty hand in the other. "One, two, three," we count under our breath. "Run!"

We cover the short distance in record time, while trying to keep our rubber flip-flops from slipping off, fear and adrenaline making my whole body tingle. We collapse, heart pounding and light-headed, behind the second closed door. "Safe!" Our quiet neighborhood is a war zone that exists in our fear. In bed, I rehearse in my head how I might kick and scream and bite any deprogrammer who might leap out and try to kidnap me. I know an adult could easily overpower me, but my eyes narrow as I stare at the dirty roof tiles. *I won't go quietly*, I say to myself.

Eventually, when no kidnappers show up, the hysteria dies down. It feels good to walk slowly again, pausing to sniff my favorite rose-bush. If I'm honest, I'm just a teensy bit disappointed that no real kidnappers showed up to test our defenses. I guess the grandparents decided it would be too much hassle and went back to ignoring us. The scare reinforces that Systemites, even, or especially, relatives, cannot be trusted. They don't understand. They are outsiders.

While Grandpa encourages Family members to write home and maintain a good relationship with their relatives to keep them from becoming enemies, our real family can only be the Family. I know my mother sends her parents monthly newsletters, telling testimonies about our mission work and asking for donations, but I don't hear if they write back.

Safe now to roam about, Patrick and I race to our favorite tree, the spring sun beating down. I swing my way up, curling my bare toes around the branches, and Patrick scrambles behind me. Even when he stops to catch his breath, I keep going, straight to the top. The highest branches bend and sway under my weight, and when there's nothing left to climb, I pretend I'm a bird, looking out over the tops of trees, far above everyone else.

The adults can't reach me here. Not even my brothers can climb this high, because the branches are not strong enough to hold their heavier weight.

All the tiny people on the ground don't matter. There's nothing ugly, nothing painful. I reach my hand up as if I could touch God.

7

A CHANGE IN ATTITUDE

In three years, we have fixed up four houses and are our own little village inside the village. The Cottage, where Patrick's family lives; the Main House, which is still mostly our family; and the Pink House, attached to the Main House by a hallway, where my mother and other helpers live. Our latest rental is the Stone House, a squat house built with one-foot-square granite blocks that is twenty meters along a path behind the Main House. We enclosed the patio, which is now our schoolroom—a big improvement on the wooden shack behind the temple.

As we fix up more houses, more Family members come to fill them. Ching-Ching moves here with her father, Zacky Star, and his two wives, Auntie Hope, a kind, round, American Jewish woman with long, straight black hair to her bottom and a big nose, and Auntie Kat, one of the first Chinese disciples who joined in Hong Kong. She has a cheery smile with chipmunk cheeks and freckles. They have five daughters and one son, with Ching-Ching the oldest (a year younger than me). Patrick and I are thrilled to have more kids our age.

While we still mostly live with our own families, during the day the children are put into age groups and cared for by one or two caregivers per group. This frees the parents to do their assigned work for the community.

I've never bothered to keep track of all the aunties and uncles;

even before moving to the Farm, they have been coming and go-ing. Some stay for three months, six months, a year, depending on how many times they can get their tourist visas renewed and whether they feel "called" to a new mission field. We fit them into rooms as tightly as we can. Sometimes a family of two adults and two kids might sleep in a ten-square-foot room.

Our lifestyle has greatly improved since we dug a sewer pit and built a tiled indoor bathroom onto the Main House with a sit-down toilet and separate shower. We used our connections with the Por-tuguese officials to get the city government to pave the main road coming into the village, plant electric poles, and hook us up to proper metered electricity, so we will only have to use the noisy generator for backup.

My mother is relieved, as she won't have to carry car batteries back and forth to power the computers she uses to edit the Mo Letters. Since Hong Kong had the latest pagers, cell phones, and laptops made in Japan and India long before they were available in the US, she always had the first Apple, IBM, and NEC personal computers.

We've cemented the pathways connecting all the houses, planted flowers along the borders, and even pestered the city officials until they reluctantly added our village to the weekly municipal garbage collection route. It's quite a different place from when we moved in a few years ago, and the Chinese villagers express their apprecia-tion for how we've improved their standard of living by dropping off small gifts of food.

And my father finally found a solution to our poisonous-snake problem. Though so far, God has protected us and no one has been bitten, the snakes have been showing up when we least expect them—dropping from the roof or nestling into our beds. My father brings in three dump trucks' worth of sharp-cut gravel rocks and spreads a layer of granite around each of the houses at least eight feet wide. He figures out that the snakes don't like slithering across the sharp rock edges with their soft underbellies. Though some of the aunties and uncles shake their heads, the plan works. No longer do we have to do nightly cobra bed checks.

With all the new families, there are more kids, so school has changed as well. We now have three classes: older children, younger children, and nursery.

Nestled on Auntie Hope's motherly lap, I focus on sounding out words and am not embarrassed to make mistakes when I read. It took me longer to learn than many of the other kids, but eventually it clicked, thanks to help from Auntie Hope. Now I speed through multiple Peter and Jane readers in a sitting and begin reading the *Kidz True Komics* and *Picture Bible* for myself, thrilled with the new way to entertain myself during our boring naptimes.

A few of the adults take turns teaching us for a couple of hours each morning after our two hours of Devotions. They don't need any teacher training; they just read from the *Childcare Handbook* curriculum or copy out problems on the blackboard. Family Care, under Auntie Sara Davidito and Mama Maria, released the *Childcare Handbook* in 1982. Now, parents don't need to use System educational materials and are no longer allowed to attend outside Christian schools. At almost seven hundred pages, the educational volume has everything Grandpa thinks a child needs for a Godly education on the mission field. One chapter has the history of the world, starting with Creation. Another is math up to multiplication tables and division, plus a little geometry for the boys who will need it for carpentry. Science and biology are another chapter, also starting with Creation, including a long section on debunking the evil lie of evolution. My complaint is that new teachers always start at the beginning, so we've done the first part a dozen times without getting to the end.

The opening page sums up what our leaders deem most important for us to know. Grandpa writes, *"I consider for our children right now, the best education you can possibly get is in the Word, in the Bible and in the Mo Letters. As long as they can read and write and figure the 3 Rs, Reading, Riting and Rithmetic. The best education they can get is an education in the Word and faith and survival and mobility and preaching the Gospel, right now!"*

The preface continues with an explanation as to why we have taken this view: *"We are not against education, at least not our kind! . . . A little of the world's education sometimes can help in a few instances where you deal with the world and meet the System on its own grounds. How much formal education should we give our children to enable them to live in our present-day society? Our children need only what is known as basic education up to 6th grade education."*

Grandpa says our lessons should always be based in something useful to serving God. We practice our letters and grammar by writing witnessing letters to the Sheep who write into our radio show or who we have met while out witnessing. Our Chinese teacher, Auntie Kat, writes witnessing lines on the chalkboard in Cantonese or the lines to Family songs translated into Cantonese for us to memorize.

More important than any scholastics is our spiritual education.

"Turn your toes out more. No, arms higher. Your thighs are supposed to be turning, too. Straighten your knees. Straighten your elbows, but curve them slightly." My mother is trying to teach me ballet, but nothing I do is right.

"I can't!" I cry, throwing up my arms.

The burning frustration in my chest is forcing my eyes to leak embarrassing tears. I won't cry. I'll get angry instead. Whenever my mother tries to teach me how to do something—how to read, to write, to draw—it's the same. We've been through this scene over and over.

"Yes, you can!" Her voice is high and frustrated. "I've decided," she tells me. "From now on, you are forbidden to utter the words 'I can't.' What does the Bible say? 'I can . . . ,'" she prompts.

I sniffle. "'I can do all things through Christ which strengthens me,'" I quote dutifully.

"Right, so this 'I can't' attitude is against the Bible. It's a dirty word. Any time you say 'can't,' I'm going to wash out your mouth with soap. And you are going to memorize every verse and poem about '*I can*' that I find, so we can turn around this bad attitude you have."

There is nothing I can do but nod. It's hard at first. Really hard. I didn't realize how many times I say "I can't" in a day. Every time I do, I have to quote a verse from the Bible or a famous quote or a poem about persistence from *The Good Thots*. *The Good Thots* is a compilation the Family made of System short historical stories, parables, poems, and quotes that Grandpa and Mama Maria approve of as teaching good lessons in line with our Family beliefs.

I memorize two dozen. I like reciting part of Winston Churchill's "Never Give In" speech. I make my voice low and gravelly and quote, "Never give in . . . Never, never, never, never . . . except to convictions of honor and good sense."

But my favorite poem is about a tiny cork that pops right back up no matter how many times an angry whale lashes it with his big tail, taunting, "You never, never can keep me down, because I'm made of the stuff that is buoyant enough to float instead of drown."

Over time even I notice the difference. The familiar sinking suck of failure is replaced by an "I can" attitude. I begin to believe that with enough stick-to-it-tiveness I can overcome any challenge. (I can even beat my brothers at pull-ups.) My mother praises my new determination.

"Faithy, wake up." I'm woken abruptly from a deep sleep to my father shaking my shoulder.

"Faithy. Come on, get up now!" It's dark, but suddenly a bright light blinds me. I spring up, scared. It's just a flashlight. "We need your help. You're going to have to be very brave. Can you be brave?"

I nod, getting more nervous by the minute.

"We need you to help Sheba have her puppies. Do you think you can do that?"

We have had a lot of dogs over the years, but Sheba is our favorite. Sleek black and brown with intelligent, patient eyes, she has watched over us kids since before I can remember. Sheba's had six puppy litters over the years, which we sold or gave away. Her puppies are always well-fed, licked clean, and cared for.

I knew Sheba had been in labor since yesterday and only one puppy had been born. "There's no way to get a vet to come out until morning," my father whispers.

"Yes. I'll help," I say, proud to be called on to help at such an important time. I crawl out of bed and follow my father in the darkness to the barn stall, where Sheba lays panting on bloody newspapers. The metallic smell of blood, newspaper, dog, and dirt assaults my nose. Illuminated by the light of a single naked bulb dangling from a ceiling wire, poor Sheba looks at me with such pleading in her soft brown eyes. Nehi and Hobo are standing next to her, clearly worried. My father gently helps her up onto her feet and holds her upright, as she can barely stand.

He points at a red plastic bucket filled with water and a soap bar on the floor next to it. "Scrub your hands to your elbows. One of the puppies is stuck in the birth canal. I've tried and your brothers have tried, but our hands are too big to reach in and get it out. We need you to do it. Your hands are the only ones small enough to fit."

I look at Sheba's swollen vulva with bloody mucus dangling from it and want to back out the door. But my father and the boys are looking at me expectantly, even Sheba with her sad brown eyes. She's in pain. I breathe deep, past the shallow tightness in my chest. I set my face. I won't let them down.

My fingers reach into her sticky, hot vulva, feeling for the puppy inside. She doesn't move, just hangs her head lower. She knows I'm trying to help. "Daddy, I can't get my hand in any further." I'm afraid to push too hard; I don't want to hurt her.

"Just keep going, you're doing great."

I feel her muscles clamp down and squeeze my hand painfully. "Daddy?" I whimper.

"It's just a contraction. As soon as it lets up, push your hand in further."

I wait for a minute, gritting my teeth against the pain in my hand, I say silently in my head, *I can. I can. I can do all things through Christ, who strengthens me.* Then I inch my fingers forward.

"Okay. Can you feel the puppy?"

The tips of my fingers brush fur. I feel a tiny nose, a head. I nod.

"Good! Now try to get a hold of the head and slowly pull it out." Easier said than done, as another contraction squeezes my arm 'til I think it will go numb. As it lets up, I inch my fingers over the puppy's head and gently pull him forward. It seems to take forever. I pause and breathe with Sheba through the pain of each contraction, my hand stuck inside her. At last, I pull him out.

He's soft, warm, and slick. His black body is no bigger than my hand. He's dead.

My father takes him from me. "He has been trapped in the birth canal too long. The others should be alive," he says soberly.

I look at my arm in the orange light of a 20-watt bulb barely flickering. It is covered in blood and mucus. *Ick, gross.*

"Can you do it again?"

My whole body shivers. But, of course, I nod. Again, and again. I try to ignore what I'm doing.

"Don't think about it," my father coaxes me. "Just do it." It's a useful technique when I need to do something gross or painful.

I look over Sheba's head into the darkness beyond as all my focus is on finding the next puppy. I painfully and slowly pull three more pups into the dim light. They are alive.

"That's enough for now, Faithy. Let's hope Sheba can birth the rest on her own now that the ones that were stuck are out of the way."

Shaking, I walk back to the bucket and dip my red, sore arm into the icy water. I scrub and scrub at my arms and under my nails, but the smell of blood won't go away.

I want to stay and hold vigil with her. I sway on my feet, and my father catches me.

"Go back to bed, Faithy. You did good. We have done all we can for her right now; let's just pray she makes it."

Dear Jesus, please help Sheba to be okay, please, please, Jesus, help her to live, I repeat over and over as I lay in my bed.

The next morning no one comes to wake me up, so I sleep late. I wander into the dining room, where everyone is finishing breakfast, the bright sun streaming in through the windows, just as my father walks in through the front door. "Boys, come here!" The solemn look on his face tells me before he speaks. "Sheba has gone to be with Jesus. She's gone to dog heaven."

Fourteen eyes fill with tears.

I stare at my hands. *I failed. I tried so hard and she died anyway! Why didn't Jesus answer our prayers?* My chest is so tight I can barely breathe.

"We did all we could for her. The vet said she had fourteen puppies."

Our jaws drop. I'd never heard of a litter of fourteen!

"Sheba just didn't have the strength to birth that many." *If the vet had showed up yesterday, it might have saved her,* I think resentfully. "Faithy helped us save some of the puppies last night. We got out five puppies; one was dead, but the other four are still alive. Praise the Lord!"

Uncle Michael puts the four surviving puppies in a box with a blanket. He bottle-feeds them every two hours, even through the night. I pray silently all day, *Jesus, please help the puppies to live.*

My father takes Sheba's body and puts her in a gunnysack. We all pile into the van and drive up Eucalyptus Hill two miles away—the sharp, medicinal smell of the trees tickles my nose. We stand around while my father digs her a proper grave off the side of the road. It is my first funeral. We erect a small wooden cross over her grave, and each of us kids steps forward to say goodbye and give her a present—some ribbon, a ball, a tattered collection of cheap treasures from kids who have little to give. Tears wetting our cheeks, we try not to look at each other. I carefully place my offering on her grave—an empty glass perfume bottle that Mommy Esther had thrown away; I'd kept it so I could enjoy the lingering fragrance. It is the saddest day of my young childhood, losing our beloved Doberman. Whenever I smell eucalyptus, I think of her grave.

In a few days, the first puppy born is the only one still alive. She had been able to nurse from her mother for one full day and was stronger than the others. We name her Shebina—daughter of Sheba. Unlike the rest of the dogs, who are rarely allowed in the house anymore, Shebina is raised in the trailer Uncle Michael shares with his new wife, Auntie Crystal.

"She thinks she's human." Uncle Michael laughs as Shebina jumps up on the bench to sit with the family at the table.

She is the worst guard dog ever. She genuinely loves everybody—friends, strangers, neighbors. She bounds up to each passing person, tail wagging, expecting to be petted. We love her with a touch of melancholy. She can never take the place of our first love, Sheba, but she does her best to make up for it.

8

MY SISTER IS A JESUS BABY

As the Farm evolves, so do the Family's witnessing practices. With the AIDS epidemic sweeping the world, Grandpa starts to rein in Flirty Fishing. "We can't have this disease of Sodomites spread in the Family," he says.

You can't miss a single Mo Letter, as you never know what life-altering revelation might be on the horizon. Several years earlier, a Mo Letter insisted that women should be willing to suffer STDs to save souls as Jesus laid down His life. (The accompanying picture made me wince—a woman nailed to a cross with a stake through her pum. Yeek!) But the consensus among the adults was that most are okay with STDs that they can treat, but *not* herpes. That is the *incurable* disease, like leprosy. Once you had it, you were tainted forever. Some of the adults had herpes, but we knew which ones, and we asked that they wipe down the shared toilet seat with Lysol after they used it.

As Grandpa tells Homes to wind down FFing and find new ways to support themselves, women who had longtime Fish who supported the Family could continue the relationship, but everyone else needed to stop. After a few more years, the FFing ban became final—*no one* was allowed to sleep with Systemites, on pain of excommunication.

Grandpa's call to curb FFing gives my mother the excuse she wanted. She spends one last night with Uncle Ashok to say goodbye.

While she does not seem distraught that this will be their final time together, I'm worried. I love going to his apartment in the city. He gets me treats and lets me cut out shapes in the chapatti that he cooks me in his kitchen. But mostly I like that the attention he shows me makes me feel warm and safe. I'm worried all this will end if they break up.

But we have a bigger surprise coming.

Three weeks after their breakup, my mother discovers she is pregnant.

I'm going to be a big sister!

The question we are all wondering is who oh who is the baby's father? My mother said it could be my father or Uncle Ashok or another uncle living with us at the Farm who has bright red hair. This is not uncommon in the Family; with all the "sharing," it is not unusual for children to not know who their fathers are. We're told there is no shame in it, not like in mainstream society, where such a mystery is taboo. All children belong to the Family and Jesus first. At least with these three options, the baby's coloring will surely tell us.

My mother tells me that having a little brother or sister is like having a life-size doll to play with. I am excited. After so many years as the littlest one, I am excited for my new role as big sister. I must learn all I can about pregnancy and childbirth so I can help. I study the first volume of the *Childcare Handbook*, which is about babies, and watch the *Miracle of Life* documentary many times. It shows *everything*: the little tadpole sperms shooting out of the penis and into the woman's vagina, the hard swim upstream in the fallopian tubes, the egg getting fertilized and growing into a fetus, and the birth at the end, which looks gross, so I usually turn it off by that point.

Natural home births are common in the Family, and my mother decides she wants to have her baby born at home with a midwife instead of in a hospital, where she had me. It will be a teaching moment for us kids.

When the big day arrives, we all cram into the Dodge van and head to our old apartment, which we still lease in Macau so we can host Family visitors. The Macanese midwife my mother hired is also the head nurse at the hospital. She insists we need to be in the city near the hospital just in case something goes wrong.

My mother is on a double bed in one of the two small bedrooms. As the midwife and Mommy Esther help her with breathing, all of us kids sit or sleep in the living room, listening to the rhythm of panting and crying out with contractions. We are dressed in identical, brand-new gray tracksuits. Esther says we need to be clean and not wear any farm clothes so we don't bring germs that will hurt Mommy or the new baby.

The seven of us try to sit still and read our *Kidz True Komics*, but this is taking hours longer than anyone thought, and we are tired and cranky in the chilly apartment. It is December and cold, and we are all bundled up in our winter coats and hats because the only electric space heater is in the delivery room and the rest of the apartment is not heated.

Every once in a while, we get an update, but when I try to peek in, I'm shooed away. After twenty-seven hours of labor, Mommy Esther finally calls us in from the living room: "Kids, it's time."

All of us pile into the small room and stand quietly at the end of the bed in shock, looking on as the midwife directs my mother to "keep pushing," even though she already has been for nearly two hours.

Like I have, my siblings have all seen *The Miracle of Life*, but none of us are fully prepared for this. My mother's vagina is stretched so wide, and a big hairy ball is coming out of it. I've seen animals give birth, and I keep telling myself this is just the same. But it doesn't sound or look the same. There's blood on the bed, and

Mommy Esther is looking between my mother's legs and saying, "That's good, you're almost there. Let's have another push." The midwife is urging her in Portuguese. My mother makes a long grunting sound and scrunches her face up, and then bam! The baby shoots out. Across the bed! Thank goodness my father is standing there to catch her before she lands on the floor! He gets sprayed in the face with mucus, and we all laugh uncomfortably. I look away. It's gross.

When I look back, I see Mommy Esther cradling a baby girl with black hair on her head, a fuzz of dark hair all over her tiny white body, and a small blue mark on her lower back.

Right away, the midwife calls the doctor. He shows up to give my mother stitches and cut the umbilical cord, because in Macau, a baby can't get a birth certificate unless a doctor cuts the cord. Silly, I think; if you show up with a baby, it was born, wasn't it?

My mother is exhausted, but my father doesn't notice. "Praise the Lord! Let's all gather around for pictures!"

My mother weakly waves her hand in protest, and I step in. I brush back her sweaty, frizzy hair and open her small makeup compact, trying to put some on her. I know she hates to look bad in pictures, and she doesn't look very good right now, with her face all red and puffy and her hair sticking up everywhere.

Mommy Esther makes us all wear surgical masks when we take turns holding our new little sister, so we don't get her sick.

When we get home, my mother settles in to recover in her room.

She tells herself and anyone who will listen that baby Nina is my father's because she is so white, but we all know better. Even I know what that blue mark means. Most Asian babies have them, though they go away after a year.

Her fantasy is shattered when Acrisio, a longtime Fish of Mommy Esther's, stops by to see Nina. He is a tall, elegant man with silver hair, older than most of the System men who come over. He walks into my mother's bedroom, takes one look at Nina, and exclaims, "She looks just like Ashok!"

Mommy Ruthie bursts into tears, screaming, "No she doesn't! She looks like Ho!"

I'm shocked by her emotional outburst. I can tell from Mommy Esther's embarrassed looks when she's hurrying Acrisio out that it's not a very Revolutionary thing to say. I know Mommy Ruthie wants the baby to be my father's because she's in love with him, not Uncle Ashok, but I think she is being silly. It doesn't matter to any of us whose sperm made Nina, including my father, who is bouncing around, showing her off to the neighbors.

Each of my older brothers, starting with Nehi, who is fourteen now, spends one month as Nina's full-time nanny. "This is great training for you boys when you become fathers," my mother declares. They don't mind playing with Nina, but they hate washing the poopy cloth diapers. I'm too young to be responsible for her full-time, but I get to play with her every day. In a secret fear I won't admit to anyone, I'm a little worried that Uncle Ashok will love Nina more than me because she is his actual little girl. But when he visits the Farm, he still slips me treats or a little money to buy ice cream. On my birthday, he pulls me aside and gives me 100 patacas ($14). It's our little secret. I've never gotten so much money from anyone. I hide it away and don't spend it. It's not like ice-cream money. It's real money. I need to have something I really want before I'll spend that. I'm still his special girl.

Before long, my mother is proud of having a Jesus Baby, a baby born because of FFing. A lot of families have one or two kids who don't look like the rest of their family, and you always know they are Jesus Babies and are considered a special blessing from God. She says baby Nina is her reward for FFing Uncle Ashok for years, even though he didn't end up joining the Family.

"Nina is a Jesus Baby, just like Davidito!" she boasts.

Wait, I wonder, the reality setting in. *Does that mean that Davidito isn't actually Grandpa's child?*

I ask her how come Davidito is Grandpa's son if he is actually a Jesus Baby?

She explains that Davidito's biological father is a Spanish hotel employee named Carlos who Mama Maria FFed while she and Grandpa were living in Tenerife. "Davidito is still Grandpa's son. Jesus just used a different man's sperm to bring him. Esther is still your mommy, isn't she?"

"Yes," I say, unsure. I know I'm not supposed to question Davidito's place. He is Grandpa's chosen son and heir. *But still*, I wonder, not for the first time, *what about my father? Why has Grandpa never called for us kids to visit him? Why is Davidito the heir to the throne when he is not even Grandpa's child?!* I've read the begats in the Bible; I understand the succession of kings.

But I know better than to speak any word that might sound even a little critical of Grandpa or Davidito, so I keep my questions to myself and try to make sense of the adults' actions. Davidito was sent by Jesus. It doesn't matter who his father is. But I still think it's unfair that my father and Aunt Faithy are not the prince and princess anymore.

Even though Davidito is the heir to the throne, I'm reminded daily by my parents that my siblings and I still have the responsibility of being members of the original Royal Family. Our history is not our own—it belongs to everyone—as do our daily lives. The *Kidz True Komics* illustrate our family line back four generations. Even our first steps were recorded in international newsletters, and every landmark since has been chronicled, photographed, and mailed around in *Family News*: "Faithy, 7, introduces you to Rachel, our cow," "Faithy with the pretty marigold flowers she and the other children planted on the path," "Little Faithy loving up a beautiful Chinese waitress in the hotel's restaurant!"

The Family is our destiny, and carrying on the Family legacy—saving the world—is our purpose. Everyone looks to us to set an example, and nothing brings my mother more happiness than sharing a note from Grandpa that she received in response to one of her newsletters, which reads, "You good grandkids make me a very happy Grandpa."

Every day we're told that we need to set an example because we're Grandpa's grandchildren. But then we're told, just as often, "You're not special just because you are Grandpa's grandchildren. You're just the same as everyone else." We're told to be exceptional, and then we're punished doubly so that we know we're not.

9

FARM LIFE

At 4:30 a.m. the birds are beginning to chirp in the darkness. I pop out the plastic mesh screen on the window of the Cottage, crawl through the frame, and silently slip inside Patrick's room. We take turns waking each other, depending on who gets up first. Sometimes we meet in the middle, at the window, with one heading in and the other heading out. We wouldn't dream of starting the long day without each other or leaving the other to oversleep and get yelled at or spanked.

I seem to do most of the waking these days. When it's Patrick's turn, he'll shake my shoulder, then jump back out of reach. A couple of times he's been too scared to wake me, and we were nearly late. He tells me I throw punches or kick him in my sleep. What's a few punches among friends? I say. I'm not doing it consciously.

I shake Patrick, but he's in a deep sleep. I drag him by his arms until he sits up, eyes closed, bobbing like a kite. I threaten to pour water on him, but there's no response. We must get going or we'll be late, and if we're late, we'll get yelled at. As I head to the bathroom for some water, he grunts and climbs out of bed. It takes only a minute for him to pull on a worn singlet and red shorts, and then we're out the way I came in, through the window.

It's still dark when we enter the dining room for breakfast. My older brothers look like the living dead. But life returns when Uncle Michael carries in a tray of soggy French toast. They say he used to be a chef before he joined the Family, but I don't see much sign of it. I join hands with Patrick, and a chorus of wavery voices starts singing grace to a fast tune. It's really a medley with two songs squashed together, the first tune a little slower, then the second tune speeding up faster and faster.

"Thank the Lord for the food, thank the Lord for the Family, thank the Lord for another day of life. Yeehaw!" I always "yeehaw!" with gusto. It's my favorite part.

Halleluuuuia, Haaalleluia, Halleluia praise the Lord. Praise the Looroord.

moves smoothly into

Thank You, Jesus, for this food and for our home so fair.
Help us, Lord, to do some good and keep us in Thy care,
and bless our loved ones ehhhveerywhere,
in Jeeeeeesus naaame, weeee pray.
AMEN!"

I wouldn't dream of not saying grace; it's a magic wand that will kill worms and germs.

But I much prefer singing grace to listening to the adults say a long boring prayer. Sometimes they insist on doing both, which I privately think is overkill. God heard you the first time. Being smarter, we kids have crafted our own prayer that suits all eating occasions, particularly when we're so hungry we start gobbling before remembering to pray:

Dear God, thank You for what I already ate,
and thank You for what is still on my plate. Amen!

After breakfast, Patrick and I dash down to the Farm to start our chores before 6:00 a.m. Now that the summer is here, we have about three hours before it's too hot to work outside. Our flip-flops slap against the cool tiles as we whir past Mary, who is doing dishes in a red plastic bucket. She's given up trying to fit in with the boys and prefers house chores rather than farm chores with us. I yank open the heavy wooden door that leads to the outside and step into the light gray of early morning.

Uncle Michael walks slowly down with the key to unlock the padlock on the big chain link gate to the farmyard. It is a double gate, eight feet high, made with metal pipes welded together as the frame and wide-hole chain link mesh as panels. The holes in the chain link are about two inches in diameter—perfect to wiggle a few toes into to clamber up and over the gate if Uncle Michael is too slow.

Shebina is not much of a guard dog, but she is always the first to greet us, stub tail wagging. I pet her as she bumps my stomach gently with her head. Rex likes rougher play, and the boys play tug-o-war with him carefully to avoid his long teeth.

We have been steadily adopting more and more animals, recreating my father's idea of a Texas ranch. Most Family Homes wouldn't dream of putting so much effort into raising animals as a hobby, but when our father has an idea, he bulldozes forward, and most people are too intimidated to say anything. My father's vision is justified by the hundreds of people who visit our informal petting zoo each month and leave with posters and Jesus in their hearts. "Now we don't have to go out to witness; the Sheep come to us!" he boasts.

To the left of the Farm gate is a vegetable patch—Uncle Michael's pride and joy. He planted it not long after he arrived in Hac Sa, and it's been providing us with greens, tomatoes, cucumbers, and hot peppers. It's fenced off on all sides, with a roof to keep the pesky goats and birds from devouring the bok choy and tomatoes. It is only ten feet by four, so give a few goats ten minutes in there and nothing is left but stumps poking out of the furrowed soil—as we learn from personal experience, many times.

Once inside the gate we grab our rubber farm boots from the tack shed, a structure we built from concrete cinder blocks, that sits to the right of the gate.

Patrick is a year younger than me, but at seven years old, he's strong enough and a good partner to work with. Our first stop is the goat pen: a roof made of corrugated metal siding, a concrete floor with a drain, and a chain link fence surrounding our herd of brown, black, and white splotchy goats. After the great goose tragedy, my father trucked twenty live goats from across the border in mainland China. He told the adults we'd get fresh goats' milk from them, not realizing it takes a special breed of goat to produce enough milk to collect. We never got to make goat cheese, but we did get an occasional goat barbecue. I learned from my pet goose to never get attached to an animal that might end up on the dinner table.

With our shepherd's staffs, we herd the goats to a field next to the farmyard by the Big Tree—a hollow fiscus tree hundreds of years old. Shebina often tags along to protect us from mean neighborhood dogs. This is our favorite part of the day. For two hours, all we need to do is make sure that none of the goats wander too close to the neighbors' vegetable patch by the creek. Other than that, we have complete freedom. No adults.

Out here, under the morning sun, we can talk about whatever we want, laugh, jump off rocks, slay dragons, call down fire from Heaven to burn our enemies, fight pirates—and there is no one telling us, "Stop laughing. Are you being foolish? What are you talking about? That's foolishness!"

I make up wild pirate tales, and Patrick willingly acts out his part. Our staffs are excellent props; they can be anything from pirate swords to Moses's rod to a royal scepter. Also, they're good for digging under rocks to find squirmy bugs. But our favorite story to play is *Heaven's Girl*, a series of comics that Grandpa's written especially for us children.

Heaven's Girl is our superhero and teen model. In the illustrations, Marie Claire, aka Heaven's Girl, is fifteen and dressed in a see-through toga that barely covers her bum. She's beautiful and carries a shepherd's crook—an End-Time prophetess with supernatural powers. We wait with eager anticipation for each monthly installment, which arrives with the adults' Mo Letters. The story begins a few years into the future, in 1989, at the start of the Great Tribulation described in Revelations, a final reckoning whose date has been prophesied by Grandpa. Heaven's Girl is captured and gang-raped by a troop of Antichrist soldiers before they toss her into the lion's den:

"It sure seems like a waste to feed such a pretty girl like this to the lions!" one of the soldiers said to his companions.

"You know what, I was just thinking the same thing," another one added.

"Yeah, why should the lions get to enjoy her before we do?" several of them piped up! "What do you say, Commander, how about if we have a little fun with her first?"

Heaven's Girl submits willingly to the rape and whispers in the soldiers' ears about Jesus, which makes two of the soldiers feel guilty. They come back to rescue her from the lion's den, but when they arrive, they find her unharmed. Jesus gave her the strength to lift the heavy stone that covered the exit and escape. The soldiers convert on the spot and join her as disciples, helping her escape into the wilderness.

Over and over, Heaven's Girl escapes the Antichrist, using sex to survive and gain influential protectors, leading God's people and performing the miracles of Moses: starting storms, calming storms, calling fire, blinding her enemies, all with her shepherd's staff. Thrilling! Patrick and I read each story over and over until we nearly memorize them. They are much more exciting than the *Picture Bible* we've read a million times.

After we role-play the latest installments, it's time to bring the goats back from grazing. Then the real work begins.

Patrick and I grab a heavy shovel and bamboo broom and drag a dirty wicker basket that's as high as our waists. The shovels are as tall as us and made all of iron, so they are hard to lift when empty, much less when full of cow manure. We have the least coveted task of mucking out all the animal stalls.

Some of our rich System friends bought a donkey and pony for their kid but soon discovered they were not equipped to handle them, so they gave the animals to us.

Sammy, our unusually large pony, is easy enough. Patrick, Mary, and I have been learning to ride on him. But our donkey, Don Quixote, or Mad Max as the boys now call him, is no little burro that went to Bethlehem, no sir. He is all muscle, with a tummy like a barrel. His back is higher than my head, and he has short, rough gray hair. And he is mean as a snake. He'll bite anyone who gets in range.

We also have three Australian quarter horses that my father got from the Macau Jockey Club when they retired. Shadow, a sweet, calm horse; Marcus, cantankerous and crafty; and Taurug, a huge dinosaur of a beast who enjoys taking an occasional nip at passersby.

We don't enjoy mucking stalls, but we don't dally. We are racing the sun; after 10:00 a.m., no one can work outside in the blistering heat without getting sunstroke. We quickly shovel out poop from the horse stalls and lay fresh straw for them. But handling the cows isn't as simple. They don't poop out neat little balls of grass like the horses. They always have the runs. It comes out in a dark liquid stream that spreads into a round, ripple-y patty the size of a big pancake. If they've just done their business, you'll never scrape it up. Just turn the hose on it full blast. But when it sets for a while, it forms a crust on the outside that holds it together. If the cows don't step in them or smear them around, they'll form into nice round patties, and we can test our skill.

Spotting my target, I tip the edge of my shovel under the lip of a patty, making sure the center is right in the middle. Then I scoop, with an unhesitating, smooth move, like ripping a tablecloth out from under a table of dishes. *Shkeerrit.* With the satisfying sound of iron moving across concrete, I have the entire patty in the shovel. Patrick cheers as I dump it into our basket, which we drag around after us, cow to cow.

When Patrick and I finish, we haul our baskets into a corner, where they'll sit until the Friday manure run, using a cart that Uncle Jeff and Uncle Ashok built for Mad Max to pull. The cart has two big wheels, a front bench seat for the driver, and two hard wooden benches in the back along the sides.

On Saturday and Sunday, we take the donkey cart to the main road in front of Hac Sa beach, where the city's #21A bus arrives, and give out free rides. Most of our passengers are locals from the city escaping to the beach for the food stalls that pop up along the road with ice pops and meat sticks. When people get in the cart, we give them posters about Jesus and try to get them to say a short prayer to ask Jesus into their hearts. It's not easy to talk to people about Jesus when they are squealing with excitement at the cart's movement; for most of the local children, this is the closest they will get to a live animal. So, we just give them posters and tell them to pray later.

Patrick and I have finished our chores and are just about to head back to the house when I'm knocked onto my butt by a gallon of water. Blinking my eyes open through the streams, I see Nehi and Caleb on the roof with an empty horse barrel, laughing themselves silly. I spot Patrick running for cover, which leaves me alone, exposed. Locking my jaw and squinting my eyes, I plot revenge. Water fights are frequent and have the bonus of keeping us cool in hundred-degree heat. No crappy squirt guns for us. The holder of the farm hose was king, but we will fight with jugs, buckets, and horse barrels.

Today is different. The farmyard has five full-grown guava trees, and we wait impatiently all year for them to ripen. The guavas are small, the size of a child's fist, soft and sweet. Some are white inside, but the strawberry guavas are pink. In the summer, we eat our fill of the soft, sweet fruit—whole guavas, guava shakes, guava ice cream—often giving ourselves diarrhea from overindulging. Once the guavas start dropping from the trees, overripe, our moment has come.

I collect the fallen fruit and load them into my shirtfront. When I can't fit any more, I crouch behind a big blue barrel and give Patrick the signal. "Guava fight!" the cry goes up. The attack begins, all-out warfare, no sides. It's every man for himself, kill or be killed.

The missiles are flying. Josh jumps up to throw a guava at Patrick, so I leap up and let fly. *Darn, just missed him.* I crouch again as Josh retaliates. My position is compromised. I dash behind the corner of the barn wall. Nehi sneaks up behind me, and *splat.* The fruit squishes between my shoulder blades, sticky and wet. With nothing left to lose, I run into the fray, sacrificing myself to the cause. I see my target and hit Josh square in the neck. Revenge is sweet. That just leaves Nehi. As the fight reaches a frantic pitch, we are popping out from behind barricades and throwing without even looking first. Auntie Crystal decides at this moment to go wandering into the farmyard. *Splat.* An errant guava smacks her upside the head.

"Boys!"

We freeze. Fear pulses through my veins like fizzy water.

Auntie Crystal is skinny and short, American and high-strung. She arrived at the Farm a year ago, and within months her and Uncle Michael were married and moved into a trailer next to the house. I'm puzzled why she doesn't dress like the other adult women in flowy hippie skirts. She bounces around the Farm dressed like a teen girl in tube tops, ruffled short skirts like a tutu, and bobby socks. With her frizzy, light brown hair in two pigtails on the sides of her head and a huge pretend smile on her thin lined face, she fairly buzzes with energy. Unless you get her mad. Then she strikes like a snake—with a hard slap across your face.

But Uncle Michael likes her, so we try to stay out of her way and not make her mad. I feel a little sorry for her. She told me that before she joined the Family, she had lost custody of her kids for being a drug addict. Good thing Jesus saved her. Most of the adults in the Family have an interesting story about how God saved them from drugs or suicide. How they were searching desperately for the Truth, for love, for somewhere to belong outside the corrupt world that spawned the horrors of the Vietnam War. Whenever a new adult puts us to bed, we beg to hear their testimony—the story of how they joined the Family. The System is a scary place. "You kids should be so grateful you don't have to suffer what we did without Jesus and the Family." We are so glad to be born into God's kingdom.

Well, right now I'm scared.

Maybe if I keep my head down and stay hidden, I will be overlooked. "Come here! Come here right now! All of you!" Auntie Crystal shrieks. "Boy are you going to be in trouble when I tell Uncle Ho about this. Now, you just march on up to the house," she says, grabbing Josh's ear.

I emerge from hiding to join the five other convicts (of course Mary is not present), and Patrick melts away. I view the battlefield. Guava flesh covers the farmyard, white stains of sticky seeds splattered on the walls and ground, their fleshy bodies split open, stepped on, the pink insides spilling out, casualties of war.

We're frog-marched up to the house, where our father is summoned.

He lines us up, and we stare at the floor, awaiting our judgment. Under other circumstances, he might have taken little notice of a fruit fight—he's started a few himself—but not with Auntie Crystal yelling about hooligans throwing guavas at her. The rules are clear. You can *never* raise your hand to an adult.

My father's face stretches into the grimace that he gets when he is mad. "Who hit Auntie Crystal?" he growls. I can always hear it in his voice when we are going to get it, low, intense, and angry. Our eyes fleetingly glance around, but we remain silent. We don't know whose ill-aimed missile hit her.

"Well," Auntie Crystal huffs. "I think they're all to blame."

Father barks, "Nehi, bring me the Rod of God."

A shiver ripples across the wall. I've been hit with many things—hairbrushes, bent coat hangers, long shoehorns, belts, flyswatters—but never this. I have seen this used on Mary and Josh, but I have never done something bad enough to be included in the punishment.

When Nehi returns, my father tests the weight of the weapon in his hand. Then he goes down the line, making each boy turn, pull down his pants, and place his hands against the wall. I can feel the rush of air as the paddle swings by, three times each. *Thwack, thwack, thwack.* The boys hold back tears as they rub their red, hot bottoms and gingerly pull up their pants.

Finally, it's my turn. I look at my father, hoping he'll relent. There's no point trying to justify myself; talking back just leads to a slap in the face or a quotation from a Bible verse.

I stand there, unable to say a thing. A tear trickles down my face. Crying is mortifying, but usually the adults take it as repentance and back off. But not this time. He tells me to lift my skirt and turn to the wall. As my fingers meet the cool, unmoving wall, I think of my brothers standing next to me. They didn't cry out, I won't cry out, crying is sissy.

Thwack. The force is so strong that I don't feel anything, just the sensation of being lifted off the floor and thrown against the brick. I plant my hands more firmly to regain my balance as I wait for the next two blows. Shock. Impact. Burning turns to an ache. I never get over the shock of being hit; the fear of it is often worse than the pain itself.

In a roar like rolling thunder, our father tells us the same things he's told us hundreds of times: "You kids are a disgrace. When I was your age, I was already a leader. I was preaching the gospel in churches across the United States. I was starting the Family with Grandpa. We were traveling around the country in our motor home and gathering disciples for Jesus. I committed myself to witnessing, preaching, teaching, and saving souls every day. We had no time for such foolishness!"

We all know this to be true. We've been raised on life stories about Father David, the Prophet Mo, Grandpa, and how the Revolution was started in the *Kidz True Komics* we read daily.

When he finishes his speech, I hurry out after the boys, swiping at my eyes and nose. I'm shaking all over, and my breath is high in my chest. It will hurt to sit down for a few days. But along with the throbbing pain, I feel a quiet triumph. I survived the Rod of God. Although I was terrified of it, not being spanked with it separated me from my brothers. Now they can't jeer at me for getting off light because I am small or a girl. Whether it's snakes, biting donkeys, or spankings, I'm as tough as they are!

My inability to swim had long separated me from my brothers. My father would take the boys off on excursions to swimming holes and I would be left behind, silently pouting because I wasn't included. But after weeks with my mother at the small pool at the Pousada de Coloane, a former manor house that was recently converted to a hotel, I have finally learned to swim. She patiently showed me how to kick and paddle in the shallow end. I appreciated it. My father would have just thrown me in the deep end and yelled, "Paddle!" like he did with my brothers.

The next time my father calls the boys for a swim at the reservoir, he agrees to let me join them.

Yes! I finally get to go with the big boys!

I'm excited but scared. Really scared. Unlike the hotel swimming pool, the reservoir has no place to put your feet down for even a moment. Not that you'd want to. Even though the reservoir is much clearer than the muddy brown ocean, who knows what's in the murky, greenish water?

The mud squishes under my feet and sharp bits of sticks poke me as we make our way down the steep bank into the water. *What if there are snail larvae here?*

We've been warned by Mommy Esther, "Stay out of still pools of water. The snails lay their larvae and they will burrow into the soles of your bare feet and nest there."

I lift my feet as quick as I can, trying to make as little contact as possible with the mud and not slide off the edge.

The boys sail past me, leaping in. I lose my balance and land on my butt, sliding down into the water. I kick out to the middle, away from the mud and worms, and relax a bit. I can tread in place, touching nothing, just kicking my legs and doing a dog paddle. *I'm doing it. I'm okay!*

I beam as my father says, "Good job, Faithy."

Aaron grins at me, and Hobo gives me a wink.

"Let's jump off the dam!" Caleb shouts.

I look up. There is a concrete wall fifty feet to my left with a big "No Swimming" sign. Occasionally, a local dies out here. They get drunk or don't check for rocks under the waterline before they jump off the dam wall.

It's terrifying, but I clamber up the muddy bank behind my brothers. Hobo reaches a hand back to help me up the slippery slope, before the boys run to the top.

"Go carefully, boys," my father cautions.

The boys patter out onto the hot gray concrete wall. There's a sixty-foot drop to the rocks on one side and a thirty-foot drop to the water on the other.

This is madness.

I hesitate. The top of the dam wall is perhaps two feet wide, with a metal pipe railing at chest height down the center. I must walk on one side of the pipe with barely enough space to put my feet.

"Come on, Faithy!" the boys call.

I've waited for years to go with the boys to the reservoir. This is my chance to show I belong in the special adventure club that my father has with my brothers. If I show any weakness, whine or cry, or can't keep up, I won't be invited back.

"Make sure you don't dive. A belly flop from that height could kill you. Go feet first," my father instructs.

No worries there. I don't know how to dive; I can barely swim. I'm certainly not going headfirst. With my wet arm wrapped around the sun-steaming steel pipe, I inch my way along the wall out to the middle. *Never, never give in.*

"You have to go all the way out to the middle of the dam, and make sure to jump as far out as you can, otherwise you'll hit tree branches hidden under the water," my father warns. "They can rip you right open." *Now you tell me.*

I look back down the wall to the land. Josh is already making his way down the wall toward me. I must jump to make room for him.

"Just do it!"

"Jump!"

"I'll count, one, two, three!"

I won't be a coward. I'll never live it down.

I refuse to seem weak in front of the boys or my father. He admires toughness. *One, two*—deep breath—*three. I can. I can.* Though every instinct is screaming not to, I jump.

Falling. Takes. Forever.

Bang! The water slams me, and the shock carries me down, down, down. It's dark. I'm gagging. Water shoots into my nose. Madly, I kick my legs as hard and fast as I can. My arms pull. I've heard that sometimes when you are underwater you don't know which way is up and you can swim down and drown instead of up to air. I see a faint glow. *Keep swimming. Don't pass out.*

I explode up, into the sunlight, sputtering and gulping grateful breaths. My father swims over and plucks me up. I'm rubbing my eyes and shaking. And very happy to be safe in his arms. For once, the pride in his eyes is shining on me.

The boys cheer.

I did it!

Josh's head bounces up in the water next to me. "Let's do it again!"

I jump three more times that day. The fear is just as sharp each time, but I go home a hero and, best of all, accepted.

10

———

BURN AFTER READING

In the six years since we arrived in Hac Sa, our renovation projects have transformed our once barely livable residence. What started as a collection of small, traditional Chinese farmhouses or shacks for my immediate family and a few others has grown into a Family community of roughly fifty people, as Family members come and go. We are now considered a Combo, which is a large Family Home with a resident population of fifty to two hundred people.

My parents are still the Home Shepherds, but now we also have department heads, adults who oversee certain areas of responsibility like childcare, the cooking and cleaning schedule, and fundraising. Life in a Combo is more regimented, run much like a kibbutz.

We no longer live in family units; children are in their groups full time, like boarding school. The little kids have fully equipped classrooms with handmade teaching aids and are often taught by the teens. They spend one hour in the evening with their parents for dinner and family time, but if their parents are busy, they can stay with their teachers. My father never does family time, but I see him at Devotions or on the Farm.

Uncle Ben is the main teacher for our older children (OC) group of eight kids, and a singer-songwriter, the latter a talent he puts to good use. I've been memorizing Bible verses since I could talk, "to brainwash ourselves (the good kind) with God's Word." Depending on the teacher, or punishment, I might have to memorize anywhere from one to three Bible verses a day. I don't have a photographic memory, so that means hours of repeating phrases over and over, trying to get them to stick. I'm determined, as I don't want to miss movie night. The highlight of our week is the one System movie we are allowed to watch, chosen from the short list of movies "approved" for our age group. But we can only attend movie night once we have recited our verses for the week. There is always some kid outside the living room door memorizing madly, either to triumphantly skate into the room as the opening credits roll or to be sent tearfully to bed to finish his verses. That won't be me.

But Uncle Ben changes the game by setting the Bible chapters to a catchy tune, which makes them a zip to memorize and review. He does the same with multiplication tables and holds memory tournaments, pitting us against each other. I love the rush of winning, and we all push for first place on the tally board. For the first time, school is not a chore to avoid.

And our larger population means more mouths to feed—we've long since exceeded my father's small stipend. We rely ever more heavily on provisioning. Each week Uncle Michael and one of the boys, Josh or Caleb usually, will take the van into Macau for the provisioning pickup trip. They spend the day going around to different shops and supermarkets whose owners are receptive to our message and who save the nearly outdated food for us.

Every dollar is stretched until it's threadbare. Thankfully, the Farm is making enough money to support itself with visitors paying for horse-riding lessons, using our three Australian quarter horses, Shadow, Marcus, and Taurug, and our pony, Sammy. My father has Chinese John and my brothers building a riding ring to use for the lessons, so we don't have to walk riders around the open fields.

We continue to raise donations each weekend through busking and selling CDs of Family music created by Music with Meaning, the Family's music writing and recording home in Greece. Some of the new people help support themselves through monthly donations they receive from family and contacts back in the US.

All the money we receive is used for overhead or sent to Grandpa. None of the adults in the Family give a passing thought to things like retirement, savings, or property ownership. Jesus will come back in the Rapture long before any of that is an issue. After all, according to Grandpa's End-Time prophecy, the seven-year Great Tribulation of Revelation is supposed to have started about a year ago, sometime around 1986, with Jesus set to return in 1993. As we can't yet identify the Antichrist, though there is lots of speculation, Grandpa suggests he is ruling in secret behind the scenes. Of course, God could change His mind and give us more time if He chooses, but because we cannot know, we must stay vigilant.

Even though it doesn't *seem* like the start of the Tribulation, every month, new Mo Letters arrive to remind us of the impending rise of the Antichrist's one-world government and point out the signs of the times from the news. The October stock market crashes around the world are evidence that Grandpa is right—the world is teetering on the brink of collapse and the Antichrist will step in to save it. We live every day in preparation. We have lots of canned food, and our flee bags are packed. A flee bag is not just for persecution, but also in case of a natural disaster, fire, or war. It has the few essentials that we would need to grab when it came time to escape: a change of clothes, flashlight. My father is responsible for throwing the family's passports and a little money from the safe into his flee bag. Sometimes we have drills where everyone grabs their flee bags and runs to a designated meeting place in the nearby field.

The bigger the home gets, the more preparation we need. With everyone following God's command to "be fruitful and multiply," the kids now outnumber the adults, often two to one. The Family demographic is shifting as hundreds of the early children are becoming teenagers. To address the challenges of this age group,

Family teens around the world are given long questionnaires about every aspect of their lives. One of the things that surfaces from their answers is that many teen and preteen girls feel traumatized by sexual encounters with adult males.

In response to these questionnaires and to all the police raids and court cases against Family Homes, Auntie Sara, Davidito's former nanny, who has graduated to a top WS leader, sends out a new, adults-only "Burn After Reading" letter, *Liberty or Stumbling Blocks*, shifting the policy of sex between adults and children.

While not an absolute ban from Grandpa, Auntie Sara's letter makes clear that sexual relations between adults and young teens seem to have a damaging effect, especially on girls fearful of getting pregnant. Without rejecting Grandpa's earlier teaching, Auntie Sara says that due to this and considering the persecution the Family is facing worldwide because of child abuse claims, adults shouldn't have sex with kids who are underage in the country they live in, which is around fifteen or sixteen in many places. While all things are lawful for us under the Law of Love, all things are not expedient (1 Corinthians 10:23). Kids and young teens can still have sex with each other if they want, but must be discreet to avoid attracting the notice of law enforcement.

The adults read this letter in a closed-door session, but I don't hear about it until some months later, when my father holds a meeting with us teens to explain the new policies.

Whew! That's a narrow miss! I am relieved, though I won't admit it to anyone. Even though I am only ten, I have been very nervous about becoming a woman at twelve and having sex with adult men. None of the older girls have spoken to me about being initiated, so I sense it's something bad. Just the thought of an adult male touching me in that way makes me feel sick to my stomach.

Fifteen is still years away. I take in a deep breath and let it out with a smile. Finally, I can be around the grown-ups again without having to worry.

My anxiety lifts, and not a minute too soon. Uncle T, as everyone calls him, shows up at the Farm with a suitcase and a guitar. Uncle T is a musician and minor celebrity in the Family, particularly in Latin America. He sings on the Music with Meaning music tapes we sell when we go out witnessing, and he stars in a Family-produced kid show called *Uncle T Time* that we have watched for years. He is a tall, dark, handsome man and a rocking inspirationalist.

It's been a few years since he last passed through, and my eyes follow him in adoration as he leads inspiration at Devotions. I haven't seen him take much notice of me, so when he stops me in the kitchen and calls me over, I search my brain for anything I could have done wrong. *Was I fidgeting too much during Inspiration?*

Mostly I get in trouble for forgetting to say "yes, sir" and "yes, ma'am" or for trying to explain myself on the rare occasion I get caught doing something I'm not supposed to. "Stop justifying yourself!" Auntie Crystal will scream. "The Bible says, 'If I justify myself my own mouth will condemn me.' Job 9:20." I shut up, knowing a slap across the face is next. But I can't hold it all in. When I'm backed into a corner, bursting with rage and the unfairness, I know silent tears will begin rolling down my cheeks, even though I clench my jaw to hold them back. I *don't* want the other kids to see me crying.

I approach cautiously. Uncle T takes me by the shoulders and bends down so that we're eye level. I brace myself for the correction, but he kisses me smack on the mouth. Affection is encouraged in the Family, and we're all taught to give hugs and kisses, but a kiss on the mouth is different. I pull back.

"Have you ever French-kissed?" he asks with a knowing smile. I don't know where to look or what to say. I stare at his shirt and say nothing. I know what French kissing *is*, but I've never actually done it.

"Look at me," he insists.

I tilt my eyes up as he leans in and again presses his mouth against mine. I feel a wet tongue pushing against my lips and press them more tightly together.

He pulls back and looks into my eyes. "Kissing and being affectionate is how we show God's love. Are you going to be unloving?" His voice drops on the last question, and I hear the displeasure that signals punishment. There's nothing I can say. *Of course I believe that I should show people God's love. Of course I want to make Jesus happy.*

"Open your mouth," he orders.

Like a robot, I open my mouth, and he pushes his tongue inside. I try to hold still and not gag, making my mind as blank as I can. After moving his slimy tongue around like an eel for what feels like an eternity, he says I can go. I run outside so fast I lose one of my flip-flops. I rush to the hose and wash my mouth over and over to get rid of the taste. My mind flashes back to the bed with Uncle Jeff. *Is that what Uncle T wants?*

All my hero worship turns to disgust. I'm in a loop of confusion and distress. After that, I walk around the outside of the house to avoid passing through the kitchen, where Uncle T might catch me alone again, until he leaves six weeks later. I try to brush it off. *Gross, but it's over, he's gone.*

A few months later, I'm alone in the schoolroom, collecting a sweater that I left when we ran out for Get Out. I feel a big hand on my shoulder, and I shudder, and then laugh when I turn and realize it's just Uncle Bill, one of the teachers for the group of five-year-olds. Uncle Bill is a towering, skinny, mellow man with a funny mustache and blond receding hair. I've always trusted him. But before I know it, he kneels in front of me to hug me, then gripping my shoulders, he shoves his tongue inside my mouth. I can't move. *Him, too?* I don't know what to do, or who to tell, or if this is Godly or wrong. I'm even more confused when a few months later the adults have an exorcism over Uncle Bill to cast out the demon of homosexuality.

After that, I try to make sure one of the other kids is always with me. The age limit for sex with adults has been raised, but maybe French kissing doesn't count?

There is no one I dare ask.

Whenever new folks arrive, the dynamic always changes slightly. Will the new adults fit in smoothly or have tense arguments requiring serious prayer sessions? Will their kids be friends or foes? A cute boy to flirt with, or just more girls stuffed into the same bathroom? There is also the possibility that contraband will find its way to the Farm.

I don't know how the strange book arrives.

I see it peeking out of a pile of old clothes to be discarded and pick it up, curious. *The Secret Garden*—just the name thrills me! Checking to make sure no one is looking, I slip it under my jacket and walk away, my heart beating like a trapped sparrow.

I find a quiet corner and begin reading. From the first page, I'm in love. Systemite literature is forbidden, but I can't turn in something so enchanting. Instead, I hide the book in the loft, and when I have a few minutes between my tasks, I steal away to read. Afraid of discovery, I don't turn on a light, instead reading by the sun that sneaks through the dusty skylight. I ignore everything but the sound of approaching footsteps as I'm swept into a wonderful world of country estates, hidden doors, and secret keys.

It's tricky, getting away in a commune overrun with kids and adults, and whole days pass before I can return to my other world. But I think about it all the time, during class, during chores, and even during grace. The story is even better than the cartoons about Grandpa's home that I've read a thousand times, or the Bible stories that I can repeat in my sleep.

This is new, my very first novel. The rich descriptions transport me, and I see every detail in Technicolor. I live with each scene for days before I can sneak back and read the next one. I walk about the Farm in body, but in my mind, I'm wandering English manor grounds. My hands push aside the morning glory ivy growing on the farmyard fence, as I search for the secret door in a stone wall.

Mary, ever the burden, grows suspicious and follows me around. It doesn't take too long before she catches me in the loft. As soon as I hear the ladder creaking, I slip the book under the blankets, but it's too late. Mary, sure that I'm hiding something, digs around until she finds it.

I'm dragged before my mother to answer for my crimes. She taps the volume against her palm, waiting for me. She had read the back of the book and fixates on the word "magic."

"Where did you get this book?" she almost shouts. She's just found out she is pregnant again, and she's even more emotional than usual.

"I found it," I mutter quietly.

"I caught her hiding it in the loft!" Mary announces with a self-righteous expression. I'd want to punch her smug face if I wasn't so desperately concerned about my own safety.

"Faithy, this book is about witchcraft! That is the Devil's work trying to get in and influence your mind. You should know better than this!"

"But, Mommy, it's not real magic or spells. It's nature and exercise that heals Colin. Positive thinking is really just like prayer . . ." I trail off.

"Quiet!" she snaps. "I've heard enough. The Devil disguises his work to suck you in. We can't allow these worldly influences to corrupt your heart. You obviously knew it was wrong or you wouldn't have been hiding it! I'm confiscating this. Don't let me catch you reading something like this again, or I'll have to tell your father."

"Yes, ma'am," I agree, my eyes downcast to look subdued and sorry. The truth is, I'd just finished the book when Mary found me. No point in arguing. I don't want to see the flat end of my father's

Rod of God, so I go quietly. My mother is not a disciplinarian. Her heart isn't in it, unlike other adults, who are eager to hand out retribution. But she'll call my father if she thinks the offense merits it.

I walk away disappointed the book has been taken and I can't read it again. *Where can I possibly get my hands on more novels?* I discover that Ching-Ching's parents are not quite as strict as ours. They have *The Lion, the Witch and the Wardrobe* by C. S. Lewis, which Grandpa approves of, since it's a retelling of the story of Jesus; we've all seen the cartoon a dozen times. But the other books in the series, like *Prince Caspian*, don't have such an obvious parallel and would be suspect. I don't dare take the books home, afraid they will be confiscated by a stricter adult. Curled up in the corner of Auntie Hope's couch, I read as fast as I can. All too soon, I finish the few slim volumes. By the time I leave Auntie Hope's, I have a desperate hunger in my belly to return to the fantasy world the books created for me—I must find more, but I have no idea how.

My reading material is not the only point of conflict between my mother and me.

Her frustration with me is mounting. She's been getting complaints from a few adult men. "Why can't you be more loving?" she asks. "You're too proud."

My behavior around men has changed since the French-kissing lessons. I pretend not to notice them, and offer no warmth, no smiles, no encouragement, and try to never be caught alone with one. This standoffish attitude frustrates my mother, who doesn't understand where it is coming from.

I shrug and say, "I'll try to be nicer," but I know I won't. The instant any man starts being nice to me, I get a sick feeling in my gut and blast them with as much frosty distance as I can. I manage to look down my nose at them from my great height of four-eleven.

My mother nicknames me the Ice Queen.

It embarrasses me when she calls me that in front of people, but the truth is that when I imagine ice in my veins, I feel a little stronger, harder, and safer.

It seems that as I grow more distant from my mother and withdraw more, the more yielding Mary becomes.

I pass my older sister in the hallway one afternoon, and she says, "Faithy, I want to speak to you. Can you come with me?"

I give her a sideways look, wondering what she's playing at. "Fine." I shrug, following her into the empty kids' bedroom.

She smiles at me and pats the mattress next to her on the single bed.

"Okay. What do you want?" I ask suspiciously. After Josh, Mary is the naughtiest kid on the Farm, but far worse, she's the number one tattletale. *What is she going to get me in trouble for this time?* I'm still sore at her for turning in my book.

"I just want to say that you're my sister, and I love you. I want to apologize for fighting with you all of our childhood and for telling on you."

I try to speak and realize my jaw is hanging open. *She must be building up to something,* I think. *No way this is genuine.*

"I'm turning over a new leaf and apologizing to those I've hurt. Our relationship will be different from now on," she continues with a serious look.

I'm not sure what to say. Is this a setup that I haven't seen through? I give her the obligatory hug and mouth, "I love you, too."

I walk away, waiting for an ambush. But it doesn't come. Instead, every time I see Mary, she smiles at me and says, "I love you." It's a nice relief to not be fighting, but this is weird. Can a naughty, bickering, rule-breaking girl change into a calm, loving, yielded woman overnight? Like flipping a switch, the sister I've known my whole life is gone, replaced by a perfect disciple. Always positive, always willing, always praying and praising God. I keep waiting for the mask to crack, but it never does. *How does she do it?* I wonder.

In the strangest turn of events, Mary is now held up as a shining example for me to follow. As I hear the adults compliment her and see her happy (smug) face, I am resentful and jealous, and then I feel bad for being so. Maybe I'm wrong to be suspicious. Maybe Jesus really did transform her. But I feel further away from her than ever. The only explanation I can come up with is that she's been paying attention to Josh and the ever-harsher punishments befalling him.

I've noticed that despite the consequences, Josh, at fifteen, is defiant as ever. He can't seem to keep his mouth shut or his hands out of trouble. He's sarcastic and rude, and he even sneaks alcohol and smokes cigarettes with Lok Keen's teens, whom I rarely see these days.

Esther keeps making us have exorcisms over him, even having him fast for three days prior to make sure he is taking it seriously, agony for a hungry teen boy. My father keeps sending him into isolation at the Stone House, where he's kept in a locked room like a prisoner. Someone brings him his meals, and he's allowed to read only a prescribed list of Mo Letters. I wonder if the isolation is more for the adults' benefit than for the redemption of my brother; it keeps him out of their way and from derailing the delicate balance of communal living. Over the past three years, he's spent nearly a year total in isolation.

Fortunately for the adults, the other boys have fallen into line as best as lively teen boys can; though there is much the adults don't know. Caleb still follows Josh around when he's not in isolation, but he knows how to keep quiet. Hobo is doing his best to be a good example and follow orders. He struggles quietly with an inability to read; he sees the letters backward, so he thinks he's dumb, which is very hard on his pride. Nehi is off in his own dreamy world with his Nikon and guitar. Bones is still a clown, always goofing around and making weird faces, trying to get a laugh.

With the exception of Josh, it seems the Farm is a good place for whipping teens into line.

In fact, some government officials and police have serious issues with their teenagers taking drugs and bring us their sons so we can be a good influence on them. Their boys work with us on the Farm, mucking out stalls and riding horses, kind of like a halfway house. I don't know if our rehabilitation efforts are successful; the boys don't usually stay long with all the hard work.

But my father boasts to anyone who will listen, "We know that the Family way of life is right because of our good fruit, our children." While other families are desperate, struggling with children who are on heroin or cocaine, we live a clean life with hard work and discipline. As he likes to say, "A good tree cannot bring forth evil fruit."

I feel sorry for those poor teenagers who are killing themselves with drugs and destroying their lives. Sometimes when we drive around Macau, I look out the car window and see System people going about their days, to work or school and home in an endless circle, and I wonder how they can bear the empty pointlessness of their lives. How terrible to live without the purpose and truth that we have in the Family.

My parents have become good friends with Macau's chief of police, and he knows we don't break any laws. But if he gets an anonymous tip about drugs, he is duty-bound to check it out. The anonymous tips are usually that we are growing illegal drugs on the property, which is utterly ridiculous. In the Family, taking drugs or even smoking a cigarette is a cardinal sin. I can't imagine how horrible the consequences would be if one of us were caught with drugs or cigarettes.

When Lynne Watson's articles came out and we were blacklisted in Hong Kong, we didn't have the connections we do now. Over the last few years, we've built roots in the community by helping our neighbors, so when the newspapers in Hong Kong still occasionally publish negative articles about the Family, the police chief defends us. Sometimes he even gives us a heads-up call before the official white vans arrive for the occasional fake police raid. It's done for show, as they know we don't have drugs on our property.

These happen a few times a year now and typically involve my mother running into the dining room of the Main House, waving her arms to hurry us. "Police raid!" she'll shout. "Gather up and hide the Mo Letters! Then go sit in your rooms. No one go outside!"

We'll all rush around, grabbing any Mo Letters and *Kidz True Komics* we spot, especially the ones that have sexy pictures, and shove them into drawers and under our mattresses. Then we all go to sit on our beds. It's hard for me to keep from giggling.

The policemen crawl around in the bushes outside our house, and after an hour or so, the police chief apologizes and the men load back into their vans and head out. Up goes the "all clear" call.

In other countries, the raids are no laughing matter. Government agencies launch extensive investigations into allegations of child sex abuse, raid disciples' Homes, and take their kids away and house them with social services while the situations are being investigated. Some Family Homes just disappear in the night, the kids stuffing their belongings into suitcases and garbage bags.

In the Philippines, the VHS tapes we made to follow Grandpa's instruction of "glorifying God in the dance" had been confiscated. But that was just a filthy interpretation of evil minds to think that the beautiful dances and pictures of naked women and kids were somehow evil or wrong, like our *Asian Angels* videos. An example of how the Devil wants to turn what is beautiful into something dirty, according to Grandpa.

After the raids, the adults are sharper with us than normal for the rest of the day, but soon the usual grins and "Praise the Lords" flow back into conversation. I'm relieved but frustrated. It's like we get the downside of being part of the Royal Family without any of the advantages.

I'm always more afraid of reporters than I am of police. As we learned from Lynne Watson, reporters will twist whatever you tell them into something nasty and make everyone hate you for doing nothing wrong. Sometimes we see them wander up the road with their big cameras and microphones, and we all run inside and lock the doors until they give up and go away. Even our Chinese neighbors refuse to speak with reporters about us.

The reporters think that because my father is Grandpa's oldest son, he is a big Family leader, the next in line, or at least that he knows where Grandpa is hiding. But even if he wanted to, there is nothing he could tell them. Grandpa's location is completely *Selah*, even to my father.

"Why do they keep hounding us? I don't even know what he looks like!" I complain to my mother after a recent reporter scare. I'm sitting next to her on her big bed, something I rarely do these days, as I'm always with the teens.

"I've got an idea." She has that naughty glint in her eye that usually means something fun and not totally approved by my father or the Family is about to happen.

"Can you keep a secret? You can't tell anyone what I'm going to show you."

"Of course," I reply, nearly indignant. I've been keeping secrets all my life. It's my mother who can't keep secrets.

She takes me into my father's dimly lit office. It's stuffy and too dark, with heavy drapes blocking the hope of sun, all decorated in black and red. In the far corner is a small metal safe. My mother makes sure we are alone, then works the combination to open it. Homes are supposed to keep sensitive material locked up, especially if it has to do with leadership. I have no idea what we keep in the safe other than our passports. She pulls out a couple of photographs.

"How would you like to see what Grandpa really looks like?" She is bursting to share her secret.

Boy, do I ever! Grandpa's appearance is the best-kept secret in the Family other than his location. All images of Grandpa and Mama Maria are supposed to be destroyed. Doesn't my father know this?

Maybe, because he's Grandpa's son, he isn't held to the same rules? Or maybe he's breaking a big one by keeping these.

I stare eagerly at the two photos my mother holds out to me. One is Grandpa by himself, gazing into the camera. The other is him with a few women. Mother points to a plain-faced auntie sitting next to Grandpa. "That's Mama Maria," she whispers.

I stare for a minute, trying to memorize both of their faces, then she whisks them out of my hand and back into the safe, afraid someone will catch us. She hurries me out of my father's room, reminding me to keep the secret. I nod solemnly.

I'm quiet with my disappointment. Grandpa doesn't look nearly as magnificent as all the drawings I've seen of him in the Mo Letters. Instead of the full, imposing beard, his is thin and wiry as weeds. He has deep-set eyes like my father, but not the all-knowing power portrayed by the cartoons.

Mama Maria is an even greater disappointment. Grandpa has written letters about her sexiness and beauty as long as I can remember. But instead of the flowing locks and perfect symmetry illustrated in the Mo Letters, she has limp, mousy hair, buckteeth, and glasses. I feel lied to. I ball up my fists but then let the anger melt through my fingertips. Grandpa is a prophet. He speaks directly to Jesus. I guess the artists must change the way they look for security, I reason to myself.

As I walk through our village, I look at my friends, siblings, the other adults, and I know none of them have seen Grandpa's or Mama Maria's real faces. I feel special. I know something powerful, something dangerous.

My mother has trusted me with our first big secret.

11

IT'S A TEEN REVOLUTION!

There are whispers, whiffs of excitement about the Farm becoming a Teen Home. The only other Teen Home I know of is the huge Heavenly City School (HCS) in Tateyama, Japan, a mountain town about five hours' drive from Tokyo. The school is named after the Heavenly City described in Revelation. Grandpa has visited the Heavenly City in spirit and described its buildings and delights in our full-color posters. He says the Heavenly City was traveling through space to Earth, like a spaceship, but we can't see it in our earth telescopes because it's currently hidden in the moon, waiting to be revealed at the Rapture.

Homes with special ministries, like Teen Homes, are larger Combos with a hundred or more people, but they are rare. The HCS is a training and reeducation center where Family teens are taught revolutionary discipleship and strongly encouraged to declare their personal commitment to God and the Family, separate from their parents; overcome their spiritual problems or Needs Work On (NWOs); learn practical life skills, like cooking, handyman work, and childcare; and find marriage partners.

We've been tracking with envy the stories, testimonies, and videos coming out of the HCS. And while every continent has a Music with Meaning recording studio to create Family music tapes in the native languages for sale, the HCS's recording studio is turning out new Family teen stars who are writing and performing

Family songs and making their own music videos like, *Watch Out for 666* and *Cathy Don't Go to the Supermarket Today* about the Antichrist, and *Watch Out for the Green Door*, based on a dream Grandpa had about Hell.

Macau is viewed as a relatively safe haven because of my family's strong relationships with the local government officials—and our Farm has room to grow—so it is declared a good place for teens from the Philippines, which has been hard hit with persecution from allegations of child abuse.

Soon we receive fifteen teens between the ages of twelve and sixteen who have been living in Family Homes in the Philippines. They are mostly girls (my brothers are downright giddy) and just a couple of teen boys, so my options are limited. Jacob is six feet tall, reed-thin with a long face, and barely says a word to anyone. Eddie, his younger brother, is his exact opposite, fat and impossibly annoying, who tries to make up for his lack of good looks with teasing, cutting comments.

The teens are excited to get out from their old Homes, away from their parents and come to the Farm—a place they have long read about in the *Kidz True Komics* and *Family News*, where testimonies, photos, and stories about my siblings and I have been publicized. We are used to new people expecting that, as Grandpa's grandkids, we will be little angels. I think my brothers enjoy squashing those assumptions.

I beg and plead to be allowed in the teen group with my siblings, even though the official age to be a "teen" in the Family is at least eleven or twelve and I'm still ten.

My mother goes to bat for me. "She is much more mature than most kids her age, because she has always had to keep up with her older brothers. We shouldn't separate them now," she tells my father, and after a little pushback, he agrees. *I've earned my place.*

Almost overnight, my tight sibling group balloons with testosterone and estrogen. The teen girls are moved into the large room at the Main House, where my whole family slept when we first arrived over six years ago. The teen boys add a couple of bunks to my brothers' room. We pack 'em in dorm room style. There are no closets in these old Chinese houses, so everyone keeps all their belongings in a small suitcase under their bed.

As a welcome party, my father decides to take the whole group of teens camping at the beach for a week. These teens need to get a taste of survival skills and roughing it, he tells Esther, who is trying to dissuade him. Some of the other adults are concerned about the trouble twenty horny teens can get up to. My father believes in instant obedience to his commands, but he's lax on supervision.

Esther's concerns are valid. The teens spend the week sneaking into each other's tents and hooking up. My brothers have been sexually active for years. Nehi even had an intense, two-year relationship with one of the adult women starting when he was fourteen. I overheard the adults whispering that she was heartbroken when the leaders broke them up, something about them being in love, which meant they were putting themselves first. *What on earth did an adult woman see in my skinny, dorky brother anyway?*

But this is my brothers' first time having sex with girls their own age instead of adult women. Even though we don't have condoms, the boys work extra hard to not get the teen girls pregnant. The adults have made it clear that a teen pregnancy means marriage, but even without a pregnancy, there are still lots of broken hearts to mend after the sex spree.

Of course, I don't find out anything is going on until the end of the trip, when a tropical storm blows down all our tents in the middle of the night. I wake alone, batting away wet canvas sticking to my face and wondering where my tent mate, Joan, has gotten to.

I don't find the new teen boys attractive, but I want in on the excitement and attention. I try to model myself after the older girls, swinging my hips and flipping my hair. I watch Joy with envy. I've never seen such a beautiful creature in real life, with her long dark hair past her fully formed breasts and small waist. My brothers are of the same opinion. I don't understand how anyone can be so feminine and delicate. She moves gracefully and speaks softly, her eyebrows raised at our loud farmyard ways.

Everything Joy wears looks cute on her. Her miniskirts and button-down shirts tied at the waist to show a few inches of flat tummy. I copy her, but nothing looks the same without breasts. I am willing mine to grow with all my might, but they are barely little swollen nubs.

As we sit under the trees outside our drying tents, she tries to help me. "I did some modeling in Japan. When you take a photo, try sucking in your cheeks a little."

"Like this?" I turn into a fish face.

"Hm, no, not quite."

I try again and again and again. "How do I smile and suck my cheeks in at the same time?!"

"Perhaps just try pressing your tongue on the roof of your mouth."

After an hour, we both give up. Whatever special beauty skill she has doesn't seem to apply to me. Secretly, I keep practicing my fish face, hoping for the miracle that will make me pretty.

After the camping trip, we have our first big teen talent night. Typically, Family talent night performances involve singing, dancing, dressing up, and playacting. Bones does a great impersonation of Gandhi while wearing just a white sheet diaper, with all his skinny ribs showing and an Indian accent and head shake. It busts us up laughing.

But the arrival of the teen girls turns our talent night into sexy dance performances. Most of the girls pick System songs from *My Old Favorites*, which are three cassette tapes of Grandpa's favorite secular System music. Because Grandpa approves of them, we can listen to them for special occasions like dance nights. They are mostly songs from the fifties like "Hot Diggity" (1956, sung by Perry Como) and "High Hopes" (1959, sung by Frank Sinatra). Some other favorite songs to perform to are "Fire and Ice," a sexy Family song about FFing, and my brothers sing "(Let Me Be Your) Teddy Bear" by Elvis Presley.

The girls move their hips and arms to a hypnotizing rhythm in a coordinated striptease. Their matching jean skirts with snaps down the front are perfect for ripping off to end in their bras and panties, and the teen boys applaud and whistle.

As the Farm adjusts to becoming a Teen Home, Aunt Faithy arrives from Latin America, where she's been demoted from Area Shepherd. She now dubs herself a Teen Shepherd and announces that all the teens are now required to have buddies. The buddy system has been around in the Family since the Texas Soul Clinic Ranch, because Jesus sent out the disciples two by two: "If one falls down, the other shall be there to lift them up" (Ecclesiastes 4:10). That is interpreted to mean that your buddy is there for your physical safety, if you run into a snake, and your spiritual safety, if you're tempted to misbehave.

Normally, we must have a buddy only when we leave the commune property. The new system, copied from the HCS, is much more rigid. We're supposed to go everywhere and do everything together. We cannot leave each other's side unless the Shepherds say we can. It gets a little awkward sometimes, especially if someone wants to have a romantic rendezvous.

We are reminded, "Your first loyalty is to Jesus and the Family. If you see one of your brothers or sisters in Christ being disobedient, it's your responsibility to report them for their own good, or you are just as guilty as they are. If we find out you knew about it and didn't say anything, you will also be punished."

I know this is true, but I can't bring myself to tattle—especially on my buddy Joan. Joan is fifteen years old, blond, and *very* developed. But she doesn't act disappointed that she's stuck with the youngest, least developed girl in the teen group. In gratitude, I do my best to be an easy buddy, which includes trying to look the other way if she goes off on her own occasionally. Reporting on Joan is the last resort. We all know we should report on ourselves. Otherwise, our sins will separate us from Jesus, and He won't be able to bless us or speak to us until we confess it. I hope Joan will report on herself if necessary. I like Joan and don't want to get her in trouble.

To help us become more honest, we fill in daily Open-Heart Reports (OHRs) each evening before bed. The OHR is preprinted on a small slip of paper that is passed out to us after dinner. We fill out our name and the date, tick the box for whether you had a BM, fill in how many glasses of water we drank (I always put eight, though I don't really know how many I had. How am I supposed to remember? Does milk count?), and which verses we memorized.

Then the dreaded final question: "What NWOs are you working on?" Five blank lines to write about any mistakes we made, corrections, or bad character traits that we are trying to overcome. The first week is easy: "I'm learning to be more obedient, more yielded, etc." The usual sins. But soon I'm staring at those five blank lines, thinking, *What do I put here?* I don't do something bad *every* day. Plus, I'm not going to say anything about balancing the basket of leaves on top of the bathroom door with Bones. . . . I try to come up with something new that won't get me in trouble. Creative writing at its worst—trying to create things that are wrong with me. "I need to be tidier." "I need to listen more." "The Lord is teaching me to not be foolish." "I need to pay better attention in Devotions." Okay, that one is true.

With the arrival of the first group of teens, we get another surprise. Mene, a Family celebrity, comes to live with us. Even better, she is our real cousin, my uncle Aaron's daughter.

I've never met any of my cousins or Uncle Aaron, who has been dead since 1973, when climbers found his body at the base of Mont Salève in France. It was never fully determined whether it was a hiking accident that killed him, but Grandpa said that God had called Aaron home to Heaven; like Ezekiel, he went walking with God.

I've read about Mene in the Mo Letters and watched videos of her performing on the Music with Meaning shows for years. The whispered rumor is that she's been living at Grandpa's Home since she was eleven, so she must be extra special. I'm jealous and study her to see what she has that I don't. Why did Grandpa choose her? Perhaps if I'm extra good, he will send for me.

She is different than I expect. At fifteen, her long, wispy blond hair floats about her face, but it's her expression that's different. She seems far away, childlike. She wants to laugh and play with us, but she doesn't seem to understand our jokes. Sometimes she helps Mary in the kitchen, and Mary must show her how to do simple cooking tasks and then must remind her again the next day.

Soon, strange things start happening around the Farm. A beam falls from the roof in the stables, nearly hitting our horse Taurug. People are having more accidents. Then one morning we learn that the night before, every single teen had sleepwalked into a different bed.

We are gathered by the adults for an emergency meeting and reading. "This is a spiritual attack," we are told. "We wanted to spare you teens having to find out. We had hoped that the Farm, without the stress of Grandpa's home and with more young people her age, would help Mene. But the Devil has his claws in her too deeply. She is plagued by a demon who speaks to her and whom she can direct to do harm. That is what has been happening."

"Yes, I do remember Mene staring at that beam, and it looked like she was muttering under her breath," someone pipes up.

We all shudder. She is using a demon to cast spells.

At Devotions, we read the Mo Letter Grandpa wrote about Mene.

If you can't resist (the devil) then get rid of him yourself, wake up somebody that's with you and tell them to pray with you. And if they have to use a rod to beat him out of you, fine, you've got my permission. (Sara: Yes sir I'll do it!) If you've got to slap her to wake her up and get her out of that kind of spirit, slap her! Slap her good! Knock her around! Let her have it! . . .

Now get out, you damn devil, and leave her alone, or I'm going to whack the daylights out of her! (Mene cries.) Thank God that's the first time I think I've seen tears! Are you sorry? (Mene: Yes sir!)

You think you're going to make it up there (in the system) somehow? The only way you could make it is to be a whore, that's all! You wouldn't even be an FFer, you wouldn't even be doing it for God, you'd just be doing it for a living. You'd probably end up on drugs—a drug demon possessed, alcoholic, diseased whore and soon dead! Now is that what you want? (Mene: No sir!) . . .

You're dirty, you're filthy, you stink! Your self-righteousness pride stinks worst of all, like stinking dirty menstruous rags! . . . And we're not going to stand the stench of it anymore, is that clear?

As far as I'm concerned your father Aaron died failing God. . . . Do you want to die like that knowing you failed God and you disobeyed and hurt your family, your grandfather your father your foster father all of us? (Mene: No sir!)

I glance over at Mary and my brothers. As the reading continues, their expressions change from puzzled to terrified. *Who could have guessed?* Mene seems so nice. Simple and strange, always staring off and spacy, but not evil or demon-possessed. But Grandpa can't be wrong. Shows you never can tell about people.

And Uncle Aaron died failing God? Psychological issues? Suicide? This is the first I've heard of it. Grandpa said God took him to Heaven because he was too spiritual for this world.

"Demons are giving Mene violent visions. She's babbling about harming herself and others. For everyone's safety, we are going to quarantine her in the Stone House with Michael and Crystal," my father tells us. "They are going to live with her and try to help her exorcise the demons." I feel bad that I was jealous of her.

Mene disappears into the Stone House, and I don't see her for months. A few other "problem teens" are soon sent to live there as well. It's now called the Victor Home, as the teens who are there are supposed to be working on getting victory over their issues. It acts separate from the rest of the home and is very secretive, reporting directly to WS. No one is supposed to stop by to visit, even my parents.

I'm so caught up in my new world of teens, I try not to think much about Mene or the other teens in the Stone House, other than as a very scary warning of what could happen to me if I stray. I do my best to not end up a Victor, devoting myself to the Teen Shepherds and my new job, teaching the toddlers for two hours every morning while their regular teacher has Devotions with the adults.

Only the teens who haven't completed the basic education in the *Childcare Handbook* are given a few hours of study time each week so they can try to reach a fifth-grade level. With Uncle Ben's memory techniques, I'm in good shape, but many teens are still struggling to learn their multiplication tables. If they don't want to study, which they often don't, they can volunteer for more chores—after all, life skills, cooking, and caring for children are more useful to our futures as missionaries.

We also give weekly Bible classes to System young people who come to the Farm to ride the horses. Nunu is a handsome Portuguese nineteen-year-old who has been coming regularly to study the Bible with Joan. All us girls think he is cute, but we know the rules—we can flirt to get them interested in Jesus, but we can't touch.

I love my new grown-up responsibilities, but the one downside about being in the teen group is that I don't see Patrick much, as he is in the older children group, and we don't do farm chores together anymore. Our old jobs of mucking stalls are now reserved for the delinquent teens who are in the Victor group.

When I see the Victor teens sweeping the village streets or shoveling rocks, I feel sorry for them, but I don't say a word. I don't want to risk getting sent there, too.

12

THE SILENT COUP

Funny Family fads come and go, triggered by a Mo Letter or visiting Shepherd from another country, whether it's adding bleach to our drinking water or wearing sarongs to, as Grandpa promotes, let our privates air properly in the tropical humidity. Sometimes trends are not so funny, though. In recent months, the tone of the Mo Letters has become more militaristic about putting God first. *How?* I wonder. *We live for God every day.*

I hear my mother and Esther discussing the new Letters, and my father telling them not to worry. But the Farm has just grown too big not to draw attention from the higher-up leadership.

When my mother is around five months pregnant, an Australian couple, a heavyset woman and a skinny little man, arrive at the Farm from WS. As the days go by, my mother becomes more skittish. I hear her whisper to my father that the Family is going through another big change in leadership. Loyalties have been called into question, and things have tightened up. Apparently, the top Family leadership thinks certain Homes, like those at the Farm, are too independent and want to rein them in, so they sent WS leaders to consult and assist.

I spy on the couple from Australia. They seem quiet and unassuming, not leading Devotions or giving big speeches. I would have barely noticed them. Just another auntie and uncle, one fat, one skinny.

After they've been here a few weeks, I notice they begin having lots of closed-door meetings with the adults, including my parents. I ask my mother what they're discussing, and she tells me they just asked about how her relationship is with Dad and how things at the Farm might be improved.

We've been reading about Grandpa breaking up marriages of top leadership in the recent Mo Letters but don't expect that wave to hit our small beach village. How wrong we are. At Devotions, the WS Shepherds announce to us all that people need to put the Family and Jesus before their own personal families, which means that certain couples may be required to break up. They task my mother, as one of the Home leaders, to break the bad news to the couples who need to separate.

On the outside our schedule goes on as normal, but tension is tearing the community apart. Everyone is angry or sad or fearful.

Before I register what's happening, the visiting Shepherds turn their crosshairs on my family, and my mother starts getting blamed for all the problems at the Farm and in her marriage. She's brought by the WS leaders before the Home Council for prayer. Like sessions she's presided over, the adults sit in a circle around her, listing her faults, and she must confess, before they all lay hands on her for a two-hour prayer to beg God for mercy on her and to deliver her from her sins.

She is quietly stripped of her Home leadership role and separated from my father as part of her breaking. She spends more and more time in her small bedroom at the End House, our latest acquisition on the far side of the Stone House. When I see her occasionally at family time, her eyes are red and swollen. Why is my father letting this happen?

I know the Shepherds are a bit scared of him. Not only is he Grandpa's son, but he's famous for his trigger-happy temper. I've seen them flinch when he raises his voice. It's still the "Ho Farm." I suspect he's using his usual tactic of agreeing with everything and waiting for it to blow over and the WS Shepherds to leave so things can go back to normal, so I'm not too worried.

But that strategy won't work this time.

In the middle of my mother's trials, we have a bright spot: the birth of my baby brother! Or rather, two new brothers, as Auntie Jeannie is also having my father's baby. Auntie Jeannie is about the same age as my mother, but the two women look nothing alike. Auntie Jeannie resembles a thin-boned, freckled bird topped with a cloud of red curls. But she sizzles with nervous energy like she's been plugged into a light socket.

Their babies are born two days apart, and Auntie Jeannie and my mother end up side by side in hospital beds. I'm later told that when the doctor came to check them for release, he picked up Auntie Jeannie's chart and checked it, then picked up my mother's chart and paused.

Recognizing the confusion on the doctor's face as he spotted my father's name on both charts, my mother commented, "They were almost twins!"

She loves to tell that story. Of course, a good disciple is not jealous.

My mother names her new baby Jondy, after my father's nickname. When she comes home from the hospital on my eleventh birthday, she calls me to her and hands me my baby brother. He's wrapped in a small patchwork blanket that we teen girls sewed for him. His little fist pushes out, and his mouth opens in a big yawn. He is the cutest, goofiest baby I've ever seen. I kiss his fuzzy forehead and smell his baby skin.

"It's your turn now. When Nina was born, your brothers took turns raising her. Now you are old enough to take care of Jondy," she tells me. My teen job of taking care of the toddlers has prepared me for this.

I'm delighted. He's mine.

"Make sure you bring him back to me every two hours to nurse, at least until we get him on a bottle," she calls after me as I carry him out of her room.

I now have two, nearly twin, baby brothers. Although we don't really consider Auntie Jeannie one of my father's wives in the same way Esther and Ruthie are, she's kind of been adopted by our family, so Andy becomes our little brother. He is the fattest baby on the planet—his fat rolls have fat rolls. He doesn't cry or fuss much, like the other babies do. He just lays in his bouncer like Buddha, his fat cheeks resting on his shoulders. Jondy is the opposite. Wiggly and wiry, he wants constant movement. His big ears, like mine, stick out from his pixie head. His goofy, drooling smile lights his eyes with pure joy when I cross my eyes and stick out my tongue. When my mother can't calm his fussing, I rock him to sleep. There is no off-the-clock time with him. Even in the Family where we are used to always caring for younger children, eleven is young to be in charge of a newborn. Having this responsibility makes me feel like a real teen, and I can't help but feel self-important whenever my baby brother spits up on my shoulder. It proves I'm not a kid anymore.

My father seems proud of his two new sons, though he is too busy with the teens to spend time with Andy or Jondy. He and Aunt Faithy have been loving running the new teen group. They have a willing audience to listen to their stories of the early days of the Family. But his talent for ignoring things he doesn't want to hear doesn't sit well with the Shepherds from WS.

A few weeks after the births of his two new sons, my father is sent to Japan. The visit is supposed to be a few weeks long, so no one makes a big deal when he takes my two oldest brothers, Hobo and Nehi, with him and brings them to the HCS. The boys are sixteen and seventeen, and it's time for them to leave home. But my father is privately hoping that this invitation is more than a simple visit. After all, he knows that Grandpa is secretly living in the HCS.

At first I barely notice my father's disappearance. In recent years, he'd been spending more and more time on his real love, the animals. Overseeing building projects and witnessing to and cementing relationships with our key System friends took the rest of his time. When I stopped working with the animals, I rarely saw him, until he started taking on the teen activities. Even then, I interacted with him only as a Shepherd, not as my father. Now, in his absence, other adults quickly fill the power vacuum left, and our daily regimen continues the same. Until an unexpected visitor arrives.

13

THE GRAND EXPERIMENT

Shortly after my father's departure, we get word that someone from Grandpa's house is coming to visit the Farm. There is huge excitement and even greater speculation over who it might be. I secretly hope that I will finally meet Davidito, but I hardly dare to think it might be Grandpa coming.

Turns out, it's Auntie Sara, who has been living in hiding with Grandpa. Boy, are we excited to meet her, someone we've read about in the comics and the Mo Letters for our whole lives. The fact that someone so important is coming to our faraway village feels like we've won the lottery.

Auntie Sara arrives in secret, as the leaders always do. The first glimpse I have of her is at Devotions. There is nothing dramatic in her appearance. She's a rather plain auntie with long, straight, thinning brown hair. She wears the same shapeless long dress as the other aunties. But there is nothing subtle about her impact.

Her first night, she gathers all the teens together, except me. I'm not told about this meeting until I hear the shocked whispers from the teens afterward, and I'm cruelly disappointed that I missed out. Apparently, Auntie Sara did some kind of public sex demonstration with one of my brothers, in front of all the teens! I couldn't tell if what I'd heard was true, false, or mashed up in a game of broken telephone, but whatever it was, nothing like that had ever happened at our Farm before. There's always been plenty of sex, but always behind closed doors. *What does this mean for the rest of us?*

At teen Devotions the next morning, Auntie Sara explains that we are going to try out some experiments in how to raise Godly, dedicated, Family young people.

"Though younger teens under sixteen can no longer have sex with the adults, you are still strongly encouraged to have sex with each other," Auntie Sara tells us. "I'm going to implement an experimental teen program here before introducing it in other countries."

She explains that teen girls are ready to get pregnant and marry at fifteen or sixteen, and in the big Homes they do. But many teens in the Family live in small Homes, with few in their age range. With Homes spread out around the world, the teens are in a tough spot: they are taught to have sex, but they don't have the chance to interact with many other Family members their age to find marriage partners.

This is the real reason the leadership has decided to create teen training centers, where teens can learn to be better soldiers for Jesus and meet other Family teens to find marriage partners, settle down, and be so busy having babies that they won't have time to get into trouble.

Our Farm is going to be the grand experiment.

One of Auntie Sara's main changes to our routine is the introduction of a rotating "sharing" schedule for us teens, like the adult sharing schedule. During our Get Outs, we have already been pairing off in boy-girl couples on Walkie Talkies, walks to get to know each other. Now, it's time to take it to the next level.

In addition to finding marriage partners, we're expected to have sex in our own age group, but not to get selfish or cliquish, like in the System high school movies we've seen at movie night, where the hot guy gets with only the hot girls. In the Family, everyone is supposed to share sex with each other, even if they are not attracted to the person.

Children twelve and under are exempt from participating, but the age lines are blurry and ever-changing. Now the adults are saying twelve is considered a teen. I've just turned eleven, but I'm put into the teen sharing schedule. Once a week our names are put on the bulletin board next to someone else's, and after dinner, we are supposed to get into bed with them for an hour. They are called word dates. We're told that we don't have to have sex with the person we're paired up with, but we all know it's expected that we do *something* sexual. We're not given condoms because if we get pregnant, it's God's will.

I'm a tough case. The Shepherds can't pair me with my brothers, so there are few other teen boys they can put me with. At least that's their excuse when I get put with Eddie, who, at fourteen, is one of the youngest teen boys, which is probably why I'm stuck with him.

After dinner, sweaty, chubby, annoying Eddie comes to my single bed in a room I share with five other teen girls, who are all away on their dates. We get under the covers, fully dressed. *It's no big deal, I can do this*, I tell myself. I try to focus on the mechanics of it, ignoring my feelings of disgust. We talk about any old thing, trying to make this seem normal and not so embarrassing.

I hate his breath in my face, and I don't want to kiss him. He is eager, though, and keeps talking. I can feel him pressing his hard-on against me through his pants. If only he would shut up, I might be able to do this. I remember the lessons my mother and Uncle Jeff taught me. I put my hand on the bulge, and he shuts up. He unzips his jeans and pulls it out, and I try to ignore any emotion about what I'm doing, while still figuring out how to do it.

I grip it and move my hand up and down, copying the motions I remember being shown. He starts making noises and adjusts my hand a few times. Okay. I make a mental note. It doesn't take long, but it seems like forever before he grunts, and the sticky stuff comes out.

I jump up, grossed out. "I gotta go wash my hands," I say as I make my escape to the bathroom.

I pray he'll be gone when I return, and I take my time drying my hands. When I creep back in, I'm relieved to find that he left. *Okay, I survived that*, I think as I push away the feelings of revulsion and bury them down. It's just because I think Eddie is gross, I tell myself. But tangled in my disgust, I have a sense of pride. I did what all the other teens are doing. I deserve to be with the older kids.

A year ago, I only cared about being faster, tougher, and smarter than my brothers, or at least keeping up with them. Now I'll do anything to look and act like the older girls. I want the teen boys to notice me.

The girls brought cool clothes from other countries, like stretchy, short tube skirts and tube tops. How do they know that the yellow tube top will match the plaid shirt with the yellow stripe and the white stretch skirt? I try to take note of the different outfits and how they combine them to learn the secret.

I become a regular at the Free Store, the hot, stuffy room at the Farm where everyone throws all the clothes and things they don't need. I pick through the castoffs and try to look sexy and cool but can never get it quite right. My tube top doesn't look the same as it does on the other girls; it keeps slipping down because I barely have any boobs to hold it up. I need something to help.

I tell my mother that I'm getting breasts and need a bra now. She looks at the little swollen nubs under my T-shirt and tells me I don't need one yet but promises to look. Why would I want a bra anyway? Her motto is "Come on ma, burn your bra!"—the title of another Mo Letter. I walk away, cheeks burning. I'm embarrassed to talk to my mother about these things, because I know she'll tease me about them in public, thinking she's so funny: "Oh, look at Faithy, she is getting little breasts!" *Ugh*.

I stand in front of the mirror and carefully catalog each feature on my face, trying to determine why I cannot get the teen girl "look." Plain brown hair, brown eyes, straight nose, medium-size mouth, straight teeth, round cheeks. I realize that I am plain because each feature is boringly normal. Nothing stands out. Not like blue eyes or blond hair or a tipped-up button nose. Well, if I can't compete on my looks, I'll just have to act sexier. I practice walking with my hips swaying from side to side, like Grandpa talks about in the Letters. *"A woman should walk like the pendulum on a clock,"* he says.

My whole worth and acceptance into the teen group seems to hinge on being able to attract a guy. It doesn't matter that I don't really like any of them, and the few who are not repulsive are not interested in me. No matter how I try, I feel like the older teens are in a bubble, and even though I'm swimming as fast as I can, they just keep floating further away.

I miss the easy fun I had with Patrick, but he's beneath me now in the kids' group. Now that I've crossed the line into the teens' world, we don't mix. Unsure and self-conscious, I don't fit in with either the kids or the teens.

My father is still not back from Japan. At first, we thought his trip was being extended by a few weeks, but then a few weeks turned into a few months, and then word started circulating that he might not come back *at all.* New Shepherds have arrived from WS and are running things. Aunt Faithy has been sent back to Latin America. The Shepherds tell us only what they think we need to know, and all our communication flows through them.

Except for my mother, no one seems upset about my father's departure. My brothers nearly have a party when they find out he isn't coming back, except all their energy is focused on the new wave of teen girls. Even troublemaker Josh is starting to shape up now that he's in a relationship with quiet, pretty, pale Laura.

I can't say I miss my father, exactly, but I do miss his adventures.

Our close-knit family has unraveled, but I barely notice because I'm too busy watching the toddlers, keeping up with the teens, taking care of Jondy, and trying to attract anyone who isn't Eddie.

I'm rocking a fussy Jondy to put him down for a nap when my mother calls me into her room.

"Faithy," she says slowly. "I have some news."

I'm about to ask what it is, but she rushes on in a tumble of words.

"I've been invited to go to WS to work on the Words. It's a great honor, something I've wanted to do for years."

I stare at her. "What about us?"

She shakes her head slowly. "I can't take you kids with me. They only want me. You'll have to stay here. But don't worry," she says with forced cheer. "You'll have lots of people to watch out for you. Esther takes care of Nina so much anyway, and you're both busy in your groups."

"What about Jondy?" He's only four months old.

"You've been doing a great job with him. He'll be at the nursery, but I want you to keep an eye on him. He's going to be your responsibility."

I sit in shock. Seeing the explosion, but not yet feeling the impact. "How long will you be gone?"

"I don't know, honey," she says, brushing a piece of hair out of my face. "It could be awhile. I'm moving there."

I try hard to push down the rising panic. *Why? Why you? Why now? What about Jondy and Nina?* I dare not say, "What about me?" I'm old enough to be left. As hard as I try to act older and fit in with the teens, deep down I am just an eleven-year-old kid who is losing her mother. At least Esther is still here, even though she rarely leaves her room most days.

I start to feel pressure behind my eyeballs and will myself not to cry. After all, this isn't the first time my mother has left me. I don't remember it, but I was told she left me when I was just a few months old. Aunt Faithy sent her to the Philippines to break her pride, and when she returned a couple of months later, apparently, I was so angry with her I refused to nurse from her ever again.

"Where are you going?" I force myself to ask.

"You know I can't tell you," she says, kissing my forehead. "All WS homes and their locations are *Selah*."

Of course I know this. I'd just hoped I might be able to picture where she is and how far away, instead of dropping into nothingness.

"It's God's will," she says.

My mother always wanted to be important to the Word. And since the Word is Grandpa, she's tried to get as close to him as possible. Marrying Grandpa's son, being a secretary to my father and Aunt Faithy, then continuing to work on the Mo Letters, even out at the Farm. A few years ago, she had written to Mama Maria, asking to be sent to WS. That was the pinnacle of discipleship. But now, with Jondy just born, she's not so sure. She says, it's strange that after so many years of ambition, dreaming, and asking to go to WS, now, when she has given up that dream and doesn't really want to go, she is called. That's how God works.

Still, she knows such an offer will never come again. To refuse it would seal her forever as not being a strong, dedicated disciple, willing to give up everything, including children and husband, for God.

I can't picture exactly what WS is like. A Family Home, where no one witnesses, where you can't have a stream of Family members as visitors or go to area Fellowships, where you live in constant secrecy even from the rest of the Family, where people work in small, dim rooms on their computers, typing prophecies. Although you probably get to see Grandpa. I think my mother hopes she will be with Grandpa again.

The next week, as she prepares to go to the airport, a few of us gather to say goodbye. I sit on her bed as she packs the last items into her suitcase. There is not much to say. She hugs me and puts

Jondy into my arms. She gives three-year-old Nina a teary squeeze and passes her back to Esther.

"I'll watch out for them," Esther says.

Then my mother is gone.

She promises to call, but we both know that's a lie. Long-distance phone calls are rare to nonexistent, and anyway, we're bound to the three-minute rule. No one in the Family is allowed to speak on the phone for more than three minutes, because the longer someone is on the phone, the more likely it is they'll say something they shouldn't, which could be overheard by government forces tapping our phones.

My heart flaps around in my chest like a wounded bird. I go back to my group and my routine. It doesn't change, but there is an anchor missing, an empty space I try to ignore. I don't know where in the world she is, and I don't know how to contact her. I pick up a crying Jondy and start walking back and forth across the nursery, bouncing him rhythmically. "Shh, shh, shh," I soothe.

I'm not angry at my mother for leaving, at least not consciously. *How can I be angry at her? She must obey God's will, as we all must.*

Time passes slowly in my mother's absence. I spend every afternoon, after our morning Devotions and classes, working in the nursery so I can be with Jondy. There are six babies in the nursery, but only Jondy stays there full-time. I help take care of all of them, but Jondy is mine. I quickly become an expert at diaper rash, sterilizing bottles, and soothing cranky teethers.

During these long, exhausting months filled with work, infrequent boring classes, taking care of Jondy, and missing my mother, I have one bright spot: I'm in love!

It snuck up on me. One day while we were having Get Out together in the field, I was looking for someone to play badminton with (Grandpa says we should call it "goodminton," because we don't want to be negative about exercise, which is good for us), and Michael, one of the new teen boys who just arrived from India, smiled and offered to play with me. I didn't think much of him at first, with his straight brown hair and eyeglasses. But as we played, he laughed and chatted with me, his eyes twinkling. By the end of the hour, I thought he was the most handsome boy at the Farm. Even his glasses looked cute. I'm enjoying his company, and even more than that, he makes me feel noticed.

At the teen dance night a couple weeks later, all my self-consciousness and inadequacies bubble up. I am pretending so hard that I fit in, but the whole time I'm watching the teen girls, comparing myself to them. As I make my way along the wall, Michael walks up and asks me to dance. He dances four dances with me! And tells me how pretty I look! Just like that, I fall in love.

Walking alone the short distance back to my house after the dance, I can't feel my feet on the concrete. My heart is soaring up out of my chest. I stretch my fingers toward the stars, skipping and spinning all the way. Heaven!

I come up with every excuse I can to see Michael and hang out nearby. One day after dinner, I wait in the dining room while he is on cleanup duty.

As I wait for teen Jessica to finally finish sweeping so Michael and I can be alone, I feel pulled between two forces—desperation to run away and desperation to be near him. Finally, as I walk out to leave, Michael steps outside with me. Before I can say anything, he leans down and kisses me on the mouth. I hold my breath while a rush of pleasure sweeps through me. He loves me, too! He waves me off, and my joy is boundless. For one moment, I'm certain and unafraid.

The next day, I write him a poem, pouring out my love on a small pink piece of note paper. I slip it to him after dinner, and he thanks me. I watch the clock waiting for his response. One hour. Two hours. Six hours. It never comes. Soon it becomes clear he won't be writing back, and the humiliation sets in. I blame myself. *How could I have written something so cheesy! I'll never write another love poem again,* I think, disgusted with myself.

But I don't have to worry about my humiliation for long. Michael is leaving. He is moving to Japan. I don't know why. These things just happen. People come and people go—their visa is not renewed, their parents call them home, they are sent away as a punishment.

Despite my shame, I desperately try to find a way to be alone with him to say goodbye. We meet down at the farmyard, and he kisses me sweetly, holding my face, while I try to hold back my tears.

The next day he is gone, and everyone goes on as if nothing has changed. But my whole world has turned to ash. That night I sob into my pillow for hours until I fall asleep. I didn't know a heart could hurt this much. The pain lodges inside as I go through my chores, cleaning toilets and watching kids, sitting in Devotions. I move in a daze for weeks—slowly coming back to the present out of the gray haze that separates me from the laughter of others.

I will love you forever, I think.

After four months without a word from Mom, she returns. We're in the middle of a whooping cough outbreak, and Jondy is terribly sick. He is just eight months old, and Mom is furious that nobody told her that her kids were all sick and that her baby could die. She hugs me close for a long time, and I smell her familiar mom smell. I'm happy to see her, especially for Jondy's sake. He is struggling to breathe, and I don't know what to do.

Mom seems broken, sad, and lost, but happy to be back, wanting to be welcomed, desperate for connection. I want to give her what she needs, but I feel distant from her. I've navigated caring for my baby brother and losing my first love without her or anyone else to talk to. I try to bury those feelings, to act mature. So, I ask her what happened—why she came back.

She begins, slowly. Her experience at WS was not what she expected. She was sent to live in a small, orderly WS home run by a Frenchwoman named Abeille. There were about sixteen people, including children, in the Home, and Mom was put on childcare duty instead of working on editing the Mo Letters.

"I thought, 'Well, if nothing else, I'll get to work on publishing,' but that's not what I did. I was just so unhappy. I thought, 'Why am I taking care of Abeille's baby when I have my own baby at home who needs me?' I was crying all the time and, finally one night, something went wrong with my heart, like I literally felt it break and I could hardly breathe. It felt like some sort of heart attack," she tells me.

She thought she was strong enough to put God first, but she couldn't take being separated from her kids. She had a nervous breakdown and begged to be sent home. After a number of weeks, they finally relented. She left in disgrace, her dream of a greater path of service crushed by her failure.

The Family always had a hard-core emphasis that "whoever does not forsake all that he has, he cannot be my disciple" Luke 14:33. We were scared by the cautionary tale of Ananias and his wife, Sapphira, disciples who in the Book of Acts (5:1–11) sell a piece of property and hold back some of the purchase price instead of giving it all to the Apostles and are struck dead by God.

"When I left, Abeille told me, 'Your baby Jondy will probably die if you don't leave him behind and forsake him for God.' I was terrified it might come true."

I feel sad for my mother. She seems like a broken version of herself, and it's hard to see her struggle with everything she's left behind and everything left in front of her. I help as much as I can, and she is grateful. She tells me she doesn't recognize me anymore, that I'm not acting like her little girl. I don't know what to say. I've grown up, quickly. I don't spend time with her after dinner or seek her out to talk like I used to. I don't need her.

I feel like a traitor, but I spend more time thinking about Michael than my mother. He's the one person who made me feel special.

Whenever people arrive at the Farm from Japan, I eagerly ask if they've seen Michael. Usually I'm disappointed, but sometimes I get bits of information. My love for him and the ache of loss is just as sharp as when he first left.

A teen arrives from Japan, and I approach her right away, shy but eager. I can hardly keep from bursting out: "Do you know Michael?"

"Sure," the newcomer says, rolling her eyes. "I know Michael. That guy's a player. Always hitting on younger girls."

My breath stops in my throat, and my mouth moves wordlessly. The realization smacks me in the face: I wasn't special. I'm just like every other little girl who falls for Michael's charming smile while he makes his real move on the older girls, who are much harder for a skinny boy with glasses to impress.

I feel a toxic mix of shame and anger. What a *fool* I've been! Dreaming after him. Writing him a poem. I want to gag in humiliation at the thought of that. Never again. *Never again*, I resolve with silent fury. I will never be the first to fall in love.

I am the Ice Queen.

14

SUFFERING MAKES YOU BITTER OR BETTER

The news comes as a shock: I'm leaving the Farm.

I've never been outside Macau, Hong Kong, and China (that I can remember, at least), and now I'm moving to Thailand. I don't know who made the decision; all I know is that WS leadership said that my mother, Jondy, Nina, and I are to go, and of course, we obey like good soldiers—stepping out into the unknown to follow God's will.

Mom seems excited about the move as she babbles about new opportunities. It's taken her months to recover her strength after her breakdown. She is feeling better each day, but my father is still gone, and after her failed stay at WS and with the new leadership running everything here at the Farm, she feels useless.

A week after we get the news that we are moving, we are on a plane. I do my best to say goodbye to my siblings, the animals, and the rest of the teen group, but it's too fast to process. Esther has tears in her eyes as she holds each of us tight. I know she'll miss Nina especially; she always seemed more Esther's child than my mother's.

As we step onto the aircraft, everything is a wonder. I keep wiggling in my seat, turning front and aft trying to see everything at once. The stewardesses wear beautiful purple orchids, and they give us each one. The air smells like perfume. I stick my forehead against the cold glass of the airplane window. I don't want to miss a single moment of my first experience of flying. When the stewardess closes the door and the engine begins to rumble, I grip the seat arms. But that's nothing next to the feeling of take-off—of my stomach dropping to the landing gear as the rest of me soars into the clouds.

When we land a few hours later, my mother, Jondy, Nina, and I step to the open airplane door and are hit by a wave of hot, wet air. It takes a moment for my breathing to adjust. I thought I was used to tropical humidity from Macau, but Bangkok takes it to a new level.

After wading through the sticky airport with our luggage, we spot two white people my mom's age smiling and waving at us in the arrivals area. We hug and kiss, as is the Family custom, and pile into their van. They drive us to a huge compound with high concrete walls and barbed wire—so different from the Farm. There's no welcome party or cute animals, at least none that I can see in the dark. We're herded into a very large two-story school building, where I'm immediately separated from Mom and my siblings. Nina and Jondy are sent to live with their age groups, boarding school style, and I don't know where Mom goes. "I'll see you at family time!" she calls as I'm led away.

A man introduces himself as Uncle Steven and leads me into a twenty-by-thirty-foot room filled with bunk beds. He points to a thin mattress on the floor. "Sleep here tonight. We'll get you a bunk tomorrow." I sit down, surrounded by ten little bodies curled like shrimp, and the horror of the situation slaps me in the face. I've been demoted into the kids' group.

The following morning, I voice my frustration at the unfairness to Uncle Steven. "I've already been in the teens group for some time. Can I please be sent there?"

He just stares, shocked that I'm disagreeing with his decision. Once he collects himself, he explains that the case is settled. In Thailand, the teen group starts at age thirteen. No exceptions. I'm told to yield to my new situation. I've got zero interest in being an Older Child again, watching and discussing the lessons from the same old OC-approved movies I've seen ten times. Demerit charts, boring classes because I've already learned the fourth-grade grammar and times tables they are teaching.

After breakfast, instead of falling into line, I find some teens to hang out with in the hallway and start chatting to them. Uncle Steven sees me and gives me a warning. He sends me to rejoin the OC group immediately. I drag my feet, but I don't dare disobey a direct command.

The regulations here in the Bangkok Combo are much stricter than at the Farm. We march everywhere in single file, as if we actually are in the army that the Family is always going on about. I follow the new routine, but I refuse to smile about it. Whenever the teens pass by, my eyes turn to follow them. I deserve to be in their group. I'm better than this. *I earned it!*

But the Shepherds don't think so. Everything I did, the person I was on the Farm, is gone. They don't care that I'm Ho's daughter. It's as if I never existed before this moment.

The second time Uncle Steven catches me talking to one of the teen boys a week later, his eyes turn cold and hard. He instructs me to follow him. Back in the OC room, he hands me a big piece of white cardboard and colored markers. He tells me to use the materials to make a sign with letters one-inch tall that reads, "Please do not speak to me. I'm on SILENCE RESTRICTION! I am learning to be yielded and submissive."

I stare at him in shock, barely understanding his words. My mind is whirling, searching for a way out. *How did this happen?* I'd gotten good at judging what would set off an adult, what would push them too far. Or so I thought. I'm so confused. I'm being punished for *speaking* with teen boys, when at the Farm I was a teen!

"You were flirting," Uncle Steven accuses.

I don't understand. Not a year ago I was supposed to give teen boys hand jobs on a schedule. Now it seems the Family has gone the complete opposite direction, which is fine with me, but I still don't want to be treated like a little child.

"We were just talking and laughing about something nonsexual," I explain, trying to make Uncle Steven understand. The boy had said something funny about soccer, and I'd laughed. I wasn't shaking my ass or trying to kiss him.

Uncle Steven looks down at me with the stony face of the truly righteous. Then he points to the poster board and the markers. "I expect to see the sign tomorrow morning," he says, and he walks away.

I ask one of the kids, and it seems that no one else in the large Bangkok Combo has ever received this punishment. Great. Another experiment.

I spread out the colored markers and white cardboard on my small bunk bed. I'm vaguely aware of the other kids as they leave the room, heading to dinner. Alone in the gathering twilight, I feel all my bravado dissolve. Fear of public humiliation is far worse than any physical pain. Pain, a spanking, I can grit my teeth, duck my head, and push through. But this humiliation seeps into my bones and fractures my very sense of self.

The sight of my limp hand blurs; soon I'm gasping for breath, sobbing, tears and snot fighting to escape the injustice of this trap. My head aches with the force of my sobs, my eyes are raw red, my face is swollen. But, finally, emotion spent, like a robot, I pick up the green marker and begin to write.

The next morning, I present the sign to Uncle Steven. He takes out a thick piece of rope and attaches one end to each side of the sign. Then he hangs it around my neck. The cardboard stretches all the way across my chest, and the rough rope scratches the back of my neck. My face set, I walk into the communal dining room for breakfast, the sign blazing across my front in neon colors impossible to ignore. Sixty people I hardly know stare at me. This is my official introduction to the Home members: a proclamation that I am such a horrible person that I deserve extreme, public punishment, a breaking.

Breakings derive from the biblical story of the potter and clay: if the soft clay the potter is fashioning into a vase has a hard lump in it, the vase has to be smashed, the lump removed, and then the clay refashioned into something better (Jeremiah 18:1–4). A breaking is not the average correction or spanking; it's a crushing and remaking.

The shock of the sign is enough to keep me silent and make everyone in the Home sit up and take notice. I lower my eyes to the floor to avoid the stinging stares. I cannot even speak to defend myself. I'm only allowed to speak with the OC group's two teachers, Uncle Steven and Uncle Joel. *How can I ever hope to adjust to my new home now?*

That afternoon at naptime, Uncle Steven hands me a Mo Book opened to a Letter titled *Prayer for Magdalene*. Then he leaves, and I'm alone once again. My hands shake as I feel the weight of it in my fingers. I know what this means. This is the scariest prayer for anyone in the Family. As I sit on the bottom bunk, my neck curved to not hit my head on the wood above it, I make the most difficult request of my life: I ask God to break me. My lips tremble as I ask Him to break my pride and spirit. My eyes again burn with tears as I give Him permission to do terrible things to me. I am so scared, as I have absolute conviction that He will do it. But I don't see any way out.

For the first few days, it's hard to remember that I am not to speak, especially with all the new rules I'm expected to know. My father liked to act militaristic—two sheets of toilet paper, two-minute showers—but the Thailand commune takes the Family's militaristic attitude to a whole new level. In addition to marching everywhere in single file, the OC group is on dish duty for the whole sixty-person Combo. As we wash, everyone, except me for now, must quote Bible chapters out loud in unison, without pausing or slipping up. After we wipe down the large tables, Uncle Steven bends down eye level with the table to see if we've left even a speck of dirt. I learn to be very thorough.

If we slip up, there is the demerit chart—a large chart on the wall with everyone's name and the days of the week. If we do anything we are not supposed to, an "X," to signify a demerit, is marked next to our name. Anyone who gets three demerits in a day or five in the week will be punished with extra chores and miss the weekly movie. The cruelest invention is double or triple demerits. If you are caught "goofing off" in class, the teacher will yell out, "A demerit for you!" If you try to explain or justify yourself, you'll get another demerit for talking back. As I watch Uncle Steven hand down punishments, I'm almost relieved my silence keeps me from condemning myself.

I read the list of Mo Letters that Uncle Steven assigns me, and each day at naptime, he sits with me on the balcony, where I tell him what I'm learning from the Letters and my punishment. "Yes, I was rebellious, feeling like I was too good for the kids' group and deserved to be in the teen group. Now, I see that was my abominable pride," I confess.

During the hour of family time each evening, I sit mutely on the floor, not allowed to even speak to my mother. She looks worried as Jondy pulls on my shirt to get me to play with him and four-year-old Nina cries in her arms. I desperately miss the Farm, the animals, my friends and siblings. *What is everyone doing? Patrick? My brothers?* I have no idea and no one to ask. I have no way to communicate with them. We're allowed to write letters and turn them over to a Shepherd to mail, but doing so doesn't seem worth it.

Uncle Steven is the only person I can talk to in this unfamiliar home and country. Isolated from everyone else, I grow close to him, and he speaks to me like he is my confidant.

"How long will I be on Silence Restriction?" I finally have the courage to ask.

"Until we feel that you have truly changed," he replies.

Ten days into this everlasting silence, Uncle Steven permits me to speak for one night to celebrate my twelfth birthday. Like the bat mitzvah in the Jewish faith, this is supposed to be the biggest birthday of my life, when I become a woman. This is the only time a person gets their own party separate from the group birthday that celebrates all the birthdays in a Home under that month's astrological sign. People pray over and receive prophecies for the new twelve-year-old. The birthday person is given a personalized certificate declaring them a man or a woman.

But with the Family's decree changing the age for sex with adults and for drinking wine to fifteen or sixteen instead of twelve a couple of years ago, reaching this milestone doesn't have quite the same practical significance.

After dinner, the OCs gather in our bedroom, where Uncle Steven presents me with a cake and a laminated certificate that reads, "Becoming a Woman," along with my name, age, and the date. Beneath a small picture of me, there is a caption that reads, "'Who can find a virtuous woman? For her price is far above rubies.' Proverbs 31:10. 'Loyal and Willing, with whole hearts, we're giving our lives for the Kingdom of God!'" This birthday is such a letdown. I don't feel like a woman, just another insignificant kid.

All of us kids sit in a circle and eat a dense homemade carrot cake. I struggle to stretch my lips into a smile. I'm painfully aware of the Mo Letter Uncle Steven assigned me to read yesterday. It said that no matter how we feel, we must always smile and put on a happy face for others. Then everyone gathers to pray over me. As I kneel in the center, they place their hands on my head, back, or arms, wherever they can reach, and commit me to God. Afterward, my short reprieve is done and I'm back to Silence Restriction. Humiliation is my home.

At lights-out, because of the humidity, all of us kids line up in our underwear so Uncle Steven or Uncle Joel can rub talcum powder on our naked backs. Some of us older girls try to cover our breasts with our arms or hold a shirt over our chest as one of the uncles rubs powder on us. Then, once we're in bed, Uncle Steven comes for our underwear check. Grandpa says that in tropical countries the genitals need to be aired out, so we're not allowed to wear underwear at night. We have no air conditioning, and in one hundred degrees with 100 percent humidity, I lie under my sheet, sweating. I want to rip off the itchy cotton covering, but I'm naked, and at twelve, I'm far too embarrassed to lie fully exposed in a mixed-gender room with two male Shepherds. I've learned not to take those risks. So, every night, when Uncle Steven comes around to feel our hips under the sheet to make sure we don't have anything on, I push my underwear to my ankles, and when he leaves, I pull them back up under the sheet. My small, silent rebellion.

I try to get used to the complete lack of privacy—not that we ever had much on the Farm, but it was never like this. We all shower together, boys and girls, in one bathroom after our exercise each day—only five minutes for all ten of us. The bathroom is, in typical Thai style, a single undivided room with a toilet in the corner and a cistern along the wall filled from a spout. The whole room, tiled pink from floor to ceiling, is the shower. We crowd naked around the cistern, passing the large plastic scoopers back and forth to rinse ourselves. Then we run out, grabbing towels and drying ourselves in thirty seconds. Uncle Joel is standing outside with a watch in his hand, timing us. If we are late, a demerit.

Each day I wake, not knowing if I will be on Silence Restriction for another day. Normally, Silence Restriction might go for a few hours or days at most. After two weeks, I stop wondering. This is my life now. I learn to communicate with my eyes and hands, or I speak to Uncle Steven. My initial horror and humiliation become my new normal. I realize I can adapt to anything, no matter how terrible. People stop trying to talk to me or expecting me to answer.

I do my best to fully submit and learn my lessons, to let my pride be crushed out of me, to become yielded to God. And I feel better in giving up control. It is up to Him now; I just obey.

After a full month on Silence Restriction, Uncle Steven surprises me during our afternoon open-heart talk. "We think you are ready to come off Silence Restriction," he tells me. "You have really changed over the last month."

I stare in shock. I'm not sure what to think. I've finally gotten used to fading into the background, calling no attention to myself, observing in silence. I'm actually nervous about speaking again. *What if I say something wrong and get put back on Silence Restriction, or worse? How will I talk to the other kids in my group or in the Home after never speaking to them?* I simply nod submissively and hand him my sign.

Now I deal with the stares all over again. People expect me to speak, but my throat feels glued shut after thirty days of disuse. Words slowly come back to me, but my voice sounds like a croak to my own ears. So, I remain quiet, speaking only when I need to.

A week later, Uncle Steven calls me aside. "We want you to be the Bellwether of the OC group," he declares. The Bellwether is the most obedient sheep in a flock, the one who stays closest to the Shepherd; the Shepherd puts a bell around that sheep's neck, so the other sheep will follow it.

After being the lowest of the low, I'm being elevated to the position of class leader, of head girl. The kids who weren't allowed to speak with me just days before now must follow my instructions, and I must report on them if they disobey. After my month of iso-

lation and breaking, Uncle Steven knows I have no competing alli-
ances. He can trust me; I'm the last person to cause trouble.

Now that I'm off Silence Restriction, I try to make friends with the
two girls in the group closest to my age, Clare and Marie, but under
our smiles and small talk, we circle each other warily. No one can
be trusted not to report a wrong word to the Shepherds. And I'm
the Bellwether, so they know where my loyalty lies.

I join the OC's weekly witnessing excursion, where we tell people about Jesus, pass out posters, and ask for donations. I'm excited
to see a little of the city outside of our Combo walls.

I've been witnessing since I was three, but the sting of rejection
never goes away no matter how many years I've been walking up
to strangers on the street, asking them if they want to hear about
Jesus. I've learned to ignore the pain with a big smile plastered
across my face.

People need to hear about Jesus. How I feel is not at all important.

Chulalongkorn University in Bangkok is our regular witnessing
spot. Twelve of us pile out of the van and are paired off into five
teams with one or two kids and one adult. We walk around the
sprawling campus, saying a little prayer under our breath for Jesus
to guide us to the souls who will be receptive to His message.

I like it here. The crumbling stone paths and walls softened by
shady rain trees and bright red hibiscus blooming in the cracks.
Birds chirp as students sit alone on worn benches reading or in
groups around tables, eating the yellow durian fruit that smells like
stinky socks.

"Let's talk to him," my adult partner suggests. He points to a
young man sitting at a picnic table, textbook in hand.

I follow my partner over, and at his nudge, I blurt, "This is for
you" in Thai. The young man laughs in surprise and takes the color

poster depicting an image of the Beast and 666. I learned the phrase during our Thai lesson yesterday; I hope I said it right.

My witnessing partner takes over, and even though I can understand only a few words of Thai, it's easy to follow the conversation, because I've heard this same exchange thousands of times. Finally, my partner asks, "Would you like to ask Jesus into your heart, so that you can go to Heaven when you die?" I wait in anticipation. *Will this be a soul we can write down in victory and boast about when we get home, or a rejection that we just wasted a half hour on?* There is always a little unspoken underlying competition between the teams who go out witnessing.

"What must I do?" the boy asks agreeably.

I take his smiling nod for acceptance. Whew. I feel a sense of relief and happiness—this wasn't a waste after all.

"Just repeat after me," my partner responds, pausing every few words so the young man can parrot him. "'Dear Jesus, please come into my heart. Forgive my sins. Help me to love You and others and take me to Heaven when I die. In Jesus's name I pray. Amen.'"

The teen looks up, surprised that this is all there is to it.

"Now you are saved forever!" My partner congratulates him.

I beam a smile when the student looks at me, genuinely happy that this nice young man will be spared Hell's fires.

My partner suggests, "If you want to know more, why don't you give us your contact info? We have Bible study sessions every week nearby."

I stare off, looking for our next target as the boy scribbles down his address.

I like witnessing to the college students in Bangkok. No one turns us away. They are all so friendly, greeting us, strange foreigners, with smiles and offers of durian, which I politely refuse, though I gratefully accept the slices of guava. Guavas here are huge, the size of a softball, and hard like an apple. Nothing like the custard-soft sweetness of the small guavas from our Farm.

On the drive home, I gaze out the window, enjoying the peaceful, lush campus, until we pass through the gates into the Bangkok streets, full of honking, belching trucks, scooters, and tuk-tuks.

I'm adjusting to the new people, routines, and my position as Bellwether. But during our nightly hour of family time, I notice my mother is unraveling. We sit together on her single bed in her small room and try to read picture books with Jondy and Nina to keep them entertained. When she hugs us goodnight, she whispers that she doesn't want to be separated from us kids. I try to understand what she's going through. My mother had been a leader at the Farm; now she's not even a valued foot soldier, just a disgraced single mother doing whatever chores she is assigned to in the Home. When will she recover from what happened at WS? I watch her growing more and more unhappy and afraid, but I don't know what to do.

Several nights later, Mom surprises me when she announces that she is going to take us out of the compound for a walk.

"I didn't have Get Out today," she says when a young man spots us about to exit the big gates in the high wall that surrounds the commune. "We're just going to the park across the street." My mother shoots him a big smile as we walk through.

There is no guard at the gate, but people are always watching each other, and if you plan to leave the property, you are expected to get permission. We are told it's for our safety so that if anything bad happens, any accident, someone will know where to come find us.

Mom glances behind her as she adjusts Jondy in her left arm and her shoulder bag with her right. Then she grabs Nina's hand and steps through the high entry gates and out onto the public sidewalk of our quiet residential street. At first, she walks at a normal pace, but once we turn the corner, she breaks into a sprint and begins racing down the street. I don't know what she's doing, and for a moment, I hesitate.

"Come on!" she yells back, and I start running.

She is moving too quickly for Nina's toddler legs, and soon she is literally dragging my sister along the pavement. I speed up, snatch Nina's hand, scoop her up in my arms, and run alongside my mother, dodging cow poop that's been left by the neighborhood cows that roam freely in the streets.

"What are you doing?" I shout, puffing hard. "Where are we going?"

"Shh, I'll tell you soon," she replies breathlessly.

She keeps going, through the streets and back alleyways of Bang-kok until finally she comes to a stop on the blacktop and throws her arm in the air to signal to a passing tuk-tuk. The vehicle comes to a halt in front of us. Mom pushes us aboard, handing up Jondy, and mumbles something to the driver. As we pull away from the curb, she is shaking and I'm gasping for breath.

I try to stay calm as I balance my little brother on my lap with Nina sitting between us. But I am frightened. *What is my mother doing? Where is she taking us?* The tuk-tuk driver stops in front of a dingy, dark motel in a seedy-looking area I've never been to before. Now I'm worried. I know we are in Bangkok, but I have no idea where. I've barely been outside the compound walls except for a few witnessing trips.

I follow Mom inside, surprised when I hear her inquire about a room with two beds, which costs only a few dollars in baht. She must have picked up the money witnessing. The smell of roach spray and the shabby brown bedspreads do nothing to lessen my discomfort.

"Mom, what's going on?" I plead quietly.

After latching the room door, Mom collapses onto one of the beds and breaks down sobbing. "They are going to take you away from me!" she cries over and over. "I can't let them do that. We had to escape."

I don't know if this is true or not, but it's clear she believes it, and her fear scares me. I hold Jondy tight as I try to calm her.

"Mom," I begin gently.

"No!" she snaps. "I won't go back! That home is like a prison."

The air is heavy with the heat. The old air conditioner beneath the window doesn't do much more than make a loud rattle. I watch as my mother repeatedly pulls back the curtains just enough to peer out the window, eyeing the street for someone from the compound. She is scared we will be found, but she is also afraid of being on her own.

We have no money, no connections, and nowhere to go. We don't even have a map. There's no one we can call, and soon we won't have enough to pay for the motel with the little bit of money Mom managed to sneak out.

"What about Dad? Can he help us? Can we go back to the Farm?" I ask hopefully. He's been gone for over a year with almost no word.

She collapses onto the bed. All the fight has drained out of her. She's like a puppet whose strings have been cut.

"I've written to your dad many times since he left," she says quietly, "but he doesn't write back. I don't think he will help us." The silence surrounds us, interrupted only by the death rattle of the air conditioner. Finally, she goes on. "The new leadership in Macau broke up your dad and me even before he left the Farm. They said I was a bad influence on him. We had problems," she admits, "but we were working through them. I love your dad, but I don't know how or if we will be able to get back together."

No wonder she was so miserable and agreed to go to WS to try to demonstrate her loyalty to the Family and see if she still had a place of service. I listen in silence as my mother tries to reason through her current position. It's clear she sees everything and everyone as a threat to her family; and she's become convinced that if she stays at the compound, she'll wake up one morning to find that her kids have been taken from her. I hadn't realized the extent of her paranoia. Suddenly, I feel scared for her, and for us.

At twelve, I have no answers. The only people we can turn to are in Macau, and I don't know how to contact them outside of the Family channels. But it seems they don't want us; they sent us to Thailand, after all. Mom wants to call her parents for help. I'd met them twice when they'd visited Macau, but to me they are Systemites—strangers who stayed in a hotel and we took sightseeing. Not anyone I'd think to ask for help. After counting the baht left in her purse, she starts to sob again in defeat. We don't have enough for a long-distance phone call to America.

"Mom." I reach out to touch her shoulder. "The Family would never take kids away from their parents," I say, trying to soothe. "That's not loving like Grandpa teaches."

"Oh, yes they would," Mom sobs. "Do you remember Auntie Kat of Zacky Star?"

"Yes," I say warily, thinking of my old friends, their children Ching-Ching and Yanny.

"Her marriage was also broken up, and Zack took her two kids away to Europe."

Mom names a few more people who were deemed rebellious, or a bad influence, and lost access to their children, the spouse spiriting them away to another country.

My confidence drips away. Maybe her fear isn't so irrational after all, I worry. But what can we do? I try to reassure her, "If they try to take us somewhere without you, I'll refuse to go. I'll plant my feet and refuse to get on the plane. They can't drag me on screaming." I can be stubborn if I need to be.

My mother gives me a weak smile before she stands up again and takes her post at the window.

Three days pass, with Mom mostly sobbing and fretting. She is having a complete breakdown and has barely slept the whole time we've been here. I don't blame her for feeling the way she does. I, too, hate our new home. But at least we have food, water, and shelter. And I have a good relationship with Uncle Steven now. I hadn't heard anything about them wanting to separate us; it's probably just her fear talking, though I worry that after this stunt, they may do just that. But we don't have many options, and we have Nina and Jondy. They are fussy all the time, and we've run out of ways to keep them occupied and quiet in this tiny, hot motel room.

When we run out of money for food and the motel, as cheap as it is, I convince my mother to call the Combo from the pay phone in the lobby. Eventually, she gives in.

Somehow she speaks to a sympathetic soul who manages to calm her down and convinces her to come back. Within a few minutes, someone from the Combo arrives to pick us up.

As soon as we pull into the compound gates, I spot Uncle Steven in the driveway. I barely step out of the van when he grabs me in a bear hug.

"I was so afraid for you," he says, pulling me into his chest.

In the days that follow, I notice people giving me sidelong looks. They act nice and compassionate, but I sense they are as shocked as I feel. No one has ever run away like that. Or at least *I've* never heard of it. *What will they do to us?*

I try to ignore my heart-pounding anxiety, focus on the OC group's routine, and pretend everything is normal. But I'm ashamed of my mother for running away, and I'm afraid for her. The longer the Shepherds take to pass a sentence, the worse I worry the punishment will be. I know what they are thinking: Can my mother be broken and remade? Or will it be better to send her away, to make her someone else's problem?

Perhaps unsure how to handle my mother's volatile state of mind, or waiting for instruction from WS, no one hands down an explicit punishment. But for the next two months, she is sent out to witness and fundraise twelve hours a day, keeping her busy and mostly away from others in the Home. She doesn't speak Thai, so her role is to act as a silent partner to whomever is assigned to sell our Family cassette tapes door to door, which is good, as she moves through her days in a fog.

She is put on the sharing schedule with Big John, a hulking American she tells me she is not attracted to, but he's the only adult here I like. He lived with us at the Farm for a while and took care of us kids, though Mom says he's just a big kid himself. He would teach us funny System songs and bench-press us over his head. One time, for a costume party in Macau, he dressed up as the Incredible Hulk. He soaked in a bath of water and green food coloring, only to discover too late that the dye wouldn't come off. We all got a good laugh at him wandering around the Farm for weeks looking like the Jolly Green Giant.

But here he looks smaller somehow, deflated. He was put on a month of Silence Restriction right after they took me off it, big sign and all. I don't know what he did to receive such a harsh punishment. Perhaps they are trying to crush the kid out of him.

It's been a few weeks since our return, still no punishment doled out, and we are in Devotions, reading a new Mo Letter. It says that if you have a big family (many have eight to ten kids now), and you are struggling to support yourself in a poor mission-field country, you should consider going back to the US or another wealthy country to drum up funding from relatives and churches that can support you as a missionary overseas. Like he did in one of his earlier Mo Letters, *Have Trailer, Will Travel,* Grandpa is now suggesting some Family members return to the US and witness around the country in trailers. That way they will be less likely to get sucked into the trappings of a comfortable life in America and retain their Gypsy missionary lifestyle and zeal until they can make it back overseas.

The adults can't hide their shock. According to Grandpa, America is evil, Great Babylon the Whore. America is just awaiting God's imminent judgment for its sins and for persecuting the Family, God's true children. God is going to destroy it, especially California, which is going to slide into the sea as punishment for its sodomy and for polluting the world with its consumerism and violent movies like *Rambo*.

Is this a test to see how dedicated people are? Who would want to go back to America?

As the room clears out, my mother leans in close to me. "I've always dreamed of being a Gypsy and living in a trailer," she says wistfully. "My spirit helper is a Gypsy."

Nearly a month later, she is buzzing with excitement at family time, almost like her old self. "We are going to America!" she declares. "We leave in a week."

"But, Mom," I begin, trying to ground her. "We don't have any money—"

She pulls me into a hug. "Grandma has sent us tickets. We are going to get a camper and live like Gypsies as I've always dreamed."

This, I realize, is our punishment. They are glad to get rid of us weak links in the chain.

There's nothing to prepare and few goodbyes. Everything I own is already packed in one small carry-on under my bed. We've been here just four months, so I haven't bonded with anyone outside of Uncle Steven. On our last day, he hugs me and prays over me. I feel his sorrow at letting me go now that he has finally molded me into the perfect yielded disciple. He hints that I might stay without my mom, but I know instantly I will take my mother's side over any Shepherd. I pretend I'm sorry to leave, but after everything, I'm glad to start over somewhere else.

With our small suitcases, we board another plane. This time, to America.

15

—

THE LAND OF MUCH TOO MUCH

I am an American, born to two American citizens, and yet, while I hold an American passport, I've never been to America. It's August 1989, and I'm twelve years old.

Though my mother's father is in Indiana and her mother is in Georgia, we are flying to Miami. I don't know what to expect. The only visual I have of the United States is from the movies I've watched growing up. Most, like *Singin' in the Rain* and *It's a Wonderful Life*, are too outdated to rely on, but *Twins* and *Crocodile Dundee II* might be closer. I imagine wide streets, big cars, and lots of white people.

We board the plane and file into our seats. The stewardess gives me my first Toblerone chocolate bar, and it's the best thing I've ever tasted. So much better than the carob bar Mom gave each of us for Christmas when I was six. My parents never gave us candy, so I made that Christmas carob bar last for months by breaking off half a square every few days and taking tiny licks of sweetness as it slowly melted in my fingers. When my mother saw me, she threw up her hands. "How can you stand that? If it were mine, I'd gobble it all in one day," she said.

As I slowly eat my Toblerone, I feel excited for the plane ride, though less so about our destination. Going to live in America is worrying. I've been taught all my life that America could be destroyed at any moment. I'm hoping God will protect us.

Even though she's trying to hide it, I know my mother's worried, too. She's jumpy, looking around in case someone tries to take us kids away at the last minute. I don't think she takes a deep breath until we're all buckled in our seats. After we take off, she slumps and falls asleep for a few hours. Thank God, Jondy and Nina do, too.

Halfway through the flight, when she wakes up for dinner, she digs in her overhead carry-on bag, nearly dropping her heavy laptop on my head. She hands me a map of the US and tells me to start memorizing the different states' names. "You'll need to know this in America or people will think you're not being educated properly," she tells me. Mom hasn't been back to the States in eighteen years, and she's wondering how much has changed.

After two days of travel, including twenty-four hours in the air, I dazedly follow Mom off the plane at Miami International Airport with a mix of excitement and trepidation. The customs area seems huge and stark with white, shiny walls and harsh neon lights that burn our jet-lagged eyes as I search for signs to direct us. At least the signs are in English. When we pass through the arrivals gate, we are swept into a crowd of sweaty people; everyone is in a rush, pushing to get somewhere.

My first shock is all the colors and sizes of people—Black people in African robes and turbans, brown ladies in bright dresses and head scarves, fat people, tall people. The few white businessmen seem to be far outnumbered in this colorful crowd. Us three kids stare in awe. In Asia, we rarely saw Black people, or even fat people. Most of the people there were thin with black hair, brown eyes, and golden skin. The huge, multicultural crowd at the airport is so different than the white world of the movies that I am expecting.

It takes forever to pass through customs, collect our baggage, and reach the airport lobby. Still, when we get there, no one is waiting to pick us up. Pushing our luggage cart and trying to keep hold of the kids, Mom and I search the entire building, looking for someone with the Family member look—a smiling duo sporting unstyled, slightly graying, long frizzy hair and plain, well-worn, hand-me-down clothes and eyes that have the light of a true believer.

After an anxious hour waiting and looking around for someone from the Family, Mom changes some money and finds a pay phone. She inserts a few coins and dials the phone number for the Family Home that she was given by the Shepherds in Thailand.

"No answer," she groans.

We don't have an address or a name, just the phone number and the assurance that someone knows we are coming and will be here to pick us up. We take a seat on a bench near the phone booth and wait for a bit before trying the number again. Mom continues to call the number every half hour, but there's still no answer. *Do we have the wrong number?* The excitement of the plane trip has worn off, and fear is the only thing preventing us from collapsing from exhaustion. *Where is everyone?*

Nearly six hours pass before Mom finally leads us out of the airport. A blast of hot, humid Miami air hits me as we spill out of the rotating doors. A taxi driver rushes up to us, and after Mom explains our predicament, he says he'll take us to a motel run by his brother. Nervous about being cheated in a foreign country, Mom reluctantly agrees. We are out of options.

Mom has only the $200 Grandma sent her for the trip. When we reach the dingy motel, she peels off a bill for our driver and then continues her efforts to reach our contact person. She is doing her best to stay calm, but she can't hide her growing panic.

We must make the money stretch—$36 per day for the motel. She budgets $5 per day to feed us. At the grocery store, we can only afford to buy milk and the fixings for peanut butter sandwiches, which we live on for three days.

After the second day, we make the very expensive long-distance call to the Home in Thailand, hoping that they will provide us another phone number for a Family member in the US. I watch the pay phone gulping down our few remaining dollars, only to have them give us the same phone number that we've tried dozens of times. "Call back tomorrow and we will see if we can find you another number," the voice on the other end of the phone says.

Two more days pass and still no luck. Mom calls her mother in Atlanta in desperation; her parents don't have email yet. Grandma explains that she'll have to go to a Western Union office to wire us funds, which will take a few days at least. Mom tells me we don't have enough to cover the motel room another night—we'll be on the street tonight if someone doesn't find us. I pray desperately while trying to encourage Mom that God will take care of us. I'm terrified, but it will not help Mom or the kids to say so.

Mom uses nearly all the coins we have left to make one more call to Thailand. Finally, someone there gives us the number for a different Family Home, in Atlanta. It's a lead! Mom calls the number and is given the correct number for the Home in Florida. With our last coins, she finally reaches a Family member in the Miami Home. She breaks into tears as she gives him the address of our motel. Within the hour, we get a call from reception that our ride has arrived. I jump up and down in joy and relief, pulling Jondy into a tight hug.

We hurry to the lobby, where a tall, slender man with wiry gray hair awaits us. My entire body wants to cave in in relief as we pile into this stranger's van for the thirty-minute ride to our next destination. I watch out the window as flashes of blue ocean and palm trees whiz by. The van slows as we pull into the driveway of a big house surrounded by a high concrete wall. A few people greet us as we bring our suitcases inside. This is a communal house with about thirty people, including some teens. Someone shows us to a small room where we can set down our things, and we are given a quick tour. From the living room window, I notice a large backyard covered in short green grass. I've rarely seen a lawn—they are not common in Asia.

Our hosts let us stay while we sort out where we are going next. Although it has a similar schedule—Devotions, mealtimes, etc.— this home is much more relaxed, even disorganized, compared to the Bangkok Combo we've just come from. I'm still wary, but not much is demanded of us other than the usual chores designated for Family visitors passing through, such as helping out with dishes and cleaning.

As the days pass, I realize that Mom has no real plan except to buy a camper in which we can live and travel around like idealized Gospel Gypsies. Grandpa has been floating this "life in a camper" concept since the late 1970s, in response to the ongoing police raids of Family Homes around the world, declaring that it's harder to be caught if you're mobile. He'd also introduced the concept of furloughing, where Family members could temporarily return to their "national homes," as in birth countries, visit their parents, and witness to their families to encourage them to support them when they are on the mission field. The end goal is always to get back to the mission field (non-Western countries), so no matter where you live, you must stay dropped out of the System and remember that loyalty to the Family always comes before relatives.

Mom used this furloughing concept to escape the prison that the Thailand Combo symbolized. Normally we'd limit our time spent with System grandparents to a week or so; living overseas there is a natural barrier to communication and their worldly influence.

The Family's message about Systemites is to "spoil Egypt," in reference to when the Jews left Egypt and took all the wealth they could carry from their Egyptian masters. Our right to use Systemites and take from them what we can is embedded in the Family and that's a legitimate reason to spend time with relatives. Mom calls her parents and asks for money to buy a camper for us to live in so she can fulfill her Gypsy dream. They both agree on the condition that we come visit them. Grandma, who is in Atlanta, is closer.

When some money from Grandma arrives at the local Western Union office, we buy tickets for a twelve-hour Greyhound bus to Georgia. Mom arranges for us to stay at the Family Home in Atlanta while we visit Grandma.

I pick up on Mom's moody silence and worried looks, which she tries to cover with a fake enthusiasm. We have no idea how we will be received. I'm excited but cautious. Perhaps Grandma will give us presents! Grandparents do that in the movies.

Grandma lives in Marietta, a city about twenty minutes northwest of Atlanta, in Cobb County. She and my grandfather, Gene, divorced right after my mom left home as a teen, and she's never wanted to remarry. She was used to being alone in her marriage to a military man who was gone much of the time anyway.

Grandma is waiting for us with a smile when we arrive. She is fairly overweight, with white, short hair—something I'd never see in the Family, where women are expected to keep their hair long and their bodies in good shape to be attractive to men. My mom is always on one diet or another and stressing about her weight and her big butt. "I don't want to end up like my mother," she often tells me.

Grandma gives each of us a quick hug and steers us inside a nondescript, flat, low, three-bedroom ranch house shaded by tall trees. Her place is not particularly homey; it feels dark, decorated with muted greens and grays. I'm immediately uncomfortable, but Grandma seems happy here.

We are exhausted and relieved. I know Grandma has so many questions. I don't know how Mom will answer them. *Why are we here? What happened to her marriage to my father?* At least she doesn't ask the one question all the other Systemites in America seem to: *Why is Nina's coloring different from her siblings?* With her black hair and brown skin, she has been getting strange looks from people, looks I never noticed back home. But that's because Grandma knows about Nina from Mom's letters. She even knows about FFing because she met some of my mother's Fish when she came for a short visit when I was three. She has an unusually progressive view on things like extramarital sex and homosexuality. Her older sister, Doris, was one of the early outspoken advocates for gay rights on Long Island, and Grandma, a liberal New Yorker, has many close gay friends in this bastion of the conservative South.

"Jondy, don't touch that!" Grandma yells as my brother reaches for one of her antique glass globes on the windowsill.

I know this place will be trouble. It's not toddler-proofed *at all*, and Jondy is an active, noisy one-and-a-half-year-old, with Nina not much better at five years old. I'm going to have to stay hyperalert to keep the two little kids from breaking anything. *Who puts a bunch of glass stuff everywhere anyway?*

Grandma takes us all out to dinner at McDonald's, so the little ones can play and she and Mom can talk. I look longingly at the bouncy ball castle, but Grandma tells me I'm too big to jump in, so I quietly listen to Mom trying to put a positive spin on what we are doing in America. I notice she follows the cardinal rule by leaving out all the important details—never say anything that makes the Family look bad.

She tells Grandma that she and my dad are separated and that she didn't want the separation. She glides over what happened in Thailand and says she is looking for a new start, but she doesn't know how to do it without her husband. As Grandma has been divorced a long time and never remarried, she tries to give Mom some encouragement.

After dinner, we go to the Family Home in Atlanta. I'm relieved that we are staying there instead of at Grandma's gloomy house. The main family here has thirteen kids, some of whom are my age, plus a few other couples who stay with them. With that many kids, it's a typical Family Home furnished with the bare necessities and nothing breakable, so I can relax a little as Jondy and Nina play with the kids their ages.

I soon discover one of the best things about living in America is the appliances.

The first time I use a clothes dryer is at Grandma's house. It is a beautiful miracle. I love how the clothes come out warm and fluffy and smelling like Bounce. I hold the soft towel to my face and breath in the floral "outdoors" smell. Much better than the clothes stiff with clothesline marks, a few insects, and bits of dirt stuck on them.

But as much as I love the clothes dryer, I am even more amazed by Aunt Madeline's dishwasher. Aunt Madeline is Mom's older sister, and she lives nearby with her husband, Rick, and their two daughters, Erin and Erika, who are five and two years old, respectively.

I discover I like Aunt Madeline, even if she can be a little scary at first, loud and brash. I've never seen a grown woman yell at other adults; kids, yes, but never at adults. She always has a kind word for me, though. I'm not her enemy. But she can really irritate my mother.

Aunt Madeline's house is decorated with great care. Even her bathroom has pretty, matching towel sets, carved soaps in crystal dishes, and color-coordinated rugs. Family Home furnishings are clean, worn, and functional. No time or money is wasted on matching colors or style. Aunt Madeline's house is beautiful in a way I didn't know I was missing.

Over dinner one night, she gets into it with Mom. Aunt Madeline disapproves of Mom. She views the Family as a cult and doesn't hide her opinions about Mom's decision to be a part of it. "I don't understand why you'd want to keep your kids in the Family, anyway. At least here they can go to school," she says.

"It's my decision, not yours," Mom barks. "You don't know any-thing about it. We are happy there, and the kids do have school."

"Well, Faithy is smart, no doubt about it, but it can't be good for them to keep them away from their family and a normal life."

Mom shoots back, "What's a normal life done for your kids?"

"Don't you dare!" Aunt Madeline is building up pressure to blow.

Ever the peacekeeper, Uncle Rick steps in. "Now, now, what are we having for dinner?"

"Fish . . . and don't think you can change the subject!"

"I wasn't," Uncle Rick says with a smile. "But let's have a nice visit."

Aunt Madeline glares at Mom, and Mom puts on her innocent "don't look at me, it's you" face.

"Well, what's your career, Madeline?" Mom pokes.

Aunt Madeline, a child prodigy, is quick to lament she would have been a great concert pianist if her career hadn't been inter-rupted by the birth of her daughters.

As soon as Aunt Madeline leaves the table, Mom whispers to me, "God, Madeline makes me so mad sometimes. She's still ganging up on me. It's just like when we were kids, when she would tickle me until I peed my pants. It was torture."

After dinner, I volunteer to do the dishes, as is expected of me as a good guest. Aunt Madeline is pleasantly surprised, but I am the one in for a shock, when she shows me her dishwasher.

"You just have to rinse the excess food in the sink, then put them in this rack," she explains, demonstrating for me. "It will wash the dishes."

I don't really believe it. Washing dishes has composed a large part of my life from the time I was three years old. It would take a group of eight kids at least an hour to clean up after every meal. Aunt Madeline has a family of four; we had at least fifty people to clean up after at the Family Homes. *Why didn't we have one of these?*

I marvel at the wealth on display in my aunt's home, not realizing this is a normal middle-class household in America. While Erin and Erika are similar in age to Nina and Jondy, their lives are worlds apart. Each girl has her own room. Erin even has her own TV, and she is only five! There are toys everywhere.

"What a terrible influence for a little kid to have her own TV," I comment to my mother.

"Yes. No wonder she's so difficult, always screaming and throwing tantrums."

"They're like the spoiled System kids Grandpa warned us about in the Letters," I reply, with superiority to match my mother's. I show the expected disdain for their worldliness and lack of discipline and maturity. *Of course kids who grow up in the Family with a Godly education and discipline are better behaved.*

Deep down, though, I desperately want what my cousins have: New clothes, piles of toys, books, and movies that they can watch whenever they want. Cookies and ice cream every day. But even I can see that they are not happier for it; the opposite, it seems.

After a month or so in Atlanta, Mom is excited to start our road trip across America. She wants to feel free and in control of her life again and loves our new, heavily used eighteen-foot camper, with its 1960s orange curtains and doo-doo-brown upholstery. I think it's ugly and tacky and tell her so.

But I'm also amazed. "I didn't know you could drive! How come you never drove in Macau?"

"Oh, well, we had your dad to drive, and I didn't want to drive in a foreign country . . ." She trails off, as if just hearing how lame that sounds. Something is off, but I can't think what.

Our first stop is Indiana to see Grandad Gene.

I have met my maternal grandfather only a couple of times, when he visited us in Macau. He was warmly welcomed but, as a Systemite, kept separate from the reality of our lives. A tourist visit and a few dinners could not bridge twelve years of absence. To me, he is a friendly stranger.

Mom likes to tell the story of how I shocked Grandad when he came to visit us in Macau when I was three years old. I was sitting on the floor at his feet playing with LEGOs he'd brought me as a present. Grandad watched as I lined up the LEGO family. "Here is the daddy and the mommy and the other mommy," I explained, setting each small figure on the coffee table in front of him. Grandad's bushy eyebrows shot up, and he harumphed. He knew about Mom's arrangement, but he said nothing, preferring to avoid the topic.

From the few times my mother spoke of him, I could tell she loved her father. But before this trip to America, it was almost as if my maternal grandparents didn't exist. Now, they were becoming real people.

Grandad is like a storybook gentleman, tall, handsome, and clean-shaven with a smooth, oval-shaped face and white hair. He's well-spoken and elegant, and even though he's seventy, he has the energy and looks of a man twenty years younger. I pick up a heavy iron anchor from a shelf as he tells me about catching satellite space capsules with it before they got lost in the Pacific Ocean. He'd swing the anchor on a rope out the back of his B-52 bomber and snag the parachute as the capsule fell from space. A framed newspaper article describing this amazing feat hangs on the wall. I love his mischievous smile and sense of humor, which flashes out from under the pretend gruffness.

Barbara, his third wife, is like no lady I've ever met, with her short, brassy styled hair and fashionable clothes. A "classy, sassy, redhead broad" is how Grandad lovingly describes her. She welcomes us with warm hugs and makes sure we are situated with towels and blankets, even toys for Jondy and Nina in the basement left over from her now-grown kids.

This is Barbara's house that she bought, and she rules the roost, as Grandad says with a pretend annoyance that barely covers his "cat in the cream" contentedness. He knows he is a very lucky man to have snagged a woman like Barbara after two failed marriages. He met her on a plane and knew right away he wasn't going to let this smart redhead escape. Like a true fighter pilot, he locked on determinedly until he'd convinced her to go out with him.

Life with Grandad and Barbara is a revelation. Their lovely, modest Americana-style home has a lightness to it that comes from Barbara's spirit. It is filled with an abundance of riches: stacks of board games in the den; shelves of leather-bound, gold-embossed books; three TVs; a pantry full of snacks. Mom and my siblings sleep in the basement bedroom off the TV den, and I'm put in a bedroom at the top of the house that belongs to Barbara's youngest daughter. She is away at college, so I have the whole loft to myself. It's scary to sleep alone for the first time, yet the privacy is wonderous.

Barbara bakes pies and makes dinner when she gets home from the school where she works as a third-grade teacher. On the weekends, Grandad makes us his famous blueberry pancakes with real maple syrup. Every night before bed, Grandad and Barbara religiously watch the evening news, followed by *Jeopardy!* And *Wheel of Fortune*. I sit snuggled on the couch in the living room against my grandad's side.

Mom says to me one day, "You don't know how much it means to see Grandad cuddle you and be affectionate. I was always Daddy's little girl. He'd laugh and sing and make up silly songs for me. Seeing you together reminds me of my childhood." It's nice to see Grandad and Mom getting reacquainted; she was a teenager the last time they spent much time together.

She always felt closest to her father, she tells me. Unlike Aunt Madeline, I never hear him say much about the Family. He just focuses on the moment we are here with him.

Mom is so grateful that her family has welcomed us and is willing to help. She feels safe; no one here is going to manipulate her and try to split up her family or take away her kids.

Neither of her parents liked that she had joined the Family, but they knew that if they expressed their disapproval too loudly, they risked losing what little relationship they had with her. Truth be told, Mom admits to me, they prefer the way she is now compared to what she was doing before she joined the Family, when she was involved with drugs; at least she is physically safe preaching Jesus.

Here at Grandad's, I see Mom relax for the first time since we left Macau.

She finds an old Monopoly set in the den, and I discover she is fiercely competitive. She gleefully wins every game while I'm still trying to learn the rules, until after a few games, I refuse to play with her. Board games, card games, solitaire—who is this woman who always told me playing card games was the Devil's timewaster?

On Sunday, Barbara drags a reluctant Grandad, my mom, and three curious kids to her church, First Presbyterian of Indianapolis. I am excited to see this thing I'd only heard condemned in the Mo Letters all my life—a real church. Mom thinks it will be an interesting experience for us kids.

I stare in awe at the imposing stone archways and stained-glass windows of the cathedral-like building. We sit in carved, polished pews just like I heard about. The service begins with a choir that sounds old-fashioned compared to the rousing guitar-led inspirations Family Devotions start with. Hundreds of people sit silently in their pews, listening as the preacher begins his sermon. The kids are soon squirming, and I'm already distracted, sorting through all the pamphlets and envelopes and hymnbooks in the back of the pew.

"Shh," Barbara says to warn us to sit still for the third time, when I hear the most amazing sound—snoring. I look in shock to see Grandad on the far side of Barbara, his chin on his chest, eyes closed. The sound of soft snores is magnified under the silent high ceilings. I cover my mouth to hold in snorts of laughter. I thought he might have been exaggerating when Grandpa talked about church in the Mo Letters, but my first church experience is a picture-perfect replica of his description—including the snoring parishioners.

When it comes time to get back in the camper, I'm not excited. Our couple of weeks in Indiana with Grandad have been unlike anything I've ever experienced. Living in a System home is strange and unsettling, but I'm sad to leave. Plus, getting back on the road means a return to life in the claustrophobic, cramped camper.

For the next few months, Mom takes full advantage of her Gypsy freedom. We drive up and down the East Coast, staying at different Family Homes. We don't need much money for this, as a Family Home will always put us up and feed us. She is reconnecting with Family people she hasn't seen in years. I don't think she has a single friend from before the Family.

But life on the road is hard. We never know where we will stay next.

I'm the navigator, handling the big AAA maps that Grandad got for us. I switch between telling her which exit to take and stopping fights between Jondy and Nina in the back. I like the wide road and new places. We visit some cool sites along the way: Mammoth Caves, the Kennedy Space Center at Cape Canaveral, even a Grateful Dead concert campground, where I'm given my first tie-dyed T-shirt.

As the weather turns cold, we need a house. We return to the Family Home in Atlanta and ask to park our camper on their property.

It's here that I first see snow. Back in Macau, when I'd ask Mom what snow was like, she went to the freezer, scraped out some frosty ice, and said, "Like this . . . but different." When the first flakes fall, I run into the driveway with Nina and Jondy on my heels. Mom laughs as we jump up to catch the little wet flakes. A half inch of snow falls, and I manage to scrape enough off the parked cars to make a tiny foot-tall snowman.

After the winter, the Atlanta Family Home tells us we can't stay permanently, so we drive our camper back down to Florida, stopping off at numerous Family Homes along the way, looking for one willing to take us in as full-time Home members. Too late Mom realizes we made a huge mistake moving to America without first being accepted by a Home. When we'd left Thailand, her only thought was escape. She figured it would be easy to find a Home once we arrived. With all the Family's talk of love and caring for each other, we are shocked to find no one will take in a single mother with three young children.

At this time, the Family issues a new rule: all active members are required to live in a Home with a minimum of twelve people. Homes or families who don't meet the criteria by the deadline will be reclassified as TRF Supporters—a new designation for a person who believes in Grandpa's teachings but does not live by all the rules, including living communally. What it really means is that you don't have the dedication to be a full-time soldier of God. You are weak, unworthy.

Our life feels like a game of musical chairs. When the music stops, and there is no Home willing to put us on their Home roster, we are automatically reclassified as TRF Supporters by some nameless, faceless person in WS. We are second-class citizens and completely ostracized. We desperately need a Home, but now that we're "TRF'd," the situation is worse—no Home will even associate with us, let alone put us on their register and adopt us.

We've been accidentally kicked out of the Family.

How could this happen to us? We are completely dedicated to the Family. This is a horrible mistake! I am Moses David's granddaughter!

I am afraid. *The Family is God, God's will, God's army. Am I now outside of God's will and His protection?*

I can see that Mom is scared, too, though she is trying desperately to hold it together. She tries to get in touch with my father, but she still can't reach him. It's been almost a year since she last heard from him.

Mom's punishment is complete.

With no safety net, we start making money the way the Family does in the US, by "canning." We stand on street corners or stop people in supermarket parking lots, holding up a can and asking for donations to support our volunteer work. We would never have done this in Asia—it smacks too much of beggars on the streets—but I keep my thoughts to myself.

At 5:00 p.m., we drive to a Safeway. I grab my thirty-three-ounce tomato paste can covered in pictures of Family kids. I have a green plastic binder with printed brochure pages of the Family singing in hospitals and teaching Bible classes to teens. I feel a burning sense of humiliation knowing this is not about the good works; all I want is enough money for our little family to eat and a safe place to sleep. We don't have enough money for a campsite tonight. Mom is afraid to park us by the side of the road or in a parking lot. Afraid the police will come. Afraid bad men or drug addicts will break in.

I pray with my mother. She starts, "Dear Lord, please bless Faithy, help her to do really well today. Make her bold like a lion. Please, please, God, provide for us. You said, whatever we ask in Your name, You would give it to us. So, I ask that You bring some really generous people today."

As she pleads, I pray silently in my head. *Please, please, God. And give me courage.*

"Faithy, I'm going to be just over there fixing the camper. I need to swap out the fuses and see which one is making the blinkers go out," Mom tells me. She gives me an encouraging smile.

It's a long walk from the camper parked at the far edge of the Safeway parking lot. This is the worst part. My hands are sweaty with embarrassment that I'm holding a can. I spot a middle-aged lady pushing her shopping cart to her car. I open the brochure book to the right page. I have only a few seconds to get her attention, and I have to say the right thing quickly before she brushes me off.

My face flips on the bright, winning smile that my dad spanked into me from an early age. *I can do this*, I think as I push down the shame and shyness.

"Hello, ma'am, do you have a second? I'm raising funds for our volunteer work." I have the can awkwardly tucked under my arm so I can raise the brochure high to show her the pictures. "See, this is us singing for orphanages. Here we are working with teens to help them get off drugs. This is us singing about Jesus in prisons."

"What do you want?" she barks.

"We are just asking for a small donation to support our work."

"I don't give to charity."

"Anything helps."

"Not interested."

"Okay, thank you."

I duck my head as my cheeks burn but hurry to an elderly Black woman I see exiting the store. "Please, ma'am, do you have a minute to hear about the volunteer work we are doing?"

"Hi, child, certainly." She smiles at me.

Whew, this lady seems nice.

"Here we are teaching handicapped kids in Thailand to pray and ask Jesus into their heart. We are collecting donations to help our work. Would you be able to give just a little something?"

"What church are you with?"

I've memorized the line carefully since being in America. In Macau, everyone knew us as the Ho Family Singers. Except for busking on the weekends, I didn't have to ask for money or answer difficult questions. Still, I know that church people hate us. "We are the Family International, a nonprofit, nondenominational Christian organization." *Please, please.*

"Mm, I've never heard of them," the woman replies.

Thank God.

"Here you go, child. You keep up the good work."

A dollar floats into the can. My smile widens. "Thank you so much! God bless you!"

At the end of the afternoon, Mom and I count the money in my can, $27, enough for a campground for the night and some gas to get there.

I go into the Safeway with Jondy and Nina and grab a box of Weetabix and one of Grape Nuts. I've discovered that while Grape Nuts don't taste as good as Froot Loops, if you let them soak a long time in milk, they swell up and are very filling, so a little goes a long way to feed hungry kids.

A pack of Kraft mac and cheese costs only 79 cents. I can feed the kids on that. It's also laughably easy. Boil the noodles, strain, dump in the pack of powder, a little milk and butter, and it's done. All the food in America seems to come premade in a box, not the thirty-kilo gunnysacks of beans and rice I'm used to.

On my way to the cashier, I see something that fills me with awe. Chocolate cake in a box! For sure it has white sugar, but I'm dying to know how it's possible to make cake just by adding water. What about the eggs, milk, butter? Will it be fluffy like the picture or flat and heavy like our whole-wheat-flour cakes? Back at the Farm, our cakes were made from scratch and cooked in the microwave or the Crockpot, because we didn't have an oven.

It's after dark when we finally pull into the campground. Mom jumps out to hook up the sewage, water, and electric. I start preparing the mac and cheese.

The camper shakes as Mom climbs back in, wiping her hands.

"Well, I never would have believed it if you told me a few months ago. I never even drove in Asia. Here I am not only driving but fixing spark plugs and plumbing." We can't afford to go to a mechanic for these small fixes, so she is learning from guys at gas stations who are willing to help with her repairs.

I smile at her pride.

After we eat, I put Jondy and Nina into their pajamas. They won't stop crying. Mom picks up Jondy to comfort him, and tears start streaming down her face, her earlier confidence dissolving. "I don't know how we are going to keep doing this."

"It's going to be okay, Mom," I reply. "God will provide for us. He always does."

"Oh, Faithy. The camper needs a new alternator. The roof is leaking. I've tried caulking it, but the rain just keeps coming through. It'll rot the roof and destroy the camper. I don't have the money to get it fixed properly. We can't go back to the Atlanta Home. I can't keep dragging you kids across the country looking for a Home that will take us in, and no one from the Family has responded to my requests."

"God will take care of us," I insist. "Let's pray."

She smiles sadly. "I don't know what I'd do without your faith. Nothing gets you down."

I give her a hug. *Yes,* I think, *and I can't ever let it get me down or who will keep us up?* My stomach is in knots at the injustice of it all. How could *we* get kicked out of the Family? I blame the Family, yes, but I also blame Mom. She wasn't strong enough to do whatever needed to be done, and now we're in this mess. But I squash those disloyal thoughts and look for something to help. She is doing the best she can.

"Let's read *All Things Bright and Beautiful,*" I say, pulling the worn paperback from the shelf and handing it to Mom.

She gives me a watery grin and takes the book. This is my favorite part of the day. For both of us, I think. The stories of sheep dip and cow shots and loco farmers in the Scottish Highlands soon have us roaring with laughter. I miss the Farm and all our animals. Even more, I miss knowing where we will sleep the next night and not having the responsibility of feeding my family.

When we finish reading, I climb into my loft bed over the driver's seat, and the fear I've pushed down all day wraps its scaley fist around my stomach. It's hard to breathe in the two-foot-tall space. I close my eyes and reach for the only comfort I know. I begin silently quoting the Bible chapters I've memorized to myself: "What time I am afraid, I will trust in Thee. In God I will praise His word, in God I have put my trust; I will not fear what flesh can do unto me" (Psalm 56:3–4).

Beginning with Psalm 1, I roll through Psalms 23, 24, 27, 32 . . . until I drift off to sleep. While Mom's faith may falter, mine won't. God will save us.

Within days, I have proof that He's heard my prayers. Someone in the Atlanta Home puts us in contact with another family who has also been TRF'd, a mom and dad and their five teen daughters. Like us, they have a camper and want to live on the road, traveling around. Even together we still don't have the numbers required to qualify as a full-time Family Home, so during the spring and summer we spend a few months driving around the East Coast with them, witnessing and provisioning for food and campsite parking fees.

I enjoy being with other teen girls again. Their mom has them studying the Christian Light Education (CLE) homeschool course, which was developed by the Mennonites. When they are not studying at the campsite picnic tables, we busk and can to raise money. At least I'm not alone out there.

But for Mom, the setup is fast becoming a nightmare. The girls' father is controlling and abusive to her. He takes control of our busking earnings and our supply of Family posters and cassette tapes that we need to sell to raise money, making us dependent on him. And he insists that Mom shares with him regularly.

With no other support, Mom submits to the sex.

The situation is grim, but there's a flicker of light.

Mom still has the IBM laptop that she brought from Macau. As a leader at the Farm in charge of communicating, she'd been using the latest technology and email for years with dial-up Internet. Early one morning, I find her hunched over the screen with tears streaming down her cheeks. She's finally heard from Dad! She points to a long email. Between sobs of relief, she tells me that Dad made a trip out of Japan to renew his visa, and as soon as he could access the Internet unsupervised, he sent her an email. Apparently, they'd both been writing each other letters through the post but hadn't realized the Shepherds never delivered them.

Hearing from my father revives Mom, and she gathers the courage to escape our current nightmare. The husband of the family we are traveling with gives us only enough money for one tank of gas at a time, so it takes a few days of travel before we are within a two-hour drive of Atlanta. As soon as we fill our gas tank, Mom peels off and heads for Grandma's.

16

THE NEW KID IN THE CLASS

Back in Marietta, Georgia, Mom parks the camper in Grandma's driveway, and we unload our little suitcases onto her front stoop. The sticky heat of summer has been trailing us from Florida.

I know that going to live with Grandma means that we have failed. As long as we were living in the camper and "postering" (surviving by witnessing and donations), we were still Family members of a sort—even if lowly TRF Supporters. I still had hope.

But this time it's different. We have sold out and become Systemites—the worst of all things. This is why Mom fought so hard.

Grandma leads us to our designated bedrooms and gives me a hug. But late at night, when I go to the bathroom, I hear her telling Mom she's not prepared to have us live with her; this is only temporary. She's made her life the way she wants it to be. She is older; she works full-time; and she is not keen on having three children underfoot. I return to my room knowing that, once again, I'm unwanted.

The next day, I make a point of being as helpful or as invisible as possible, so she won't ask us to leave. Because if she does, where will we go? I notice that Mom is also on her best behavior; she even goes out to look for a job. With only a GED, there are few options, but she manages to find work at a nearby call center doing telemarketer sales.

At Grandma's insistence, Mom enrolls us in a traditional school for the first time in my life. Two-year-old Jondy will attend daycare, and Nina, at six, is going to preschool. She is far ahead of the other kids. We started teaching her to read at one year old, and she's been reading fluently since she was three.

My only idea of school comes from Grandpa's rants against it in the Mo Letters and scenes from the few American high school movies I've watched. I'm nervous. Mom tries to comfort me, telling me that even though I'm attending a System school, at least it's a Christian school, one that does not teach things like evolution.

But that's not why I've bitten my nails into stubs. For nearly all of the past year, the only schooling I'd been doing is teaching Jondy and Nina with flash cards. I've been too busy acting as a parent to my little siblings to care about my own studies. *Will I be able to do the schoolwork and keep up? What will my classmates think of me? Will I slip up and reveal something I shouldn't about the Family?*

As summer draws to a close, I'm given a test to determine what class to put me in. I'm told the results say I'm quite far behind where the average twelve-year-old should be. I've never even studied some of the grade-school topics, like history, social studies, and sciences. But the school kindly allows me to enter eighth grade with my peers.

"She seems smart. Let's see how she does and if she can catch up," the administrator tells Mom.

I'm determined to do so.

Arriving at DeKalb Christian Academy on my first day feels like landing on another planet. There are hundreds of kids bustling through white-wall hallways lined with gray metal lockers and industrial-looking beige carpet. It's so different from back at the Farm, where ten kids of all ages were stuffed into one room on the patio. Here, there are thirty kids to a classroom, all of them the same age.

I don't know how to behave in this kind of setting, so I move quietly and watch everything. I enter my assigned classroom, and the teacher introduces me as Faith Jones, a missionary from China. They stare at me, and I stare at my hands. I've never been called by my surname before. It sounds like they are talking to someone else; I even forget to answer the first few times I hear it. I sit at the desk the teacher points me to, waiting, my shoulders stiff and straight.

I hear a rustle of papers and see all the students pull out their three-ring binders, with the class name printed on a sticker along the spine, and their history textbooks. All I have is one notebook and one pencil in my otherwise empty backpack. The teacher spots me staring straight ahead. She looks at my bare desk and then walks over.

"Here, you can use my textbook, until you get your own."

I'm grateful, but I feel my ears burn with embarrassment.

My first class goes by in a blur, and too soon I'm spit back out into the beige hallway that smells of rubber carpet and new paint. I awkwardly weave my way around the clusters of students standing in front of the lockers, laughing about their summer vacations, as I search for the next classroom listed on my assignment sheet. I have nothing to talk with them about. I've never had a vacation. I spent my summer keeping my family alive.

It's nearing noon when a bell rings again, and all the kids dash to the gym with their bagged lunches. As I walk into the cafeteria, I'm lost in a bobbing sea of kids I have nothing in common with and no connection to. I miss Patrick; we would have whispered and giggled together at all the strange clothes and habits—he could always bring out my silly side. Even with Family kids I'd never met before, there would be only a few minutes of initial awkwardness and then everything would feel comfortable, as we had a whole shared history. I have no one to talk with here, so I walk silently and stay out of the way.

My mom and I had prepared a lunch for each of us early that

morning, laughing at doing something we'd seen only in movies. Now the wrinkled brown paper tears in my sweaty fist. The long walk across the shiny hardwood basketball court feels endless; I'm so exposed and small, yet massive at the same time. All the kids are chatting in groups on the bleachers, and I worry about where to sit. I feel their eyes on my skin, judging my clothes, my body. *What are they thinking?* I wear a long, baggy, green-plaid shirt that covers my black stretch skirt. Now, just like Mom, I'm very self-conscious of my growing butt.

I discreetly study my classmates to learn how to dress like them. The girls all wear slacks and collared shirts, sharp colors with bold designs. It's so different than in the Family, where women are expected to wear provocative, floaty clothes. There, we welcome sexual flirtation; here, if a boy snaps your bra strap, you can report him to the teacher.

I listen to their conversations, like I'm trying to figure out a code. They talk about going shopping or TV shows. Nothing deep or important like saving the world, sacrifice, lessons, caring for children, not even the Bible. *What is there for me to say?* There is nothing from my past or my life that I can share; anything about the Family must remain a secret, as Mom needlessly reminds me, or we could get booted out of this Christian school and lose our financial scholarships.

After a few weeks, I grow accustomed to the daily class schedule and the after-school routine. I don't have playdates or hang out with my classmates; I must be home to take care of Jondy and Nina since Mom doesn't get home from her telemarketer job until 6:00 p.m.

We are not supposed to disturb Grandma. She likes the house quiet, so it's my job to keep the kids out of her hair when she is home. She's away at work most of the day, running the programs for Head Start across Georgia, so when she returns in the evening, she likes to park herself in the one comfy reclining chair in the liv-

Dad with his two wives, Ruthie and Esther, in Hong Kong. My mother, Ruthie, holding me at three months old.

The Ho Family Singers. My siblings and I perform for the Vietnamese refugee camp in Macau. (Two years old.)

At three years old, I begin years of washing dishes.

Fidgety kids.
Devotions with Dad
in our apartment
in Macau.
(Four years old.)

Passing out Gospel tracts
with my brothers Nehi
and Bones during the
Chinese Lantern Festival
at Hac Sa beach.
(Four years old.)

My mother in front
of our new home
in Hac Sa village,
a hundred-year-old
traditional Chinese
farmhouse with an
outhouse.

Bath time! With no indoor bathroom, we use a wooden barrel that our father found washed up on the beach. (Four years old.)

Our Chinese grandma helping us kids clear the garbage and weeds from the field that became our farmyard. (Five years old.)

Ashok celebrating his birthday with my mother and me. (Six years old.)

After watching my mother give birth, us kids welcome our new sister. Esther holds baby Nina while we gather around in face masks and clean, new tracksuits so we don't spread farm germs to the newborn. (Seven years old.)

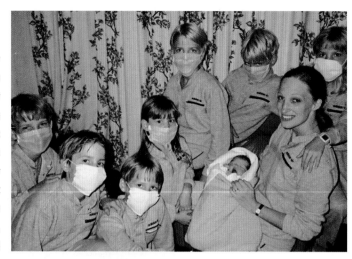

Best buddies. Patrick and I are inseparable at eight years old.

Daily farm chores. Patrick and I take the goats to graze.

Our donkey, Mad Max the biting menace, gives donkey cart rides while we pass out posters about Jesus and the End Time. My brothers, baby Nina, and Uncle Michael.

Performing for elementary school students who are taking a field trip to our farm / petting zoo. (Nine years old.)

A kids' homeschool classroom built into the enclosed patio of one of our houses. (Ten years old.)

"They were nearly twins!" My two new brothers. I hold Jondy and Mary holds Andy, born two days apart. (Eleven years old.)

Our family singing group grows up. (Eleven years old.)

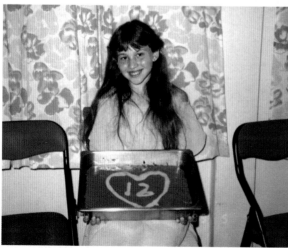

My worst birthday at the Bangkok Combo. I'm let off Silence Restriction for a few hours to celebrate becoming a woman. (Twelve years old.)

Mom, in Atlanta, Georgia, with the decrepit camper we lived in during our months on the road in the US.

Exercising one of our riding school horses back in Macau. (Fifteen years old.)

Passing out religious posters to crowds in Almaty, Kazakhstan. (Eighteen years old.)

I'm a teacher. Instructing three-year-old Emily in Almaty, Kazakhstan. (Nineteen years old.)

Hiking the Great Wall in China on my infamous trip to Beijing after two years of living in mainland China. (Twenty-two years old.)

"Should I stay or should I go?" In Taiwan, deciding to leave the Family at twenty-two years old to get an education in the US.

I did it! Barbara, Grandad, and my father come to my graduation from Georgetown University. (I'd just turned twenty-eight.)

ing room, where she watches TV and eats her dinner. I am happy to join her, quickly getting hooked on *Star Trek: The Next Generation*.

Weekends are a new concept. I never had a day off from daily Devotions and chores unless I was sick, but now we cannot keep up with Devotions as well as school. Mom is laying down in her room, too tired on her first day off from work to take us for an excursion. Jondy and Nina are getting bored cooped up in the house all morning and start squabbling on the floor in front of the TV. Grandma sets down her knitting with a thunk.

"Faithy, let's take the kids to the library," Grandma says. "We can pick up some picture books to keep them quiet."

I drag Nina and Jondy away from *The Flintstones* and bundle them into the car, grateful to get out of the house. I've never been to a library before. I think of the few novels I'd managed to read back at the Farm and wonder what it will be like.

The old brick building with colonial columns is a short drive from Grandma's house. The strange smell of old paper and new carpet hits my nose when I walk in. I stare at shelf after shelf of books, more than I have ever seen in my life. *How did so many books exist that are not about the Bible? How could people make up so many stories?*

"Faithy, I'm going to take Jondy and Nina over to the kids' section," Grandma tells me. "You can go over there and pick out some books for yourself." She points to a section under a sign that reads, "Young Adults."

I wander the aisles in wonder, the tips of my fingers grazing the spines as I read the unfamiliar titles. My whole life, I've never been allowed to read System books—will that change now that we're in the US? *What will Mom let me read? Whatever I choose, I'll have to be able to make a good case for it.*

I walk back and forth, back and forth. My head spins with the options. Suddenly, I realize I have no idea how to pick a book for myself. The few novels I'd read back at the Farm were the only ones available to me, so I didn't actually choose them. The names, the titles, the authors, are all new to me. How can I make the right choice?

I spot *Black Beauty*, a familiar friend in a sea of strangers. Though I never read the book, I've seen the movie many times. Dad always let us watch horse movies because we had horses: *Black Beauty*, *The Black Stallion*, *National Velvet*. This, I realize, is my ticket. Mom can't disapprove of these books when the Family has already approved the movies.

When I reach for the book, I notice that it's surrounded by an entire shelf of books with *Black Beauty* written on them. I gasp in shock. *What! Black Beauty has sequels! How come no one told me?*

I jump when I hear Grandma calling me from the front desk. I grab the book and hurry over to her, before I lose my courage.

Seeing the single book in my hands, she says, "Is that all you want?"

"How many can I take?" I'm almost afraid to ask. I don't want to seem greedy.

"As many as the library will let you check out. They're free. You just have to bring them back before the deadline, so only take as many as you can read in three weeks."

I have no idea how many I can read in three weeks, but I won't pass up such riches.

I run back to grab five more horse books and hurry to the counter.

Is this really okay? Is someone going to take them all away any second? For a moment, I'm transported back to the stuffy, hot loft at the Farm where I first discovered a new world in *The Secret Garden*. Even though the book was confiscated, I lived in that English countryside for months, adding my own stories.

Grandma looks at my selection, nods, and we check out. Triumphant, I walk out with my bounty. My next challenge is to convince Mom not to take them away.

When we get home, I find Mom in her room with the lights out. I open the door slowly, and she waves me over.

"Mom," I begin carefully. "We went to the library today. Grandma let us get some books."

"Bring them here," she says with a sigh, turning on the lamp. "I need to check them to make sure they won't have any bad influence."

I hand her the stack of books. "I got horse books. I'm sure these won't have any bad influence."

Squinting, Mom takes a book and reads the back in detail. She nods, recognizing the title. She passes it back to me and opens her hand for the next. When she's finished with the stack, she leans back on her pillow.

"Okay, these look fine. Just make sure you're doing your schoolwork and reading your Bible before you read any of these."

"Yes, Mom!" I sing back to her, my heart thumping with excitement.

I hurry through my homework, trying to ignore the stack of stories calling to me only a few feet away. As soon as I finish the last long-division problem, I pick up *Black Beauty*. The spine cracks as I open it. I'm careful not to bend it back. I know that can hurt the book. The spicy smell of musty paper held by a hundred other readers tickles my nose. I suck it in deep. *"The first place I can well remember was a large pleasant meadow with a pond of clear water in it. Some shady trees leaned over it, and rushes and water-lilies grew at the deep end. . . ."*

I don't stop reading.

A gray light seeps through the windows; birds twitter in the bushes. It's morning. My heart jerks painfully in my chest. *How could I have stayed up all night?!* School begins in an hour. But even that worry cannot spoil the deep satisfaction I feel as I close my eyes for a few minutes before Mom bangs on my door: "Wakey, wakey!"

Despite my bleary eyes, I say not one word about being tired. I know I'll pay for it at school, but I can't care.

This nighttime reading becomes my pattern. I fall in love with the *Dune* series, which I keep hidden under my bed. Mom may let me read horse books, but sci-fi is too far outside her Family comfort zone. The stories of monsters and heroes give me the strength to withstand the alien landscape of my school. As I walk between classes, I silently repeat the mantra against fear: *Fear is the mind-killer. . . . I will face my fear. I will permit it to pass over me and through me.* That day, I doze off in my Georgia History class again.

I'm startled awake when the teacher knocks on my desk and hands me a sheet of paper with a big red D scrawled on the front. My very first exam. I don't know much about school, but I know a D is very, very bad. I can hardly swallow. How did this happen? I read the chapter. How was I supposed to know to memorize the colony's major sharecrops? It seemed so unimportant.

Determined to figure out what went wrong, I compare the textbook chapters with the questions on the test to understand the types of things the teacher will expect me to memorize. I pay attention to what the teacher emphasizes in class and ask questions. I stop reading all night.

By the next exam, I'm prepared; when I get the test back, I see a big red A. So, this is school? A system in which they give you the answers and reward you for how well you spit them back out? It's the same thing I did in the Family, just different topics. *I can do this.*

Now that I know how to play the game, I excel.

At lunch, Katie, a petite brunette with bangs and glasses, invites me to sit with her and her friends. She's eager to hear about my life as a missionary overseas. I tell her bits and pieces, trying to analyze in real time what's "safe" and what's *Selah*. I stick with stories of our animals and Chinese customs. But when she and her friends talk about their Girl Scout troop and soccer team, I have nothing to add.

After five months in Marietta, I finally have the hang of things. I'm getting straight A's and speeding through as many library books as possible. My teachers love me, and finally, I feel seen. But things begin to feel tense in the house. Grandma said we could stay six months so she could claim us on her taxes and Mom could get on her feet, but now she is ready for us to leave. We have no plan, and Mom is scared.

I trudge home from school one day in early November, not wanting to return to a house where I know I'm unwelcome. But to my shock, Mom greets me with a sunny energy she hasn't had since we moved into Grandma's. She hurries me into the living room, where Nina and Jondy are waiting, and tells us we have a surprise. We sit on the couch, not sure what to expect. The last time Mom surprised us, she'd bought a camper.

But here, in walks our father with a big grin. When he wraps his arms around me, my heart feels like it's about to pop out of my chest. Nina launches herself at him, and he pulls her to the floor of Grandma's living room, tickling her under her arms. Three-year-old Jondy stares in awe. "Is that my daddy?" he asks. Our father left when he was a month old, and he has no memory of him except for the photos Mom showed him.

Behind closed doors, my parents have long conversations. I piece together that something important happened to him in Japan. He only left to bring his niece, Mene, from Macau to Mother Eve's house in Houston, Texas. After he dropped her off, he took a Greyhound bus to Atlanta to see if he and my mom can work things out and get back together.

Two days into my father's visit, my parents tell me that we will return to Macau after the school semester finishes. Dad promises that things will go back to the way they were.

Mom, who has been weepy for months, has got her pep back, but my heart doesn't know which way to break. Mostly, I'm happy for my mother because she's just so pleased and relieved my father is back. And while I'm glad to see him, he has been gone for three years and still seems like a distant, somewhat scary figure. But with him back, perhaps I won't have to try so hard to hold things together as the other "adult" in our little family.

I have rosy memories of our life on the Farm, filled with our animals, my friends and brothers, and lots of new people and activities. Things have been pretty terrible since we left the Farm—the tortures in Thailand, being kicked out of the Family and losing the only security and community we know, the struggle to raise enough money to survive, our uncertain living situation, even the huge cultural adjustment to life in America. I want security, our own home where no one will kick us out. We know how to survive in Macau. We have friends and supporters. And I won't have to go back to begging in parking lots. But I also won't have school, which I've started to enjoy, or access to a public library to bring home stacks of novels. And I will miss the dishwasher, dryer, oven, and television.

Grandma is not happy we're going back to the Family and Macau, but she's been clear that her house is no longer an option and we have nowhere else to go.

As we're trying to figure out how we're going to pay for the journey back to the Farm, Grandma pulls Mom aside. Apparently, her maternal grandfather, Warren Smadbeck, had left her some money in real estate stocks. He and his brother, Arthur Smadbeck, were New York real estate developers and together built residential real estate developments all over the country. They had quite the entrepreneurial flair. Someone once called them the Henry Ford of real estate. After building a new development, the brothers would take one of the large handcars used to fix the railway tracks and load a barrel of beer on it and roll down the railway through downtown New York City, where people would jump on and they'd take them out to the new brownstone developments in Queens and sell them real estate—consumer marketing for the early 1900s. My great-grandfather also owned El Presidente Hotel in Havana, Cuba, where my mother remembers visiting as a seven-year-old, shortly before it was nationalized by Castro's revolutionary government.

I'm in shock to learn that my family was wealthy, and not a little wealthy—but national real estate developer, New York skyscrapers owner wealthy. How can this be? I've known nothing but scraping by my whole life.

Before I get too excited, Grandma holds up a hand. In the hon-ored tradition of old men marrying young women, most of the fam-ily wealth got siphoned off. After my Jewish great-grandmother, Madeline, died, Warren married a much younger woman, Violeta, and most of the family fortune ended up in hers and her children's hands. It reminds me of Grandpa and Mama Maria, and I'm slow to suppress the disloyal thought.

Still, a trust account had been set up for each of Warren's grand-kids, and my mother holds a few shares of the Dakota building in New York City. It received a small sum of money every year from rental payment dividends. But because my mom had joined the Family, Grandma never told her about it. Instead, she had used the money to buy herself a car and to give her two other daughters financial assistance.

Mom is furious when she finds out, and so am I when I think of our desperate situation and the suffering we'd endured over the last year.

"If I'd given it to you, you just would have given it all to the Fam-ily," Grandma says to justify herself. That is true.

There are $2,000 of dividends left in the account where the small interest on her shares is deposited every quarter, and we use it to buy our plane tickets back to Macau.

I jump up and down as I think about the Farm, the animals, and my friends. Though I was just starting to get to know kids at school, there is no one I really regret leaving. *Perhaps I would have made friends if I'd stayed a little longer*, I think wistfully.

When I tell my teachers, they look at me with concern. "Promise you'll find a way to continue your education," they tell me. I promise, determined to do so. In the Family, all victories are immediate: a soul saved, a fridge provisioned, a floor swept. But like mist, they vanish with the rising sun and must be repeated. I like the feeling of making measurable progress toward a long-term goal. The validation. Do the exercise, learn the material, get an A. This was straightforward compared to the confusing requirements of spiritual progress—breaking, humiliation, and abandoning self. After one semester of traditional school, I've discovered that I love learning. I don't want to let that feeling go.

I resolve that I will never suffer from a lack of skill and education, like my mom. The world is not certain; things happen that are not your fault and I have to be prepared to take care of myself.

Within days, we pack up our little suitcases and say our goodbyes.

We will be back in Macau in time for Christmas twenty months after we left, but it feels like we've been away for a lifetime.

17

GENTLING AND BREAKING

The tires crunch on the gravel driveway as the black cab we take from the Hong Kong Macau ferry pulls around the bend into our tiny Hac Sa village. It is quiet. Too quiet, like a city after a plague. *Where are the voices? My friends coming to greet me? My brothers?*

"They've all left," Dad explains.

"Aaron, Mary, Caleb, Esther?"

"The Shepherds moved everyone to Japan and Taiwan. They planned to close everything down and abandon the place, but I got back just in time." He doesn't say why leadership decided to close the Farm, but I suspect it's because securing visas for so many people had become increasingly challenging, especially without my dad there to help with public relations.

Auntie Jeannie and Andy have moved to Taiwan. Aaron, Mary, Caleb, Josh, and Esther have moved to the HCS in Japan. After nearly three years of separation from my father, Esther has no interest in getting back together with him. A legal divorce isn't necessary in the Family; you are considered married to whomever you claim is your spouse, papers or no. Grandpa says, "When the private marriage ties interfere with our Family and God ties, they can be readily abandoned for the glory of God and the good of the Family!" So, it's quite common for couples to break up and choose other spouses.

"What about Patrick?"

"You just missed them," Dad says, which makes me feel even worse. "His family moved to Europe. So did Zacky Star and Hope's family."

I feel left behind. Abandoned. I didn't realize how much I expected a joyous reunion—the laughs and hugs, even being buried in Esther's smothering hugs, which smell like face powder; the chance to tell Patrick about my adventures and real school; the elbow jabs and back slaps from my brothers—until I was met with silence. There was no one to share it all with—to say it out loud and weave the complex experiences into a story, making sense of them.

I run to the farmyard to greet our animals. It's quiet here, too.

My chest burns as I stare at the empty stalls. The calves I watched become cows, the goats I took to the field every day where Patrick and I would play Heaven's Girl. A Doberman jumps on me, and I pet him absently—*Which one is this? Where are our chickens?* I hear a familiar honking screech. *Mad Max is still here!*

The Shepherds had gotten rid of all the animals except the donkey, the pony, and our three quarter horses before Dad could get back and put a stop to it. The Shepherds didn't know where to send them anyway, as we were the only people on the island who have the facilities to care for horses, other than the Jockey Club. I imagine they were glad to turn them back over to my dad.

How could they sell off all our animals without asking us? I know we don't have personal possessions, but this feels very personal. The Shepherds have sold off my childhood companions without a thought or care. I was nothing to them; my dad was nothing. All we have worked for a decade to build was just an inconvenience.

Tears pool in my eyes, but I won't let them fall. I push my shoulders back and walk up to the Main House. I am afraid to see what has happened there.

I open the heavy wooden door and take in the empty living room. Dirt everywhere. Dust motes float in the air. A *Jesus Loves Me* poster lays discarded on the clay tiles, a muddy boot print on Jesus's face.

A rat scurries across the living room. Not a mouse. A foot-long fat brown rat.

How will we live in this big house, just the five of us?

It's so terribly lonely and empty without my brothers and all the people who used to buzz around, but at least there's a feeling that we're safer than we've been in a long time. I don't have to worry that we won't have a place to sleep or food tomorrow. I think of Thailand, the humiliation and breakings, the military-style marching and cleaning. If I could survive that, I know I can survive this, too.

Over the next few weeks, we get to work cleaning and rebuilding. Boy, do I miss dishwashers, carpets, a soft mattress, and countless little luxuries that are commonplace in America. I was completely baffled when I saw carpet in the bathroom at my grandad's house, but it sure beat cold tile on bare feet in the long winter nights. After living in houses built by professional contractors, I see all the imperfections of our homemade construction—the exposed pipes, slightly crooked walls, the slanting, uneven tiles covering the bathroom floor to ceiling.

My father, unflaggingly positive, says losing our animals is an opportunity. He reaches out to some old connections at the Jockey Club, and soon we are offered several thoroughbreds that need a retirement home.

Dad has me down at the stables every morning mucking stalls again and exercising the horses. I'd learned to ride our pony years before, but now I'm getting a crash course in controlling animals who weigh a half ton, leading trail rides, galloping, and jumping.

"Praise the Lord. We'll start a horse boarding and riding school," Dad says, "and we'll make money catering to the local government officials and their kids."

Our riding school opens within a month. At first, only a few people show up, but as word gets out, we soon have whole groups, sometimes forty to eighty people a week, local visitors from Macau and tourists from Hong Kong paying 100 patacas ($12) for an hour on a horse. I teach them how to sit, hold the reins, and direct the horse as the sun beats down and the humidity makes us all drip with sweat.

Dressed in his favorite outfit—a plaid cowboy shirt, jeans, leather belt, cowboy hat, and boots—Dad teaches me to roll ice cubes in a towel and put the towel around the back of my neck to ward off sunstroke. When I finish with the horses, I head to the house to help my mom with the cooking, cleaning, and caring for my younger brother and sister.

After all the trauma we went through in Thailand and the US, we're okay with being on the fringes, preferring to be forgotten rather than cut off. We are back in the Family, but neither of my parents accepts everything the leaders say as gospel anymore. We no longer take pride in being the most dedicated disciples on earth. Our "accidental" excommunication broke my mother's faith in the Family, and those cracks are showing in our everyday life.

We still have daily Devotions, but they are much shorter so Dad can get on with farm chores. If people come to our Farm to ride horses, we still give them posters and talk to them about Jesus. We participate in parades with our horses for events and holidays, but we don't have to be a daily on-call singing group or even busk every week.

We read the new Mo Letters that arrive in the monthly Letter packets, and Dad still receives his allowance of $1,000 from Grandpa every month. We survive on that and the earnings from the horse riding, though Mom complains that Dad spends every penny he makes giving lessons on saddles and tack.

More than the little luxuries of American living, I miss my novels. On my day off, I go to the local library in Macau, but the only English books are for learning English, and those are dumbed-down versions of classic literature meant for a child, like *Charles Dickens in 35 Pages for an English Learner*. I don't have money to buy books at the bookstore, and most of the shops keep the books covered in plastic wrap, so I can't sneak off and read them in the aisles.

I write to my grandmother asking her to send me books, and seven weeks later, a small, weather-beaten cardboard box arrives. My mother cuts open the tape and pulls out ten books, and once more I inhale the smell of temptation and adventure, of escape and discovery. I wait, hands clenched, to keep from grabbing them.

Mom runs her thumb along the spines and finally says, "I'll read them first, and if I think they're appropriate, I'll give them to you." I breathe a sigh of relief. This becomes a pattern. She seems to be following the Family rules now more from reflex than from zealous devotion.

Every few months, another box arrives: *Moby Dick*, *Ivanhoe*, the *Anne of Green Gables* series, and novels by Jane Austen. I snoop until I discover where she hides the books that she has not yet reviewed, and I secretly read the books before she does. That way, even if she decides that some are inappropriate for a Family girl, I've already read them.

To manage the boredom of having no big group of Family kids to play with, I live in the fantasy world of my books, imagining myself as a heroine in each story. The first time I finish reading *Pride and Prejudice*, I sit with the book clutched to my chest. It's 5:00 a.m. Once again, I've stayed up all night and feel a profound sense of completion in its perfection and a deep sadness that it's over.

The more I read, the more I want to know. I'm insatiable. I read each book in the growing pile under my bed over and over, but there are months of waiting between book packages.

In Dad's old office, there's a room with a whole wall of old VHS tapes categorized by child, teen, and adult. The room used to be off-limits, with a constant dehumidifier running, but it's unguarded now, and many of the tapes are white with mold. After living in America and watching shows daily with Grandma, I miss television.

At night, once my parents go to bed, I sneak out a video from this home library. I've preemptively oiled all the doors so they won't squeak, and thank God we have a concrete-and-tile floor instead of creaky wood planks. I creep to the television in the living room. After wiping mold off the tapes, I feed one into our old VCR player. There's a loud crunching noise as the tape goes in, and I cringe, convinced my parents will hear. After waiting a beat, I put the volume down to 1 percent, and with my ear pressed against the TV speaker, I look up to see the pictures.

Night after night my activities go unnoticed. I start to grow bolder. I sit a little further back; turn the volume up a notch higher. I stop looking over my shoulder at every squeak in the night and stay awake later and later. I'm watching *Overboard* with Goldie Hawn and Kurt Russell when I hear a noise that makes my heart stop. The living room door opens. I whip around, turning off the TV as I do, but it's too late. Dad has caught me red-handed.

My body braces for the yelling, the slap, the Rod of God. I don't know what will happen. It's been years since I'd been disciplined by Dad, but the fear is just as fresh. Lying, begging for forgiveness, and running all flash through my mind, but each idea is immediately dismissed as futile. I stand stock-still and wait for my father to whip out his belt. Fourteen has never been too old to get a spanking in his house.

Instead, he sits on the couch and motions for me to sit beside him. Then, quietly, he asks me what I'm doing. *Is this a trap?* I wonder. "I wanted to see a movie," I whisper.

He nods. "You know you're not supposed to be sneaking movies at night, right?"

"Yes." I nod, waiting for the blow, but he isn't losing his temper. He must notice my terrified face, because he pats me on the leg and says, "I'm not going to punish you, but I don't want you sneaking movies at night. You won't have energy for your work tomorrow. Okay? Now off to bed."

I stare in shock for a second before making my lucky escape.

His patience strikes me harder than the Rod of God. I actually feel guilty instead of resentful, as I would have if he punished me.

The following day, he asks if I'll get ice cream with him at the little Chinese corner store by the beach. I am surprised. The only time he's ever taken me for ice cream was on a special occasion or when I'd "earned" it.

He doesn't seem angry, but I've seen how fast that can change. I glance nervously at him from the corner of my eye as we walk.

He awkwardly tries to ask me about myself: "How are things going? How do you feel about being back? Is anything bothering you?" I stare at him incredulously.

"I really want to know," he insists. Then he waits patiently for me to speak, instead of just preaching at me.

Who is this man?

"Not much," I reply, unsure what he wants me to say.

He waits. "Well . . . ?"

I am touched, even though I'm too scared tell him the truth about things that might bother me—anger at Mom, a desire to date, missing my novels. I've learned through painful experience to keep quiet about anything that isn't acceptable Family behavior, and that's not going to change with a few heartfelt attempts at connection by my dad. But as we eat our ice cream, I slowly start to feel more comfortable talking with him. These outings become a regular occurrence—without anyone to report on them, Dad, like Mom, seems less concerned about the evils of white sugar now. Not like when he spanked Mary a hundred swats for stealing coins from Esther's purse and buying candy.

Whatever the Family put him through in Japan has changed him. I'm seeing a *third* side of him. He is subdued. He speaks *with* me rather than just *at* me. This is the first time he's ever asked me how I am and waited for me to gather my thoughts and speak. My father doesn't say much about himself, but over time I gather the story in bits and pieces.

When my father left for Japan three years before, he had been so excited, thinking he was finally going to be allowed to see his father after being separated for ten years. When he'd tried to visit his father not long after my birth, Mama Maria denied him entry. She told him his visit was "unauthorized," meaning he had not sought clearance in advance, and he was turned away. Dad was baffled; he had never needed permission to see his father in the past. Since then, all access to his father went through Mama Maria, and he hoped this invitation meant a thaw. But upon arriving in Tokyo, Dad discovered that this was not just a visit but a coup, and new leadership had been brought into Macau to take charge of things. Dad was held in isolation for six months in a small cottage on the HSC property and was given letters that people had written about him—mostly complaints about his leadership, that he was too dogmatic, self-righteous, dictatorial, strict, bad-tempered, a harsh disciplinarian, and didn't listen to the opinions of others. That's when it dawned on him that he had been invited to Japan for retraining. Worse, Grandpa was living in another house on the property, yet he was never allowed to approach him.

For two and a half long years, my father was completely cut off from us; he was never given the letters we sent him, and the ones he wrote to us were never delivered. He was so isolated he didn't even know that we had been sent to Thailand or that we'd gone to the US. It wasn't until the end of his stint in Japan after the Shepherds decided that he was sufficiently broken that he was finally allowed to see his father, who had since moved to a Family compound in the Philippines. It was perhaps due to their father's ailing health that he and his sister, Aunt Faithy, were invited for a month-long visit.

Grandpa had long been a drinker. As God's anointed prophet, he was not subject to the same rules as the rest of us. "Great men often have great faults," he'd say of famous historical figures plagued by a vice. For Grandpa, it was alcohol, although he claimed he moderated his consumption. But during my father's last visit with him, he'd observed that Grandpa's drinking had become a full-on addiction, with Mama Maria rationing the amount of wine or sherry he could consume each day.

As they were shutting down the Farm anyway, the Asia Pacific leadership didn't see any harm in my father taking his visa trip to Macau instead of South Korea, where they'd been sending him for the last two years. But once he was back at the Farm, he refused to budge. He wrote Grandpa to say he wasn't going back to Japan. If Ruthie was willing, he wanted to try to put his family back together and live quietly at the Farm. Grandpa agreed, so he came to get us.

As the details of my father's experience slip out, I pity him and, eventually, stop fearing him as much. Since being back at the Farm, he and I have begun to forge a new relationship. Once I would have been scared to death to call him "Dad"; such a casual address would have gotten me a slap for being flippant and disrespectful. Now he is no longer "sir" or "Father," but "Dad."

When we run horses in the ring, he gives me money to bring back ice-cream bars from the beach store. We even have date nights. On Friday nights, Dad takes us all out to a nice hotel and we order dessert.

I don't know if my father has become disillusioned with the Family—he still always praises God, but I can tell his spirit has been broken. For the first time, I realize he is a human. I try looking at him with compassion and love, but not uncritically. He's flawed and figuring things out, just like me.

18

—

EDUCATION IS POWER

The biggest change I experience being back at the Farm is the absence of schooling. When I left America, I knew that if I wanted a high school education, I would have to take responsibility to get it. While the Family has created more learning resources since I was a little kid, there are no school materials for high school. The Family still disapproves of education beyond grade school.

I tell my parents that I want to get my high school degree. I've had a taste of knowledge, of being good at something, and I want more. To my great surprise, Dad is indifferent as long as I have time to work on the Farm, and Mom strongly supports my desire to study.

She sends for the CLE homeschool course from the Mennonites, the course the American teen girls used when we were traveling in the camper. Each subject is taught in paper booklets that look like newspapers, with only drawings of Mennonites—no photos. No one can say it has any worldly influence. Those kids are more restricted than we are.

When I receive my materials, I realize this is not just homeschooling; it is self-teaching. I must have the self-discipline to study by myself for hours every day.

In the morning, while Mom teaches Nina and Jondy, I sit at a scratched, gray metal desk facing the wall in our old living room, which has now become my classroom, and study. I read the instructional material, complete the exercises, then take the quiz. At the end of each booklet is a test. At first, Mom holds the answer key until I complete the test. But eventually she decides it's not worth it. "You're on the honor system," she says as she hands over all the books and answer sheets. If I am going to learn, it is up to me.

In school in America, I had teachers who could answer my questions and show me what I was missing. Here, it's me and a book with little explanation. As difficult and foreign as it was being thrust into a traditional classroom setting back in Atlanta, having to catch up to my peers in subjects I knew nothing about, I enjoyed being taught by people who were educated in the fields of study they were teaching. Teaching myself is infinitely harder. There is no one to ask if I don't understand something or if I'd like to discuss a concept or subject further. Dad never went to high school, and Mom says it was so long ago, she doesn't remember much of it. Back in Georgia, at a traditional school, I also had the peer pressure of the classroom, competition with other kids, to push me.

With dogged determination, I sit down every day. Churchill's words from my childhood "I Can" project stick with me: "Never give in, never, ever, ever . . ." *As long as I can read, I can teach myself anything*—except maybe algebra.

Plenty of days I grow bored or want to scream with frustration when I can't figure out a tough math problem and the exercise book gives no explanation, just the correct answer. But having a goal, finishing each workbook, gives me a sense of progress that keeps me moving forward. My struggles and ultimate triumphs leave me feeling more fulfilled, and I realize I'm capable of even more than I imagined.

After I start on the CLE course, Mom begins to quietly champion it within the Family. She writes to Mama Maria and WS recommending these outside schoolbooks for Family kids who might want to continue their education. The *Childcare Handbook* doesn't quite cut it, she explains, perhaps there should be an option for teens who might want to study beyond sixth grade. Even the second-grade CLE booklets she's been using with Nina could help families looking for a more structured curriculum. Mom doesn't get a response from Mama Maria or any recognition that she has even received her correspondence, but sure enough, within two years the CLE books are recommended by WS leadership and are widely adopted by Family members to teach their children.

I'm fifteen, but I feel like an adult. It's harder and harder to be deferential to my mother. When she tries to restrict me, I push back. In the Family, teens are given the responsibilities of adults but still monitored and disciplined like kids. At the Farm, I'd never seen a young person yell at an adult; we were slapped if we dared to talk back. But back in America, I'd seen the teen girls we had camped with talk back, disrespect, even yell at their mother. I begin to try it all. *Does she think that after I supported her in America, she can go back to treating me like a kid?*

Soon Mom and I are having yelling fights when she tries to tell me I can't do something that I have determined is acceptable. I know better than her, and I can prove my point.

I get so angry every time she mortally embarrasses me in public. She flirts outlandishly with handsome men she meets; talks about sex loudly in public elevators; and says inappropriate things about people, including me, only to cover it with an innocent girl grin, saying, "Oops, did I say too much?"

But still, even though we fight, our shared hardships in America have brought us closer.

A year into my studying, Mom calls me over. "Faith, I want to show you something." She is holding a color brochure. "This is Thomas Edison State University. They'll let me get college-degree credits by taking CLEP (College Level Examination Program) exams and sending in proof of my skills and the occupational work I've done over the years in the Family. With this, I can get a college degree by correspondence!"

I'm amused that she's found a way to get a degree that's a compromise between her need to feel safe and her Family beliefs, and I sympathize with the unspoken fear under her excitement.

While she still believes in Grandpa and his teachings, she no longer trusts the Family leadership. After Thailand, she never wants to let people have that kind of power over her again, so she wants to be prepared to take care of herself and her children outside the Family if necessary.

I give her a hug, and she tucks away the brochure. We're already skating a fine line with my high school education, but college is clearly prohibited as a worldly, useless waste of time. I don't say a word to anyone. Dad knows, but she keeps her school binders hidden from any visiting Family members.

This is not our only secret.

Two days later, Mom asks if I want to go with her to Hong Kong. She is vague about the purpose, but I jump at the chance to get off the Farm and see the speeding rat race of city life again.

On the ferry ride from Macau, she tells me that she's stored some money for emergencies and to pay for her college credits. As we walk into the HSBC headquarters, she whispers, "Remember, don't tell anyone about this, not even your dad."

"I promise," I assure her.

Instead of just continuing to receive the small quarterly dividends from her trust, Mom sold her shares in the Dakota building, her inheritance, to her cousin for $25,000. Much less than it was worth, but huge money to us.

"I'm going to buy a few gold coins, so we have some money when the whole economic system crashes. I want you to know where it is in case anything happens to me." Grandpa was always preaching that the great economic crash of America, and the world, was going to happen any day. "I can't face being so helpless again, like I was when we were in the US and I couldn't support you kids."

Shuddering, I tamp down the images of canning and counting pennies for mac and cheese.

Nothing has been the same after getting accidently kicked out of the Family and finding we couldn't make it on our own. I'm with her. I never want to be so vulnerable again.

19

BREAKING THE RULES

Now that the Farm is empty, I have no Family friends to confide in and find solidarity with. I try to make friends with some of the Portuguese teens who come to our riding school, but, as I learned in America, friendship is based on shared experiences, and we have nothing we can share.

As if she's reading my mind, Mom comes into the schoolroom one morning while I'm reading about the US Civil War. "Guess what!" she announces excitedly. "We are going to be getting some more girls your age! We've had word from the Shepherds that they want to send us two teen girls who have been struggling in their Family Homes in India."

Great! Finally, I won't be alone here! I can have teenage friends.

Mom confides that the two new arrivals want to leave the Family, but they're too young. "Their parents and Shepherds are at their wits' end. They are hoping a more relaxed environment at the Farm with animals will help, but if they can't make it here, they are out."

Wow, girls who actually want to leave the Family. They would have been sent to the Victors in the old days.

"You need to be careful to be a good example to them and not to let peer pressure lead you astray," Mom admonishes.

"Yes, of course," I say. I'm nothing if not the sane, responsible one in my family.

The new arrivals are Emily, fifteen, and Jen, sixteen. Everything about Em is pin straight: her short, mousy brown hair and bangs; her tall, lanky body; her thin face. She has no boobs or curves at all. She barely speaks. I can't imagine her getting up the courage to say boo, much less express a desire to leave the Family.

Jen, Miss Rebellious, is the opposite—round and loud. She throws herself on one of the beds and announces, "This is my bed." She has curves everywhere: curly dirty-blond hair, round face and eyes. She stares at the two of us and decides she is queen.

Em and I get along, and while Jen is older than us, I don't respect her. She is crazy, I think. And mean. I stand up to her every once in a while; this is *my* Farm, after all. But mostly I just let her call the shots. She cries and yells if she doesn't get her way. Even though she is bossy and loud, I can tell she doesn't have much more confidence than I do. She lifts her leg and says, "My thighs are so fat. Look at that; and look at how skinny you two are. Em, you could be a stick figure. I hate my body. I need to lose weight."

"You're beautiful," says Em.

"Yes," I agree. She is a bit chubby, but at least she has boobs, I think.

Em hates how stick-thin she is. "Like an insect," she jokes.

"At least you're tall. I'm short with small boobs, a big butt, and"— I've decided after long inspection in the mirror—"Not a single attractive distinguishing feature. I'm plain."

"No, you're not!"

"And I have weird feet. Just the other day one of the Portuguese boys coming to ride told me, 'You know the first thing I saw when we met was that your second toe was longer than your big toe.'"

"He's just a jerk. You're beautiful."

"So are you."

We lie comfortingly to each other but privately think our self-assessments are correct.

Jen loves to flirt openly and starts to secretly date a Systemite guy who works at the Jockey Club. She's pressuring Em and me to get boyfriends, but I'm still reluctant. I have no interest in the Jockey Club workers.

Every year in July, the city holds the São João festival at Hac Sa beach with a parade, food, game stalls, a huge bonfire, and dancing. This year, like every year, we ride our horses at the head of the parade dressed in traditional Portuguese folk clothes of red and green with tight black pants and boots.

As I stand leaning against a pine tree after the parade, watching Taurug eat, Nunu walks up with a big grin. "Hey, do you remember me?"

Do I ever! I haven't seen him since I was eleven, but he's just as handsome as I remember. He is a Systemite who used to come to the Farm for Bible studies, but I was too young for him to notice then. Now he's in his twenties and I'm fifteen, filling out my riding pants much better and wearing makeup. Jen shows me how to do smokey eyes, and while normally anything more than a light touch is frowned upon, my parents don't make me wash it off.

Nunu and I chat and flirt innocently, watching the local Portuguese police fill up their water guns with wine and have shootouts over the huge bonfire. Before he leaves, he invites Jen, Em, and me to a party that some of his friends are having at Hac Sa beach the following Saturday.

The next weekend, the three of us girls sneak out the huge back window of our bedroom—no lights, no flashlight—and walk down to the beach. It's a small party, a bonfire, some beer, and a handful of people who are all older than I am. After chatting for a while, Nunu guides me a little way from the fire to lean against a boulder. Cold, I cuddle into him. He leans down and kisses me. My tummy tingles in excitement.

This hot guy I liked when I was a kid likes me back!

Even though sex has pervaded my life since I was a child, I am still shy, embarrassed to show my teenage body for the first time, to have a guy touch my breasts or see them. My reticence doesn't make sense, even to me.

Perhaps I am polluted by the few romance novels I read when I was twelve? Or my grandmother's Victorian-era books?

Guys are always rushing. I just want to linger in the kiss a little longer. Time, I just want time. Time to feel comfortable. Time to know him, time to know me. As I wiggle and gently push his hands down from my small breasts then up off my underwear, he finally takes my hand and places it over his crotch.

Okay, this I can handle. I've been giving guys hand jobs since I was ten, and I'm pretty good at it.

I may not be comfortable in my own skin, but I really like Nunu. I feel like I've known him for years, so I'm willing to explore this with him.

The girls and I start sneaking out every weekend, waiting in the dark at midnight by the designated old ficus tree for our young men to come pick us up. The girls take off to Taipa to their boyfriends' apartments. Nunu and I drive up the hill, park, and spend the next several hours talking and making out in the car.

I get lost in Nunu's kisses and caresses, as I sit on the hood of his car and he stands between my knees. I love this part. But his hand awkwardly rubbing in that sensitive area more often just starts to hurt, and I move it away. I learned young that if my hand is on the guy's crotch, they're satisfied with the arrangement. I've been masturbating since I was three, when I learned from my older sister that rubbing on a pillow felt good. So far, the guys are inferior to a pillow for achieving orgasm.

Despite rubbing genitals during sex play as a kid, my hymen is still intact. At fifteen, I'm incredibly old to have not lost my virginity. I can't think of anyone who is still a virgin at my age. Heck, many of the girls were pregnant at fifteen. I am eager to get rid of this badge of shame, and Nunu is happy to help me. Even though sleeping with a Systemite is strictly forbidden by the Family, ever since we were TRF'd, I don't really feel like I'm fully in the Family. I don't feel morally bound by its rules; it's just a matter of not getting caught. And I want my first time to be with someone I choose, someone I'm attracted to.

After a month of heavy make-out sessions, the perfect opportunity presents itself when Nunu's parents leave town for a night.

I sneak out of my room well after bedtime and walk down the road to wait for Nunu. As we drive the short way to his parents' house, I'm all nervous energy and excitement.

We make out in his bed until I decide I'm ready—it's now or never—and I climb on top. It hurts like hell, but it's easier to bear the pain if I'm controlling the pressure. Once he's in, I'm too sore to move much, so he comes quickly. I'm triumphant that I'm no longer a virgin but deflated by the anticlimactic experience. "Next time will be better," he says. I don't dwell on my mixed emotions for long. I'm exhausted from the pain, Nunu from his orgasm, and we both fall sleep.

When we wake up, the sun is rising through the bedroom curtains, like a searchlight marking my doom. Damn. I'm late! My mother comes into the girls' room every morning at 7:00 to make sure we are up, which means that I need to be back in my bed before she opens that door.

We race to the car, and Nunu drives at breakneck speed. I can barely speak with fear during the twenty-minute drive. As we approach the Farm, I see my dad already at work in the stables, so I duck down in my seat as we pass by. Nunu parks behind our house, and I dash to my bedroom window. I tap the glass and see Jen and Em through the pane, freaking out. Quickly, they pull open the latch, and I climb inside. As soon as I throw the covers over me, my mother walks in and starts yelling, "What are you doing still in bed?"

Nunu is spooked by our near miss. He calls the next day to tell me he can't see me anymore. "I'm sorry. It's just too stressful to have to avoid your father."

He probably thinks Dad will go after him with a machete. With all the rumors about us, I can't really blame him. But being abandoned right after my first time stings. I hide my teary eyes and tell myself to buck up. If my parents notice me moping, they'll guess something is wrong, and there is nothing I can say. *The unfairness of it all.* Jen and Em try to cheer me up by taking me out to a bar with their Jockey Club friends.

A month after my near escape, Mom and Dad summon Jen, Em, and me into the schoolroom. "Girls, we have gotten a very serious report that you were seen sneaking out of the house in the middle of the night."

One of our Chinese neighbors has reported on us.

Not wanting to give us the chance to get our story together, they question us separately.

I follow Mom into her tiny hallway office and sit on the institutional gray metal desk facing her. "So, honey, did you have an orgasm?"

"What?" I sputter.

"Did you have an orgasm with the guy you went out with?" She looks delighted and ready to gossip, automatically assuming that I was having sex if I was sneaking out with boys.

"I— I— No, not really."

"Oh, that's too bad. You know, I've found that if you dig your heels into the bed and push up while you are having sex, that can make it easier to orgasm."

I'm staring at her like she's lost her mind. She just found out I've been sneaking out of the house with a boy, and she wants to know if I had an orgasm?!

She sighs, realizing she's not going to get much gossip out of me. "You can talk to me. I love you no matter what you've done. You know, there is nothing you've done that I haven't done myself," she reminds me with a grin.

She throws herself back in her chair, and her eyes shine as she regales me with details of a sexual encounter she had in a stream with a Native American guy back in 1969, when she was attending Woodstock. Then, just as suddenly, she leans forward, her mood taking a somber turn.

"Are you sure you're okay? Nothing bad happened?" she asks with an intensity that takes me by surprise.

"I'm fine," I assure her.

"I just want you to be careful out there. It's not like in the Family, where everyone is loving and caring. Before I joined the Family, I was raped at a photographer's studio in New York and nearly raped at knifepoint not long after that. My attacker shoved me into the doorway of the building where my old boyfriend lived, and thankfully I managed to push his apartment buzzer and scream for help. He came running and chased the guy away," she says conversationally.

"I'm sorry, Mom—"

"It's no big deal," she tells me, a lilt in her voice. "I'm fine. It didn't leave any lasting emotional damage. I just moved on."

I give her a look but don't press the matter. This isn't the first time I've heard about these rapes. She'd casually referred to them a few times when she'd shared her testimony about joining the Family, but I wasn't able to appreciate those stories until now that I've had sex. Should I be upset for my mother? It doesn't seem to bother her. Grandpa also doesn't consider rape that big of a deal. In a Mo Letter titled *Rape*, he recommends that women just submit and get it over with, even try to show the rapist God's love. I think of *Heaven's Girl* and feel a chill down my spine.

Mom smiles. "Being raped is one thing you never have to worry about in the Family, thank God."

Yeah, why rape someone when sex is on the schedule?

I think of all the men my mother didn't like but still had to share with over the years. In the camper when we were in the US, the Home in Thailand, the Farm. I shake my head. Of course, that's different. That's sharing God's love . . . right?

"Well, FFing could be a little dangerous," she continues, as if reading my mind. "I remember a time in Libya . . ." She trails off for a second.

She lets the sentence hang until I break the silence. "What happened in Libya?" Mom loves an audience.

"Well," she says, sighing theatrically. "I remember when I got invited to Libya with Aunt Faithy and your dad. I was so excited I was going to meet Grandpa for the first time. I was already in love with him from the Mo Letters. Anyway, one of Gaddafi's men who was assigned to take care of our group during our stay got me alone and nearly raped me. I pretended to be sick to avoid his advances. It was only later I found out that Mama Maria and Grandpa had invited me on the trip partly to sleep with that horrible, slimy man so that he would act as a King—a supporter—for the Family in Libya. Sayyid was his name. They were going to offer me up as his second wife." She makes her yuck face. "But before they could put that plan into effect, Gaddafi arrested him for stealing money that he was supposed to be using to take care of our team. He was thrown in jail."

Mom laughs at her near escape while I stare at her in awe and horror.

"Other than that little hiccup, I loved Libya! That's where Grandpa put your father and me together," she says, smiling. *Yes, that part I know.*

"It's also where I got to spend some intimate time with Grandpa," she confesses with a sly smile.

"What?! You had sex with Grandpa?" This is the biggest shock of the night, of the year!

She covers her mouth with her hands, like she's a little girl again.

"Mama Maria brought me to his bedroom to have sex with him," she blurts out. "It was a little strange, but such an honor."

For as long as I can remember, my mother has treated me more as a peer than as a daughter. But even though she's never had much of a filter, this disclosure is a blockbuster. My mother had sex with the Prophet! It truly is a high honor. *Why has she never mentioned it before?*

"And?" I press.

"Well . . . Grandpa couldn't really get an erection, so the two of us just petted for an hour or so. Mama Maria sat there the whole time, typing in the corner," Mom recalls.

Ahh, perhaps she never said anything because she was ashamed she couldn't give him an erection. The reveal certainly does take away from his image of sexual prowess and appetite described in the Mo Letters.

It's well known that Grandpa has no issue with incest as long as close blood relatives don't have babies together (to avoid deformity), so I would normally not think Mom's experience with Grandpa was strange. But probably because of all the System influence I've had in the past couple of years, it makes me uncomfortable to think that Mom nearly had sex with my grandfather before she became my dad's wife.

"Anyway." Mom blinks away the past. "We were talking about you and your sexual experiences!"

One confession deserves another, I reason. Besides, I am disappointed with my dating experience and I'm tired of sneaking out. Perhaps this is God's way of intervening.

I gaze at her hopeful face. She wants me to share. I could give it a try.

"Yes," I tell her, "I've been sneaking around with Em and Jen for months."

True to her word, my mom doesn't blow up or even scold me. But she does tell my father, and he reports us to the Shepherds in Japan—to the nameless, faceless people on the other end of the phone who control our lives.

If it had just been me sneaking out in the evenings, she and my father would have dealt with it as a family. But knowing that Emily and Jen were involved, teenagers the Family had entrusted to their care, they were obligated to report it, and they couldn't report on them without reporting on me. Word that I was involved would have gotten out eventually through the girls, and that would look far worse for my parents if they hid it.

The truth is, I am not really surprised. We've been conditioned to report on each other.

Within days, word comes down from on high. There will be no third chances. Em and Jen will be sent to the US and excommunicated. The Shepherds buy their tickets, and my dad takes them to the airport. We have no idea what will happen to them or where they will go, and I never hear from them again.

I'm given a choice: I can move to a Teen Home in Japan or be excommunicated like the girls. Excommunication is too scary to contemplate; we nearly didn't survive when we were cut off from the Family in the US. I may be sixteen now, but I know I couldn't survive on my own.

A few weeks later, Auntie Crystal flies in from Japan to convince me to move to the Teen Home that she and Uncle Michael run there. She is all sweetness and understanding: "I know you've been cut off out here without teen friends or good Shepherding. We have a great group of fifteen teens. We have a singing group and do lots of fun stuff. You'll love it. You'll get to be with your siblings again."

I choose Japan over excommunication. It's an easy choice, the accepted path. Japan is the pinnacle of the teen community that I'd been hearing about in the *Family News* for years. All of my older siblings left home for Japan at sixteen, and I'll finally get to see them again. Well, a couple of them. Josh has since moved to Taiwan with his new wife, Laura; Nehi and Hobo have moved to Brazil; but

Aaron and Mary are still in Japan. Esther has disappeared into WS, no one knows where.

I'm eager to escape my parents, to grow up. I suspect I'll miss my dad, the new version, more than my mom, but mostly I'll miss Jondy and Nina, my babies.

Going to Japan feels like I'm about to finally rejoin the natural flow. But I'm also nervous: *Can I readjust to the rigidity of the Family?* On the Farm lately, I'd been engaging in worldly pursuits: studying for high school, reading novels, sneaking out of the house to have a System boyfriend, teaching horseback riding, and hanging out with Portuguese teenagers.

We still studied the Bible and Mo Letters and prayed every day, but my life hasn't revolved around witnessing for years now. *Will I be able to recommit myself to God and to the Family's mission?*

In my last few weeks at the Farm, I work like a whirlwind and finish my high school curriculum. I know I can't take that—or my novels—with me. I am heading straight to the heart of the Family.

20

ALL FOR ONE MEANS NONE FOR YOU

Arriving in Japan is an unexpected culture shock. Japan is the exact opposite of China. Everything is perfectly clean and ordered. There are vending machines for whatever you might want. Things here are *kawaii*, cute, if they are small. *Maybe I'll finally fit in?*

Auntie Crystal and Uncle Michael pick me up at the airport. Uncle Michael gives me his familiar warm smile and bear hug. It's good to see him. As we drive from the airport, I dream of seeing my siblings and visiting the fabled Heavenly City School.

"I don't know when it will be possible for you to see them," Auntie Crystal snaps at my questions about seeing my family. "They live in another part of the country, hours away." *Wait. Didn't she tell me I would be seeing them soon?* We drive through wide-open tracts of green farmland. When we finally arrive at our destination, I'm in the countryside of Fukuoka, a city in the south of Japan, a ninety-minute flight from the HCS in Tateyama, looking at a traditional, Japanese building.

Uncle Michael takes me on a tour of the house. Around fifty people live in this two-story, refitted Japanese guesthouse, including the teen group. The teen girls sleep on futons on the floor in one room, the teen boys in another. The bathrooms have drop toilets—a no-flush-toilet system—that are emptied weekly by the "honey truck."

I'm led into the teens' living room. Uncle Michael and Auntie Crystal take their places at the head of the room with the teens fanned out around them. My new group.

Pretty much everyone knows who I am. They've been reading about me and my family and our life at the farm in the *Family News* for years. But I just shrug when people try to ask me about it. I would be "proud" if I discussed my relation to Grandpa. "You're nothing special, you're just like everyone else" has been drilled into my siblings and me by Shepherds for years. The truth is, I avoid the subject. It brings up feelings I'd rather ignore: feelings of resentment and embarrassment that Grandpa has never asked us, his own grandkids, to visit—especially now that I have some experience of what grandparents are after my time in the States.

Auntie Crystal's hard and distant face is not the one she had when she was coaxing me to come to Japan. She and Uncle Michael, I remember, are the Shepherds who oversaw the Victors at the Stone House, the most terrible place you could be sent. A queasy feeling grows in my stomach.

"This is Faith," she says to the group. "She has come from Macau for retraining. She is on probation until further notice."

All the teens' eyes pierce me like tiny darts. My cheeks flush with humiliation. *I've been had.* I'm not in Japan to rejoin my peers and family. I'm here for punishment.

Probation is a punishment for anything that could get you excommunicated if repeated, like sex with outsiders and, since the Family directive in 1989, adult sex with underage kids. But a Shepherd could impose it within their discretion for a consistently poor attitude, if you were too critical or doubting, or spoke back too much, snuck out of the house, or bought alcohol. Pretty much anything they didn't like.

I can't believe Auntie Crystal turned on me. During her visit, she'd been all honey and pie, going out of her way to dispel any concerns I might have had. She was the picture of sympathy, telling me it was totally understandable that I snuck out to see a Systemite, given my circumstances. She betrayed me.

Mom betrayed me.

And I betrayed myself.

The sizzle of anger running from my chest to my fingernails retreats. I have no right to blame anyone. This is my struggle. I did the deed; I pay for it.

Unable to meet the judgment of sixteen pairs of eyes, I look at my bare toes and take the stack of basic-training Mo Letters from Auntie Crystal's hand. "For the next three months, you will read these by yourself in addition to the morning two hours of daily Devotions," she tells me.

I've been kicked to the lowest rung on the totem pole.

After a sleepless night, I wake up feeling more alone than I have since Thailand. I shuffle out of bed and ready myself to rejoin the regimented schedule of the Home. I barely begin my breakfast before I'm assigned to the worst jobs and told I must do anything that anyone tells me to do—even the younger teens.

The days turn into weeks, and I am at times entertained by new experiences in a new country, but mostly I am miserable. I'm bored with reading the basic-training Letters I've read a hundred times. Where it was once habitual, I struggle with constant obedience, witnessing, selling Family CDs door to door, and cleaning bathrooms for fifty people. I miss my studies, my books, the horses. I call out to God to help me readjust to communal Family living.

Thankfully, He sends me an answer—a new friend.

Joy, a tall, gangly, half-Mexican, half-American girl with long dark hair and mocha skin, approaches me shyly. We start talking, and soon we're sitting next to each other at meals. Together we find things to laugh about, like our witnessing uniforms, flowered purple fabric sewn at home into tiny miniskirts that we wear with little spandex shorts and tops that show our midriff.

Like me, Joy doesn't really fit in; she's too tall and serious in a land of smiling dolls. I tell her she's beautiful, but she has very low self-esteem, and I don't believe her when she returns the compliment. We both wish we were cool kids: the pretty girls, or the girls confident enough to think they're pretty, the singers, and the dance troupe—the cheerleaders of the Family.

On the margins of the social fabric, Joy and I are allies, and I realize she's my first real friend since I was ten years old, running around the Farm with Patrick. We talk late into the night about how difficult everything is. I confide in her about books, my studies, and dating Systemite guys.

We maneuver to be paired together when we go out witnessing. At each store, we hand our full-color posters with a message about the End Time and 666 or Jesus's love on the back to the proprietor and talk to him or her about Jesus and ask for a donation.

Chill autumn winds are already blowing and changing the colors of the trees to red and gold. We don't have colors like this in Macau. Joy and I step into a 7-Eleven to warm up while out witnessing one day. The smell of cooking meat on a stick hits my nostrils. I'm hungry, but I dare not use any of the money we collected and come back empty-handed. We will eat when we are done in a few more hours. I flip through some of the magazines on the rack to distract me from my growling stomach, and so I look like I have a purpose here rather than just sucking up heat.

"Gross," I say to Joy, nearly dropping the violent comic I've grabbed in horror. A man is strangling a woman as he rapes her. Screams and tears spout from her face. "That's terrible!"

I pick up another and slam it closed just as quickly. More violence and horror. "How can they have these degrading comics out on a shelf where any kid could pick them up?!"

"That's normal here." Joy shrugs. "All the comics are like that. They also have vending machines where men can buy schoolgirls' used underwear."

I can barely imagine the depravity. From then on, I stay close to my buddy. I act like I can handle any threat, but I'm hyperalert, glancing over my shoulder at every gust of wind or unexpected shadow. Japan has seemed so safe, like a clean, perfect, on-time, well-oiled machine. The Japanese stand passively at a red light on our straight country road with no car visible for miles. But the closer I look, the darker it is. Scratch the surface and the rot is just underneath. Thank God we are in the Family, safe from such things.

After a couple of months of trying to fit into a new Home—and country and life—Auntie Crystal, fuming, calls me into our empty dance practice room. I'd refused to do something that one of the younger teen girls asked me to do. Auntie Crystal yells that I'm the lowest of the low, nothing and no one. No one cares about me. No one likes me. No one's on my side.

Joy is, I think silently to myself, refusing to be stomped into nothingness.

She laughs as if she knows what I'm thinking. She leans toward me until her face is inches from mine. "I told Joy to become your friend. She's been spying for me the entire time."

I flinch, and not just from the spit that spatters my face with her words. This is the cruelest blow, and she knows it. My heart cracks. I can't bring myself to meet Auntie Crystal's eyes. I learned long ago not to trust the adults, even my parents, but Joy? We shared everything. She held me up on my weakest days. She was the one person I relied on, and now she's betrayed me, too.

The next day, I force myself out of bed. I force myself to eat breakfast. And I force myself not to run away when Joy sits down next to me in the empty dance room. I'm as cold and still as marble as I repeat everything Auntie Crystal told me the evening before. The words burn like ice as they leave my throat.

When I finish, Joy reaches for my hand, but I pull it away. She takes a deep breath, and then the words spill out of her. "Yes, it's true. She did tell me to be your friend and get close to you so I could report on you. But that was only true in the beginning!" She pleads with tears in her eyes. "Since then, we've become real friends. You're my best friend! I wouldn't betray you. I haven't told her the stuff we talk about. I promise! When she asks me about you, I just tell her innocent stuff to satisfy her."

My mouth clamps together as tightly as a mousetrap. I don't know what to say. She betrayed me once—is she at it again? I watch as her sniffles turn into sobs, eyes red, nose dripping. We sit there, me a statue, her a crumpled bag. Five or ten or thirty minutes later, the tension in my jaw releases. I know how things are in the Family. Joy has no more say in her life than my parents do in theirs. The Family and God must be our first loyalty. She didn't know me when she agreed to spy on me; and she couldn't have said no to Auntie Crystal anyhow. She is mean as a rattlesnake and has complete control over our lives.

I put my hand on Joy's and tell her it's okay. The pain remains, like a scar on my heart, but I believe her. Friendship is too precious a treasure to waste.

The incident with Joy has taught me that there is no one I can truly rely on except God. He is the only constant that not even the Shepherds can control. Desperate for a connection that no one can take away from me, I develop a personal relationship with God. In a deserted room, I kneel on the bamboo tatami mat–covered floor and cry to God for help. I'm reminded of Thailand. "Please, God," I weep. "Please help me, give me strength, give me peace in my heart, make me more yielded to Your will. I will do whatever You ask of me. Please help me now. I know You are with me even though I'm all alone."

I commit myself to having a direct relationship with Jesus, regardless of what may seem like injustice by my Shepherds. Psalm 27:10

says, "When my mother and father forsake me, then the Lord shall take me up." *This is the answer*, I tell myself, *and no one in the Family can punish me for it.*

Recently, WS started publishing the Mama Letters—Mama Maria's own letters on topics like prayer and hearing from God. I feel like I finally understand their meaning and that I am walking in the path of the Letters and the Bible—no longer just reading because I'm supposed to. I'm connected to God, and they are my comfort, my only escape. *Pain and humiliation are for my own good*, I tell myself, as I've been taught.

I read the Bible with new eyes, and even though I've read the whole thing straight through more than once, and studied many of the passages hundreds of times, and memorized dozens of chapters, my new focus and analysis raises more questions. Particularly about the Law of Love.

I raise my hand in Devotions. "Uncle Michael, I know the Bible and Grandpa teaches us that God's only law is love, and that the Ten Commandments, particularly the one on adultery, are no longer valid."

"Yes. Matthew 22:37–40: 'There are only two commandments now: Love God and love your neighbor,'" Uncle Michael says, paraphrasing the passage.

"But 'All scripture is given by inspiration of God,' 2 Timothy 3:16. And the Bible says, 'Heaven and earth shall pass away, but My Words shall not pass away,' Matthew 24:35. How are the Ten Commandments no longer relevant?"

"They still give people who are not liberated a good standard to follow," Uncle Michael answers. "But Galatians 3:24–25 says, 'The law was our schoolmaster. But after faith is come, we are no longer under a schoolmaster.'"

After a few more minutes, my hand goes up again.

"Yes, Faith." There is a slight note of annoyance in his voice that warns me to be careful.

"Of course I believe in the Law of Love," I hedge. "I just want to make sure I have this straight, so that I can answer any questions that Systemites might have when we are witnessing."

His expression relaxes slightly.

"What about in Matthew, where Jesus says, 'You have heard that it was said, "Do not commit adultery." But I tell you that anyone who looks at a woman lustfully has already committed adultery with her in his heart'?"

"Well, Faith, in that passage Jesus was showing the Pharisees that it was impossible to keep the Ten Commandments, if even looking at a woman with lust is committing adultery. He was proving his point that it needs to be all about grace now."

"That makes sense," I respond. "But what about what where Paul says, 'God will judge fornicators and adulterers'?" (Hebrews 13:4)

"It's good to question to learn, but we need to be careful that our questions don't cross the line into doubting." Uncle Michael's sharp look and his accusation of doubting stop me immediately; to be accused of "doubting" God's Word is a quick ticket to punishment.

"Now to answer your question," Uncle Michael continues with irritation, "Paul still had quite a few hang-ups from his time as a Pharisee. God has given Grandpa the new and inspired Word of God, revealing new truths and interpretation to the scripture now that we, God's End-Time soldiers, are ready to receive it."

I raise my hand again, but from his place at the head of the table, Uncle Michael gives me a hard stare and in a commanding voice asks, "Do you believe Grandpa is God's prophet?"

"Yes, of course. I'm sorry. I just want to understand," I say with downcast eyes.

Of course Grandpa is correct. I try to shut out the heresy of thinking anything else, but I still don't understand. And secretly, I don't think the adults do either, at least not the ones I've questioned. *Is Uncle Michael saying that all the Bible is divinely inspired except for*

Paul's teachings? But we quote Paul all the time. Maybe only some of Paul is not correct. But then how can the whole Bible be the Word of God?

Confused, I put my dangerous inquiries to the back of my mind on a shelf marked "Unresolved questions for later."

A few days after my exchange with Uncle Michael, I'm thrilled to learn that he and Auntie Crystal have been called away by God's service to open a Teen Home in another country, which means the teen group is breaking up and dispersing to other Homes.

Joy and I beg to be sent to the same Home, wherever that may be, and to our shock and delight, we get our wish.

Our new Home is in Komae, a suburb of Tokyo. It's a converted two-story guesthouse with lots of small rooms and a central kitchen, perfect for a Family Home with six families and eight teens. Five of us teen girls sent from Fukuoka room together, and I try to make myself as invisible as possible, not wanting to prolong my almost-completed probation period.

But at dinner that night, I hear a deep voice holler my name. I jump, looking over my shoulder, and see my brother Josh. He's standing next to his wife, Laura, and their two toddlers. I had not attended their wedding, just as I had not attended Nehi's, David's, or Mary's. Weddings in the Family are small, simple ceremonies held at home or out in nature and usually presided over by the Home Shepherd. We cannot use God's money to travel for selfish purposes like attending weddings, reunions, or Christmas.

I run over to Josh and give him a hug. It doesn't matter that Josh is not my favorite brother or that he picked on me as a kid and tattled on me to the adults when Patrick and I played Heaven's Girl and pretended that Josh was the Antichrist. Josh is my blood family.

"Hey, little Faithy, look how you've grown!" he says with a crooked smile.

"You, too, bro," I say, punching him in the arm.

He always had an edge of sarcasm, and I see he hasn't lost his touch.

Laura gives a more genuine hug, and I smile to see her after all these years. "You look just the same," I tell her.

She is a thin, quiet girl with long, dirty-blond hair. I'd missed her first pregnancy when I had been in the US. I heard she nearly died from toxemia, but here she is with two healthy towheaded toddlers.

Despite her frail look, she is my knight in shining armor when she steps in with her no-nonsense attitude to teach me how to make a curry dinner for fifty people from whatever food happens to have been collected in provisioning. I've just been put on the cooking schedule and don't know where to begin.

Then, later that week, I get a brief but happy visit with Aaron. He and Mary live at the Heavenly City School a few hours away, but he's come to Tokyo to perform in the Christmas concert put on by the HCS dance troupe, which he joined not long after coming to Japan. Mary is on childcare, so she rarely travels.

I spot him in the lobby of the performance hall that the Family rented for the show, and he envelopes me in a bear hug. "Hey, little sis! You've gotten so big."

"Look at you, finally getting your dream of being a big star!" I drink in the sight of him. I missed his exuberance.

"How have you been? Have you heard from the others?" I ask.

Nehi and Hobo are doing well in Brazil, living with their wives and a couple of kids each.

I wish we had quiet time to really talk, but the performance is about to begin. We enter the hall and take our seats. As soon as the lights dim, my jaw drops. The troupe puts on an extravaganza with professional lighting, costumes, and dancing. Nothing like our humble childhood performances. Aaron is smiling like a Cheshire Cat at the center of it all. I'm proud of him and a little envious.

On Christmas morning, I am grateful to speak with my mom for the permitted three minutes. Long-distance communication is discouraged, as it's a waste of God's resources. International phone calls can cost $30 for a few minutes, so we might get permission from the Home once a year, if we're lucky. Otherwise, we write by post. Not all Home Shepherds know how to use the complex email system like my parents, but more Homes are starting to have at least one computer.

"Did you get the Christmas card I sent you?" she begins, hardly able to hold in her excitement.

"Yes."

"And what I put inside it?" she says in nearly a whisper.

"Yes, thank you."

Her card had arrived a week earlier with a photo of our family taped to the inside. I remembered her parting instructions when we said goodbye in Macau—that I should always check behind the photo—so I peeled back the tape to find the equivalent of a $10 bill.

The Shepherds read all our mail, and any money in our possession is expected to be contributed to the Home. Mom is quite proud of herself for thinking of this trick to get around the screening.

Of course, I don't spend her gift. I never do. I've saved the small amounts of cash I've been given for birthdays in a red Chinese New Year envelope hidden inside a rolled-up sock, hoping no one will find it even when they do bag searches. When the Antichrist does come and we must run, I may be on my own without a Home to take care of me.

My next call to my parents is not until Christmas the following year, 1993. I find out a lot has happened since I left the Farm. About six months after my departure, they were also given an ultimatum: move to a full-fledged Family Home or get kicked out of the Family. For my father, this would have meant losing his monthly stipend, which he relied on. He and my mother would have to depend on fundraising, which they've never been very good at, and riding lessons, which barely covered the cost of caring for the horses. So my parents agreed to move back into the mainstream Family. They sold the horses and moved with my younger siblings to a large Combo in Taiwan.

When my visa to Japan is about to expire, I'm sent on a trip to Taiwan and I get to visit with them for a few days. I'm so happy to be together after all this time, but I'm worried for them. Dad has always done his own thing, which doesn't work well in Family Homes; and Mom has her own secrets. They tell me they're planning to go to the US for their next visa trip in three months to take care of some legal business. Dad and Esther want to file the paperwork to legalize their divorce; though it doesn't matter in the Family, divorce simplifies System paperwork that requires a signature from your spouse, especially when the spouse doesn't live in the same country. Once the papers are processed, Mom will be my father's only wife.

I'm not sure what to say; I had no idea that my father and Esther are still legally married, as they'd been Family divorced and living apart for years. Before I can pose my questions, the words scatter when my parents invite me to join them on the trip.

"Yes!" I blurt, jumping up. This is a totally unexpected opportunity for me to complete my high school diploma. I'd finished all the study requirements before I left Macau—I was able to fulfill them in two years instead of the typical four because I'd been able to get through the workbooks at my own pace—but I need to take the final high school exam to get my diploma. The test must be administered by an American licensed teacher. My heart jumps in my chest. This might be my only opportunity.

I petition my teen Shepherd and get permission to take my next visa trip to the US with my parents. I count down the days until I have books, washing machines, televisions, and especially Grandad and Barbara.

Indiana is beautiful in the fall, the riot of red and gold on all the trees, the crackle of leaves in the driveway, and the smell of pumpkin pie that Barbara bakes. We sit down to eat at a table that looks the same, in a room that looks the same, surrounded by the same paintings, like the house has been frozen in time. It's strange and comforting. Nothing in my life has ever stayed the same for long.

After I lick the whip cream from my fingers, I return to my room to study. I've been brushing up on the subjects of a typical high school curriculum—especially math—since I heard I was going, so I'm as ready as I'll ever be.

Barbara has arranged for me to take the exam in an empty classroom at her school. Walking past the white walls plastered with colorful posters, I flash back to those early weeks the first time I attended public school in Atlanta. I feel the same thrill of anxiety as I take out my No. 2 pencils and the same steady confidence as I fill in my answers. Time passes in a haze, and I don't realize two hours have passed until the buzzer goes off. There were definitely questions I didn't know, but I know I'll pass. The question is: How well did I do?

My score lands me in the top percentile in English. Not quite as good in math, but I'm not surprised. And who cares? I've qualified for my high school diploma, which arrives in the mail two weeks later. My mom presents it to me like it's a royal edict, while Grandad and Barbara clap and cheer. As I hold the flimsy piece of paper in my hands, I feel the power of it run through my fingers, up my arms, and up to the tips of my red-hot ears. I finished high school at seventeen with barely six months of traditional schooling. And even if my education is considered a side hobby in the Family, and even if I'm the only teen I know who's done this, and even if the

Family has no need for high school diplomas—and even talking about one would be frowned upon as "worldly"—I stand a little taller knowing I have a diploma as a backup plan.

In October 1994, just before I catch a plane back to Japan, I have a layover in Los Angeles at a local Family Home. I'm chatting with a couple of teens after dinner when the whole Home is called to the living room. I squish myself into the corner of a worn, brown corduroy couch and sit with thirty others to hear a new letter from Mama Maria. The air is heavy. The Home Shepherd is trying to hold back tears as he begins to read.

"God has called our Prophet home to his Heavenly reward." The words struggle to penetrate my brain. My grandfather Moses David is dead at seventy-five.

21

LONG LIVE THE PROPHET

Mama Maria puts out a press release, and newspapers around the world print the news: "Children of God Founder Dies, Sect Says," announces a headline in the *Los Angeles Times*.

Grandpa's death shakes the Family. We all knew that he'd had a heart condition since he was young, and at some point, he'd been diagnosed with esophageal cancer. Over the years, calls would go out for us to pray for him, and he'd repeatedly said that Mama Maria would take over the Family in the event of his death. *"Maria is already my manager and tells me what to do,"* he admitted. She and Davidito would be the two End-Time prophets of the Book of Revelation. But he's always rallied; his death seems impossible.

If Grandpa is the Prophet of the End, how could he die before the Antichrist rose? What about all the prophecies?

Grandpa had originally prophesied that Jesus would return in the Rapture in 1993, after the seven final years of the Great Tribulation, a time of truly horrific persecution of all religions by the Antichrist. In the late '80s, when we didn't see more persecution than normal and we couldn't identify the Antichrist among the world leaders, Grandpa suggested that the Antichrist had secretly risen and was in power behind the scenes; he would only reveal himself in the final three and a half years of the worst persecution, when he will impose the mark of the beast on the world. While this kept us on our toes, I'd always thought the End Time would be a bit more obvious, what with locking up and executing Christians, like in *Heaven's Girl*.

By 1991, Grandpa suggested that the Rapture might not occur in 1993 as he originally prophesied. Because we were doing such good work, God was giving us more time to save souls for His Kingdom. God has a right to change His mind. But we must not get complacent, like the parable of the five foolish virgins (Matthew 25:1–13), as we are most certainly in the Last Days. Whatever pain or trouble or sacrifice we had to make was only temporary. It would all be over in no more than a few years when Jesus returned, and then we would be greatly rewarded. We had to do as much as possible and save as many souls as possible in the short time we had left.

The news is almost too much to take in. Over quiet sobs, the Shepherd perseveres, his voice shaking as he bravely tries to deliver the entirety of Mama Maria's letter to the group. We huddle closer together as the Shepherd reads pages and pages of prophecies extolling Grandpa, sending him to his heavenly reward, and anointing Mama Maria as our new leader to carry on in his stead. There are no details about the circumstances of his passing, the date of his death, where he died, the cause of death, or anything that could be traced to discover where he had been hiding, and, therefore, where Mama Maria is now.

When the Shepherd is finished, the whole house breaks down in tears, with everyone wondering, *What will we do now?*

I can't bring myself to cry. I am sad, but I'm also furious. *Why did I never have the chance to meet Grandpa? Why did he ignore me my whole life?*

Devastation and rage vie for first place in my heart. Waste. Too late.

While everyone is gathered, I find a telephone and manage to reach my mother, who is still in Texas with Dad finishing up paperwork. We spend a few brief minutes discussing this horrific development. Mom has no new information to share. There is little to say. Dead is dead. I ask to speak with my dad, but he doesn't offer anything more; he seems resigned to his father's passing.

Now all that we have left is what Grandpa has left behind: his numerous writings and more than three thousand Mo Letters.

Four months after Grandpa's death, for the first time, we celebrate his birthday without him here. Usually on his birthday, the whole Family fasts and prays for his health for three days. This year Mama Maria proclaims a feast instead of a fast, but she continues the tradition of everyone stopping all work to sit together for three days of prayer and reading the *new* revelations from Heaven, the Mama Letters, prophecies Mama Maria and her household have received from Grandpa and Jesus. The Mama Letters are sent around early, but they can only be opened on February 18—our feast day.

Nearly no one dares speak against Mama Maria, as even a whisper of disbelief in her as Grandpa's chosen successor is blasphemy. But as we press ahead without Grandpa, I begin to detect faint stirrings of dissent among the old-timers who have been with the Family since the beginning. Some complain that the Letters have become boring without Grandpa's fiery proclamations and crazy dreams. They are almost solely composed of prophecies she receives from Grandpa and Jesus. The more reckless grumble that they had joined for Moses David, not Mama Maria.

For us in the younger generation, who've grown up with Letters from both Grandpa and Mama Maria, there isn't much distinction in leadership. We all miss Grandpa's flair for the bizarre, but that's about it. We don't hear much about Davidito since he's become a teen. I hear rumors that he might be at the HCS, but no one really knows. I wonder how he's taking this.

When I return to Tokyo, I'm still a bit shaken, but I push aside my feelings when the Shepherds offer me a promotion. At seventeen, I'm asked to become a full-time homeschool teacher for six students, ages seven to thirteen. I use the CLE curriculum, which Mama Maria has officially approved for the children's education. I have a head start on the other teachers, as I'm the only one who has finished high school using the curriculum.

I'm busy with my pupils, but I can't help but notice all the teens around me are dating or mating. I haven't had a boyfriend since Nunu in Macau. I've gotten too used to guys making out with me and then disappearing, so now I make them wait to see if their interest is genuine. I'm looking for someone I can trust, someone I admire, but I'm also tired of being alone. Especially now that I've lost my one friend, Joy. Her parents requested she return to them in Mexico after she found out Japanese immigrations wouldn't renew her visa anymore. We write each other long letters, even make tapes, but it's not the same.

The Home Shepherd sits me down for a heart-to-heart and tells me I'm being "too picky." So, at our Teen Fellowships (gatherings of teens from the five Family Homes in the greater Tokyo area), I force myself to try to get to know the unmated boys, but I can't make myself feel anything for anyone. I find myself repeatedly running into a young man named Chris, whom I'd known as a kid in Macau. He was goofy back then, but now, six years later, he's grown up, towering over me at a height of six feet four inches. He's kind, speaks the local language, and is great at provisioning. But he's clumsy and overweight, and whenever he tries to get me alone, I come up with an excuse to leave the room.

After ignoring his attempts to date me for nearly a year, I give in to his persistence. I tell myself he's really sweet, and the fact that he was willing to wait so long means he must truly love me; that I'm just being shallow about his looks. We start "going out," and he comes over to the Komae home on the weekends. Soon, he tells me he's been given permission to move into my Home. He is on cloud nine, and I know I should be, too.

Everyone in the Family is so happy about us—and relieved that

I have finally locked in a Family boy—that I confuse their interests with my own. But no matter how hard I try, his size bothers me. I drop hints about losing weight and exercising, hoping I'll find him more attractive and be able to stay with him. But I know it goes deeper than that.

Chris is an inspirationalist, a teen leader with a big, loud personality. The Shepherds love him, but I know the truth: he has a lot of doubts about the Family, the Word, and God. He is faking it for most people. I know he is staying in the Family for me, and I feel like I'm holding up myself and him.

Very quickly—too quickly—the Shepherds tell us to move in together. "You've been dating for a few months," they say. "It's time." So, we move into an eight-by-ten-square-foot room in the house with a mattress on the floor.

After a few more months, they ask us when we are going to announce our engagement. Chris is ready to propose, but I resist. I've just turned eighteen. I don't want to be unyielded, but I'm 100 percent certain I don't want to marry Chris. I wish I had someone I trusted to talk to about this. I've learned the hard way that I can't fully trust any Family member not to report my doubts for what they say is my own good.

I need a way out. Under Mama Maria's "loving" leadership, the Family is not supposed to force people to marry anymore, but I know my refusal will be seen as one more sign of my unyieldedness, justifying eventual punishment.

As the pressure mounts, God gives me a way out—a new Family mission field. The latest Mama Letters contain prophecies from Jesus calling for missionaries to go to Russia and save the souls who have been lost in darkness for decades. With the fall of communism, the economy has collapsed, plunging the country into poverty. The people are desperate for humanitarian aid, and for the first time, missionaries are welcome.

As I read page after page of prophecy, I'm deeply moved. For the first time, I feel God's calling, something I always heard the adults talking about, a strong pull on my heart. Instead of letting me suffocate in Japan, God has opened a window to freedom, a way out. I will go and help.

I hear from Josh that Nehi and Caleb have moved to Russia with Aunt Faithy, who is leading the humanitarian aid effort. She is even working with USAID to get food into the far reaches of Siberia. She is much better than anyone they have on staff at actually getting the shipments to their destinations without losing them to bribes and corruption. It seems like another sign; my resolve is set.

Chris is almost frantic when I tell him, pleading with me not to leave. "I have to follow God's call," I tell him.

He can't argue with that, but he assumes I'll be gone only a few months. "I'll wait for you," he tells me.

Cowardly, I let him think I'm coming back. Perhaps I will, after I get this out of my system.

Once I make the decision, everything seems to fall into place, further confirming this is God's will. Caleb will help me get my visa through their contacts in Siberia. I just have to make my way to Russia. I am flattered when the parents of three of the kids I have been teaching offer to pay my airfare in thanks for all the progress their girls have made.

Where God guides, He provides!

22

MEETING THE PRINCE

As soon as I land in Russia, I feel the stark contrast to Japan. I had grown accustomed to sterility and order, but even in the airport here, everything is covered with dirt. The air is full of it. I feel the grit in my nostrils and almost wish I had a Japanese face mask. The building has cracks; the elevators don't run; the paint color is unrecognizable. Nothing is new.

I look out the window. The Soviet buildings are enormous and a lot more spread out than in Japan; the streets are three times as wide and filled with noise. Moscow looks like chaos.

In the confusion of the arrivals area, I see my eldest brother, Nehi, waiting to greet me with his trusty camera bag slung over his shoulder. We have our first hug in eight years. He leads me to his van, and on the drive over to the Home, he tries to catch me up on what to expect.

It takes hours to do things, he says. You always seem to be waiting. But that's normal here. People would be very surprised if something—airplanes, ships, buses, trains—happened on time.

The mentality of the workers—store personnel, ticket agents, flight attendants—is not one of service, either. They are often brusque or have the attitude of "You can just wait until I'm finished with what I'm doing, then maybe I'll see to you." Nehi tells me he's even heard that it's not uncommon for the tram operator to announce that he won't be stopping at the next station because it's almost his break and he is going straight to the stop where he can get his hamburger.

As we approach a residential area, he whispers to me with a twinkle in his eye that we are first going to the Home where Davidito is staying. He and a few people from WS have been traveling through Russia for the last two months, secretly visiting the Homes in this new mission field to give Davidito a chance to see how the rest of the Family lives. This is the end of the trip, and he's flying out of Moscow to rejoin Mama Maria's Home who knows where.

Nehi parks the van in front of a nondescript Soviet apartment block. My eyes are peeled wide, staring at everyone as we enter the plainly furnished apartment. I don't see anyone who looks like Davidito, but I hear someone say the group will be leaving for the airport soon. The tension is tightening in my chest. I can't get so close and miss him! I start walking through the large apartment, peeking into rooms and knocking on closed doors. I normally wouldn't do this, but I'm determined to meet the boy I've read about my whole life—the one who took our place in Grandpa's heart and life.

I come to the last closed door and knock softly. There is no answer, so I slowly push it open, expecting another disappointment. Beyond the bed, I see a dark-haired young man standing by the window, staring out into the bright sunlight reflecting off the concrete streets.

"Hi," I venture.

The man turns. Perhaps I have the wrong person; he looks nothing like the boy from the *Kidz True Komics*. He looks about my age, though not as handsome as the boy in the drawings. He'd dropped out of sight from the Letters in the last few years, so I know next to nothing about what his life is like now.

"I'm Faith," I try again. "Ho's daughter."

His face lights up with recognition. "I'm David."

We smile for a moment.

Then he returns to staring out the window. I walk to stand next to him, feeling like an intruder. His pain and sadness are palpable.

"What are you thinking?" I ask quietly.

"I don't want to go home," he blurts out.

I'm shocked to hear this. In the *Komics*, Grandpa's house is a kind of heaven.

"These last few months, traveling, meeting other young people, have been wonderful," he continues in a whisper.

Suddenly, I see his life in a new way. Trapped. Staying in one Home with little contact with anyone outside of it. My heart aches for him; he seems so lost. There is nothing either of us can do, though. He has been called home by Mama Maria and must obey.

He glances sideways at me. "I always envied you guys."

I blink in shock; it's all I can do to keep my jaw from hanging open. Throughout my life, I have both envied and begrudged Davidito for his position in the Family, for being Grandpa's chosen heir. How could he possibly be envious of us, of me and my siblings at the Farm? I never even got to meet Grandpa.

"I would read the stories about the Macau Farm and all the animals, and I begged my parents to let me visit you. But they always said no." He looks even more dejected, his gaze never leaving the window.

"I have an idea!" I say brightly. "Why don't I tell you stories from the Farm until you have to leave?"

Davidito looks at me, a spark of interest in his eyes. We sit next to each other on the bed, the only piece of furniture in some stranger's room. As I launch into descriptions of the Farm, he closes his eyes like he's trying to picture it. I sense waves of sadness like a blanket around him. I want to break through them. I don't know how I know it, but he needs comfort, touch, like Jondy did when he was a baby.

I lean back on the wall. "Come, put your head in my lap."

He looks at me hesitantly for a moment, then does so. Even

though we've never met, we've heard so much about each other's lives through the publications; it's like we've always known each other. He is family.

I gently stroke his hair, as if comforting a small child, and launch into funny tales of our donkey, Mad Max the biting menace, of guava wars and water fights with my brothers. He laughs, and I can feel him relaxing, the sadness peeling away. It is a strange moment, one I never imagined.

Too soon his WS traveling companion pokes his head in the door to say they are leaving, and the little spell of happiness is broken.

"Thank you," Davidito says sincerely, looking into my eyes.

I hug him tight, hoping to pass some of my comfort and strength into his lean body.

I'm quiet on the drive to my new home with Nehi. What a strange experience. I'm both sad and elated.

He envied us! I think in wonder.

I am in Moscow only a couple weeks when Nehi tells me that the old Russian bureaucrat woman who is supposed to process my year-long visa in Siberia refuses to help. They are shocked; Family members have been getting visas through this office for a year. *Why is this woman cracking down now?* No one knows, but she's adamant.

In a few weeks, it will be illegal for me to be in the country—a dangerous situation for a foreigner. We must figure out a way for me to get a visa or I'll have to go back to Japan. Nehi approaches me hesitantly. "I just saw this want ad in a *Family News* bulletin—a Family Home in Kazakhstan is asking for help. They have connections with the government to get you a visa. What do you think?"

I'm not sure what to think. In Russia, I have Nehi and Caleb. Now I'm being asked to consider going to a Home without knowing anyone in a country I've never even heard of. For the last two years, I've practiced hearing from God and yielding to His will.

He is my only constant in a life where we are often called to move countries and leave homes and families overnight. That night I pray, asking for God's guidance.

My favorite verse that I repeat like a litany whenever things get too painful or scary is "All things work together for good to them that love God, them who are called according to His purpose" (Romans 8:28). I know without a doubt that I love God, so whatever is happening, He must bring good out of it for me.

God has shut one door and is opening another. Who am I to say no to God's will?

"Yes, I'll go," I tell Nehi.

Little do I know how many times I'll need to hang on to that verse in the coming year.

23

———

THE BREAKING

On November 5, 1995, I board a flight from Moscow to Kazakhstan alone. As the ancient Aeroflot plane jerks and shudders during lift-off, I grip the armrests and hold on to a quote from my great-grandmother's *Meditation Moments*. *If you trust in God*, I tell myself, *you don't need to see the whole path, just the next step.*

I arrive in the country's capital, Almaty, at ten o'clock at night. It's the middle of the desert, but Almaty is still the largest city in Kazakhstan, the center of commerce, and the airport isn't nearly as empty as I'd imagined. Clutching my two suitcases, I make my way through immigration and customs and am relieved to spot two Family people waving at me with big smiles.

They introduce themselves as Peter and Esther and show me to their car. As we drive along a dark highway, I learn that they are married. He is a former decathlon Olympian from Latvia. Esther's ancestral Mongol heritage is obvious in her features and dark hair, and while she doesn't say a lot, what she does is, in good Soviet fashion, to the point. We arrive at a complex of identical yellowing Soviet buildings in the city near the botanical gardens, and the apartment door swings open to warm hugs of welcome. A young man flashes an old, familiar smile. It's Benji, one of my childhood friends. His family rotated through Macau, and even though they were at the Farm for only a short time, we remember each other.

I stare at him in wonder. The last time I saw him, we were just five years old! The little chub ball has shot up to a six-foot bean pole topped by the same shock of red curls and a face full of freckles. He picks me up and twirls me around as I squeal with joy.

"How did you end up here?!" I exclaim.

"I've been in Russia for a year now. I moved to Kazakhstan about six months ago," he replies.

"I'm so happy to see you!" I breathe in relief. One person I know in this strange new land makes me feel the tiniest bit better.

The dim, yellowish hallway light illuminates the other Home members who crowd around to receive me. I discover there are ten people all living crammed together in this one apartment.

"Welcome to our home!" Philip bellows. He's one of the Home Shepherds, a short, stocky, Italian-looking man with gray peppering his thinning dark hair.

His wife, Abigail, the other Shepherd, is a female version of him. "We are so happy you came! This is our older daughter, Stephanie, who is fifteen. And our three-year-old, Emily, who you'll be in charge of, is sleeping. We'll introduce you in the morning."

As everyone comes forward to introduce themselves, I assess my new situation: Three FGAs (First-Generation Adults) all over forty, who joined the Family in the early days. Four SGAs (Second-Generation Adults), who'd been born into the Family but are now over sixteen and, in accordance with the latest Mama Letters, considered old enough to be adults themselves. And five new disciples who'd joined the Family in the last few years from the former USSR: Tim and Dana from Poland, Yana from Lithuania, and Peter and Esther, who had picked me up, all in their twenties. Even with Grandpa's passing, membership in the Family continues to grow, although not at the same rate as the early years.

Now that I'm eighteen, I've crossed the threshold into real adulthood, and I don't have to call the other adults Auntie and Uncle. But I know I will anyway.

Abigail finally guides me down the dim hallway. "This is where you will be staying with Steph and Yana." I drop my things in the girls' quarters, a ten-by-ten room for the three of us single girls. I notice a bunk bed but not much else before I shove my suitcase under it, undress, and drop onto the mattress, exhausted.

The next morning, I awake, freezing. Yana is smiling at me from her single bed against the wall. "How did you sleep?" she asks with her thick Lithuanian accent.

"Okay, I guess. It's cold," I say with a shiver.

Yana laughs and makes a face at the same time. "The radiator in our room doesn't work, so we plug in a hot plate."

I nod dazedly, spotting the small electric burner on the floor. *I better not step on it.*

Steph swings down from the top bunk over my head. "Come on. It's warmer in the kitchen."

I pull on jeans and a sweater, the warmest clothes I have, and hurry to the kitchen. I expect to be greeted with the typical scrambled eggs, bread, and milk. Instead, there's a small gray-brown square patty on my plate.

"This is oatmeal cake," Yana tells me.

"Cake" seems like too glorified a word for the dense slab on my plate, but I gamely take a bite.

"Sometimes it is dense as a brick," she whispers. "And if the cook wakes up late, it's half-baked and gooey. When Abigail cooks, it's light and fluffy."

Obviously, Abigail didn't cook today, as I'm spitting out soapy balls of baking soda.

"This is our breakfast every day except on the weekends," Yana continues. "On Sunday, we get two eggs each! They are too expensive to eat every day on the Home's budget. I like to make pancakes with mine, but some use their two eggs to make French toast or bake a cake."

Our lunch is *tvarok*, a dry version of cottage cheese, best made into a salad with grated carrots and some raisins. Dinner is some form of meat or organs with potatoes and beets, cabbage or carrots. I hate beets and cabbage, so I discreetly avoid them the first night. And then the next night. After five nights, I realize I'll probably get scurvy if I eat vegetables only when we have carrots. *Time to grow up and stop being so spoiled*, I tell myself, as I scoop some of the slimy boiled beets onto my plate.

I'm starting to see just how basic life is here in Kazakhstan. Normally, Family Homes can raise money by asking locals for donations and by selling our music CDs, but Kazakhstan is so poor that these aren't options. I come to learn that Abigail and Philip have a supporter in Europe who sends them $1,000 a month. That sum is mostly what supports our Home, so money is very tight.

On my first weekend in Almaty, I go with Yana to the big market to shop. What we cannot get donated, we must buy. This is not like any shopping I've experienced before. The market is hundreds of people selling their wares under a flat gray sky. Their blankets spread on the cold, hard-packed dirt, piled with large striped bags filled with more wares. Some of the fancier places have a small stall instead of just a blanket.

It hasn't snowed yet, but it's in the air. Yana and I walk together, looking for warm boots. I need her to translate and negotiate for me. I've been studying my little Russian phrase book every day, but I still can't say enough to communicate.

Yana has dismissed many pairs of shoes so far. They need to be sturdy and lined with fur, she insists. I already know why. My feet feel like I'm stepping on needles they are so cold, and it's only November.

Finally, we find a pair of black leather boots with a thick, rubber sole and fur inside. They're two sizes too big, so I can wear multiple pairs of thick wool socks. Yana negotiates hard, walking away a few times in disgust. I keep quiet so I won't reveal myself as a foreigner and risk losing a good price. I know this bargain dance in Chinese, but not in Russian.

When Yana finally settles, I immediately pull the boots on my frozen feet.

"Now we will have to get you gloves," she says, eyeing my bare hands.

The boots cost more than we expected, so I don't have money left for gloves.

"Here." She thrusts a pair of gloves into my icy hands. "You can have these. I have another pair."

I am full of gratitude. Yana is different from any of the girls I've known in the Family. At twenty-five, she is older than I am, but since she's a new disciple and I've been in the Family my whole life, I'm considered older than she is. She is stocky and boisterous and wears brown corduroy pants and drab sweaters, brown work boots, and not a lick of makeup; her hair is an ambiguous shade of brown that's always pulled back into a quick ponytail. She's so different from the Family teen girls in Japan, who are laser-focused on their makeup and sexy outfits; after all, getting noticed by the teen boys is the difference between being cool and being invisible. Yana seems oblivious to her appearance.

She squints up at the setting sun. It's getting late. Yana leads me back to the huge parking lot and starts waving at a car.

Does she know him? I wonder.

She argues with the driver for a few minutes, then instructs me to jump in.

"Everyone is a taxi here. Since the Soviet Union collapsed, many people don't get paid for six months, or they are paid in bottles of vodka," she explains.

I scoot inside and take off my gloves to blow on my hands. Looking out the window, I see an old lady standing by the side of the road, shivering. She is holding up a pair of brown wool socks in one hand and a pack of cigarettes in the other.

"She is just trying to get some money for food," Yana says, following my gaze.

I ask Yana if we have anything we can give her, and Yana shakes her head. "If we give to every person we drive by, we will end up on the streets before we get home."

On my second week in Kazakhstan, Benji and Yana take me to the baby orphanage, our arms filled with donations we've managed to scrape together from local businesses and donors in Europe, friends of Philip and Abigail, who occasionally ship us supplies. We are bringing ten baby walkers and strollers and a refrigerator for formula.

The baby orphanage is where children from newborn to three years old are housed. The dilapidated public facility doesn't have any way for the babies to leave their cribs, and there aren't enough workers to help them regularly exercise their little limbs, so they aren't able to develop normally. Though the wife of the Kazakh president is allegedly involved in the Children's Foundation, no one is supporting the institutions. The staff hasn't been paid in six months, but the women who work there love the children and come to work anyway.

The matron cries when she sees our gifts and blesses us. We learn that just today three more babies arrived, discovered on the workers' daily trip to the cemetery and the nearby garbage dump.

The next week we visit an orphanage for older kids. No amount of preparation readies me for what I see. The little kids have distended stomachs and faces crusted with dirt. The workers here are less diligent. The kids are barely dressed, even in the middle of winter.

When we distribute the boxes of donated clothing we've brought with us, we don't have enough to go around, so the girls and boys have to choose tops or bottoms; they can pick only one. The half-dressed children run to me and hug me. I hug them back and braid the little girls' hair. My heart squeezes in my chest, and tears burn the backs of my eyes. I steel myself and pry their little hands from my shirt and legs when it's time for us to leave.

They cry, their dirty arms reaching, pleading for me to come back.

I understand what Abigail meant when she said that missionaries don't last long here. It's too depressing. But for the first time in years, I feel like my personal deprivations are worth it. I'm filled with a deeper sense of purpose. This work matters—bringing food and clothes to people in desperate need, not just singing for our supper in another exotic, wealthy country.

We visit the local orphanages every few weeks. When we don't have donated goods to bring, we sing songs and play games with the children, even dressing up like clowns and performing silly skits to make them laugh.

When I return to the Home, I try to shut out the anger and pain I feel over their suffering, otherwise I won't be able to focus on my daily work. I tell myself that at least we are doing something to assist, unlike most people. But I hate that I am helpless to change their situation. Songs and games won't redirect their lives, but I can't fix the economy or the government. For the first time, I'm aware that this is ultimately what it would take to help these people in a lasting, substantive way.

I have been in Kazakhstan a couple of months when Abigail summons me to her room. As I make my way down the narrow hallway, my bare feet sticking to the plastic linoleum, I sense a new tension in the air. *Is it something about Emily?* I wonder. I've been teaching her how to read and write and do basic sums. She's calmer now than when I arrived, and she's stopped throwing fits.

I knock on Abigail's door, and she waves me in. "Please sit down here on the bed."

Wary, I sit.

"How are things going for you? Are you happy here?"

"Yes," I reply, no other answer acceptable.

"What do you think about Benji?"

"He's a sweet guy. A great guy, like a brother to me."

She nods absently as she continues: "Do you think you might consider sharing with him?"

I freeze like a rabbit in the glare of headlights. Other than the FGA men my parents' age, he's the last person here I'd want to share with. *Like having sex with my younger brother*, I think, shivering. My brain scrambles for a polite way out.

"What about Yana?" I suggest. "I know she really likes him."

Abigail nods considering it as she waves me away. "Well, think about it. We need to make sure all our young men are taken care of."

No thank you, I think as I escape. I really hope it works out with Yana. She's told me she likes Benji but that he hasn't approached her. Maybe he's put off by her work boots and corduroy pants?

I continue to focus on Emily and my daily chores, hoping this will blow over. But a few weeks later, when I sit down in my usual spot in the living room to join everyone for Devotions, Philip begins to read a Mo Letter about the danger of being unyielded. This is an old letter. *Why are we reading this instead of one of the new Letters?*

When Philip is finished, Abigail looks at me.

"We all know how important it is to be yielded to God," Philip continues. "We cannot let any unyieldedness or selfishness separate us from God."

We all nod in agreement.

"Faith," Abigail says.

Ten pairs of eyes land on me, and I freeze.

"Philip and I were praying for you last night, and we got a prophecy. I'm going to read it."

I bite the insides of my cheeks. *Not good. Not good.*

"'This child of mine has been unyielded to My Word. She has refused to share my love with those who need it. She has hardened her heart against my gentle hints. Now she must throw herself on the rock and be broken, before the rock falls on her and grinds her to dust.'"

What have I done? How have I been unyielded? I search my mind, desperate. I've tried so hard to be good. I don't complain about the food or the cold, about being stuck all day with a three-year-old, about sleeping on a lumpy mattress. Yes, I was told that I needed to smile more, that my serious expression didn't show God's love. I can do that. I can smile more.

As she finishes reading the page-long prophecy, she asks, "Do you want to be more yielded to God?"

I nod silently, all eyes on me as the familiar sting of humiliation burns my eyes.

"Kneel in the center of the room."

I kneel on the gray carpet, my head bowed.

Everyone gathers around me. The weight of twenty hands presses down on my head, my shoulders, my back. I shut my eyes to hold back the tears even though my face is covered by my long hair.

"Halleluiah. Thank You, Jesus. Praise Your name. We glorify You, Jesus. Halleluiah. Praise You, Jesus," everyone repeats over and over above my head.

As the praise quiets, Philip begins, "Dear Jesus, we bring this daughter of Yours before You. She wants to be free of her unyield-edness. Deliver her from the spirit of pride and rebellion. Make her into a yielded vessel. Ready to submit to Your will, no matter the cost. Deliver her from the spirit of selfishness. . . ."

The prayer goes on and on, my back aching under the weight of all the hands. "Now, let's see what the Lord wants to tell her in prophecy."

Everyone goes quiet, listening.

"Whom I love, I rebuke and chasten," says Dana.

"I got a vision of the potter smashing the vessel with a defect and making a new beautiful vessel out of the clay," Tim adds.

After a half hour of verses and prophecies, I stumble onto my feet, my legs numb from kneeling on them so long. My eyes are red, and I need more tissue to wipe the snot streaming over my mouth. Everyone hugs me. I walk, dazed, to my room and curl against the cold wall in my bunk bed. Abigail follows me.

I feel the heaviness of her body on my mattress and her hand on my knee. "Praise the Lord for those prophecies. Remember God wants our yieldedness. We must be willing to share God's love through our bodies."

I can barely lift my head. I don't have the energy.

"I want you to take some time to pray and get prophecies for yourself about what God is asking you to do," she continues. "I feel like the Lord may want you to change your name to demonstrate that you are a new person and to remind you of your promise to be yielded to Him."

I feel a spark of resistance, but it flickers away as Abigail leaves me alone in the dark.

For the next few nights, after everyone else has gone to bed, I pray, seated at the plastic-covered kitchen table. I bow my head. "Please dear God, speak to me. I need to know Your will. Forgive me for being unyielded. Make me a better vessel of Your love. I'm here to listen. Speak to me. What do You want me to do?"

My thoughts chase each other, and I remember Grandpa's words: "Be sure what you are hearing is from God. If it doesn't sound like the Mo Letters or the Bible, it may be an evil spirit trying to deceive you." I try to clear my head until all I hear are words from the Bible. I take my pen and begin writing them in my little prophecy notebook: "Whom the Lord loves, He rebukes and chastens. This crushing and breaking is only to make you stronger, like a piece of coal pressed and crushed into a beautiful Jewel. You will become a beautiful Jewel for Me as you yield to My will."

The Shepherds had given me a copy of the prophecy that they had received for me and read at Devotions. The last line reads, "I have called you Jewel." I take these two prophecies as confirmation that God wants me to change my name to Jewel. I hate the name. It's so embarrassing and it seems presumptuous, but I want to please God more than anything. My shoulders slump as I give in, my last bit of resistance fading. I will call myself Jewel.

At Devotions the next day, I speak up. "I prayed last night, and God told me that I should call myself Jewel to symbolize becoming a new, more yielded vessel." I cringe with embarrassment.

"Praise the Lord!" Abigail and Philip say in unison. "Thank you for being yielded to His will."

In the days that follow, Abigail and Philip continue their campaign to have us share more in the Home. They read various letters on the Law of Love, including one of Mama Maria's latest prophecies, *Go for the Gold*. It reiterates the Family's views on birth control: the gold medal means having sex without a condom; the silver is pulling out; and bronze is using condoms. *"Any form of taking things into our own hands to prevent pregnancy is contrary to God's Word. It is saying to the Lord that you know better than He does; that you want control of your life, instead of yielding and trusting that He knows what's best for you."*

As we finish reading the letter, I feel my throat closing and I can't find air to breathe. In the past I would have been happy to go for the silver or the bronze. But now, after committing to yield to God in every area of my life, I know that's not an option. I grab my coat and race outside, my boots crunching in the crusty, blackened snow. I sink down next to a crumbling wall behind our massive apartment block, a deserted spot where I bite my hand to try to hold back a keening wail, but I can't keep in the tears. I'm afraid.

In Japan, Chris and I, like a lot of the teens, had always been incredibly careful, pulling out or using condoms (if we could get them). But now, anyone I shared with would see me as unyielded for doing so. More than that, I want to please God and follow His Word, to not live outside the bubble of His protection. My entire existence revolves around God, serving Him and loving Him, but I'm terrified of being a single mother or being forced to marry someone I can't stand because I got pregnant sharing with them.

I think back to the Farm, when the older girls, fourteen, fifteen, and sixteen years old at the time, talked about how to induce a miscarriage. I remember how I'd lay awake at night, terrified, planning what I might do if it came to that. *I'm good at jumping rope. I could jump rope for hours to lose a baby.* Now, all those thoughts come rushing back to me as I contemplate what I would do if I get pregnant here.

When I can no longer feel my hands, or my feet, or my heart, I stand up and walk back inside. I'd just promised God that I will do what He wanted. I can't back out now. I can't turn my back on His will as shared by His representative.

A few days have passed when I hear Abigail's voice. "Jewel . . ."

After a moment I realize she's speaking to me. I hurry to hide my hesitation and follow her into her room.

"Are you ready to be yielded to God?" she asks.

I nod.

"Benji confessed to us that he really likes you."

I blink.

"This is how you can show God that you are yielded to His will. Friday night should be good. What do you think?"

I nod again.

"I know it's hard to share with someone you're not attracted to. I've had to do it many times. I share with Tom and my husband now, because there are no other FGA women in the home."

It's not the same, I think. *You're the Shepherd, you choose to do this, you've been doing it for years, you're already married with kids! You won't be a single mother.* But I say nothing.

"You're going to need to ask Benji. He is too shy to ask you himself, and we don't want him to know that we told you. Make him feel this is something you want. He is very sensitive."

Yes, I thought, *he'd be horrified if he knew I'd been told to have sex with him and how much I hated the idea of it.*

"That's the loving thing to do," Abigail imparts before dismissing me.

My first instinct is to run to Benji and tell him everything. Sensitive and generous, he'd give me the shirt off his back. But I know if I put my faith in Benji, the Shepherds will find out and I might get put back on probation. Benji, puppy that he is, can't keep a secret.

Perhaps in some tiny way I had hoped that changing my name, being more enthusiastic and sacrificial, and helping around the home would be enough. But it's not. I know how tenuous a person's position can be in a Home. I could easily be sent away. And if I get a reputation of being unyielded, I could wind up without a Home and kicked out of the Family once again.

As I lie in my bed, I can't stop shaking. *This is silly,* says a small voice in my head. *Just do it. Grit your teeth and do it. You're making too big a deal over this.* I'm disgusted with myself. *What is wrong with me? Why is this so hard?* In Japan, I'd had sex with a few guys, including Chris. I was more careful now, because I was told if I got a guy excited by making out with him, it was my duty to "take care" of him and give him an orgasm. If a girl refused, she was worse than a tease: she was rebelling against Jesus and the Family. But if I got stuck with some guy I didn't like, I could revert to a hand job or blow job. Even those times when I hated myself for going further than I wanted, the interactions began with some small attraction, a spark of interest. Here, I was being directed to have sex with someone I felt a physical revulsion toward, to allow them inside my body, and I couldn't use a condom.

I only want to be with one man, a man I'm in love with, my mind screams in torment. *That's only in romance novels,* I scold myself, gulping for air, my head and eyes red and aching. Perhaps I have been polluted by worldly ideals of romance and monogamy instead of sex as sacrifice for the good of others.

That Friday night, I get ready for my date with Benji, which will take place in the living room. It's the only room in the apartment that doesn't have multiple people sleeping in it. Wearing my night-gown, I make the short walk through the dim orange light of the hallway. *I can do this, I can do this*, I repeat over and over. *I don't have to do anything. I won't do anything*, I think at the same time.

My feet don't want to cooperate. The living room is dark; a dim light illuminates the mattress made up on the floor. I can barely look at Benji's hopeful, eager face. Up to now, I've enjoyed and ap-preciated his friendship. But I know this, being forced to sleep with him, will change everything. He embraces me, and I try not to shudder. We sit awkwardly on the mattress side by side. I'm not eager to help him.

He tries to kiss me. I let him. *This is for God*, I recite over and over in my head. *Please, God, help me!*

Benji's hands start to roam over my breast under the nightgown. He is hesitant and unsure. He must have had sex before, but it doesn't seem like it.

God, how long is this going to take? I pull my nightgown over my head and lie prone on the mattress. I kiss him, trying to block out sound, smell, and feeling. Get outside my body and just pretend it's someone else. *I'm someone else.* He undresses quickly. Thank God it's dark so he can't see my expression. There is nothing wrong with him. Skinny, white, freckled skin, but he's not ugly or old. *What's wrong with me?*

Benji lays over me, and we fumble a bit. It hurts when he pushes in, but it always does. In a minute he is done. *Thank God.*

I hug him and give him a kiss, grateful it's over. Then I throw on my nightgown and run to the bathroom. In the shower, I scrub my body over and over, inside and out.

My joy in Benji's sunny, open nature is destroyed. He seems con-fused when nothing more comes of our sharing. Despite living in the same house, I find I can avoid being alone with him, and he is gone most of the day on witnessing trips anyway. I'm grateful for my secluded little world with Emily, who takes my full attention, so I can't dwell on things. The only time I can't suppress my dread is at 2:00 a.m., when I bolt upright in terror. The toilet and I have frequent meetings with God as I kneel on the cold black-and-white tiles and beg, *Please, please, please, dear Jesus, please don't let me get pregnant.*

And I can't leave the country without asking the Shepherds to buy me a plane ticket—not that I would seriously consider leaving. God brought me here. My suffering is my own fault. I'm not submitted enough. I need to work harder to have no will of my own so I can truly be the yielded vessel Grandpa talks about.

Abigail calls to me in the hallway several weeks later. "I need to talk with you about something serious that has come to our attention."

My heart nearly stops. *I slept with Benji. What more can I do? Please don't make me do it again*, I want to scream. But I follow her to her room again.

"We need your help. Have you noticed that Steph is hanging around Matthew a lot?"

Oh boy, I think. *Not good.*

I had met Matthew back in Moscow when some teens from a few Homes had gathered in a park to play dodge ball. He obviously thought all the girls liked him. Tall and lanky with floppy black hair and blue eyes, he walked with a lazy, confident strut. I ignored him. I knew from experience that guys like that were trouble.

We'd barely exchanged a few words, but it was enough. He thought I was proud and stuck-up, and I thought he was an arrogant ass. I didn't even know he lived in Abigail's Home until a month after I'd arrived; he'd been away on a two-month road trip, witnessing in other cities throughout Kazakhstan. Our mutual dislike upon meeting had been tempered by living together in the same house, but not by much. With my efforts to be humbler, I had tried to stop my subtle digs, but he had no such qualms.

"We are concerned," Abigail continues. "Steph is only fifteen, and he is sixteen. As you know, it's now against the rules for anyone under sixteen to have sex with anyone over sixteen."

I nod. The rules have changed once again. The age limit for any sexual genital contact is now sixteen. Sixteen- and seventeen-year-olds can only have sex with people under twenty-one, and eighteen-to-twenty-year-olds with people up to seven years older than them. Once you age out into over twenty-one, you are fair game for the older FGA adults.

Breaking these sex rules brings punishment not just to the teens, but to their parents, too. So I understand why Abigail looks desperate. A violation like this could affect the whole Home when reported to the Area Shepherds.

"Matthew is brokenhearted. He left his girlfriend in Russia," Abigail explains. "He wants consolation, but I'm afraid that if Steph keeps hanging around and comforting him, it will be more than that."

I nod again, unsure where this is going.

"Please talk to him. Distract him from our daughter. Give him a listening ear."

"I will," I promise, relieved she's not requesting that I have sex with him. I can stomach Matthew's company, as long as it doesn't come to that.

The next night, I find Steph at the table speaking with Matthew. She leans in, touching his arm, but he jumps back when he sees me. "Steph." I give her a big-sister smile. "Your mom wants you to head to bed."

"You should be in bed, too!" she snaps.

"I'll be right there."

Steph huffs off, and Matthew, disappointed to lose his audience, looks as if he might go, too.

"I'm making tea. Do you want some?"

"Sure," he says, cocking his head.

I try to be the adult. "Look, I know we've had a rough start, but I'm working on becoming humbler, so maybe we can try again?"

He watches me warily, not sure what I'm up to.

I set the kettle to boil and sit down across the table. *What in the world do I talk about?* I cast around desperately. "So how did you like Russia?"

"It was okay."

"You know, I left my boyfriend behind in Japan when I came here," I say, trying to give him an opening.

He looks surprised. "Yeah, that must have been hard. I left my girlfriend in Moscow."

I sit back to listen, tossing in encouraging questions here and there as he opens up about leaving the love of his life. Apparently, she wasn't as sure as he was that they were fated to be together and had turned down his proposal. She was also a couple of years older than him. He goes on, detailing this paragon of beauty and virtue, and like a good disciple, I put aside my nausea and try to be a friend. At least I can empathize with his pain.

When the kettle whistles, I pour water over a teabag for him and fill my mug with just water. He makes fun of me, but only lightly.

I defend my habit by saying, "Hey, this is what we drink in China."

Matthew and I continue to meet in the kitchen a few nights a week when he is not away on road trips witnessing in other cities. I tell him about Hac Sa, the Farm, the animals. We talk about our past relationships. Our pain and our understanding of the Mo Letters.

Are the two most unlikely people becoming friends?

I start to look forward to seeing him, and I notice a little bubble of excitement in my stomach when I put on my robe and casually head to the kitchen for my nightly mug of hot water.

After a month, our late-night kitchen conversations begin to change. Matthew hardly ever speaks of his former girlfriend now.

Instead, we talk about God and prophecy, and he plays his guitar so I can hear the songs he's writing. Then we hug goodnight, and we go to our separate rooms.

The routine is comforting, easy, and safe, until one evening, when I go in for the obligatory goodnight hug, I linger. His arms stay wrapped around me. My foot slips, and I end up in his lap. For a moment, we laugh. But neither of us moves. I sit on his lap longer, and before I know it, our lips are touching. We both jump back, shocked. I don't know if I kissed him or he kissed me, but I realize I don't care. Being with him is starting to feel so natural.

Kissing Matthew becomes a habit—and for the first time, a relationship feels special and beautiful and *right*. I begin to smile more; I don't even mind the oat cakes in the morning. One afternoon, as I'm floating down the hallway, Abigail calls my name. Someone's on the telephone.

I'm not expecting anyone. My mom and father just spoke with me the week before, for Christmas, and no one has the money to call long-distance on a whim. I pick up the receiver.

"Faith." I hear Chris's familiar voice. "When are you coming back? I miss you."

The phone goes limp in my hand. I haven't thought much about Chris in months. We'd sent each other a few letters, but that was it. I'm shocked that he got the permission—and the money—to call.

"Faith?" he says again.

My heart squeezes at the pain in his voice. But I must be honest. It won't help to lead him on. "I'm not coming back, Chris. God wants me to serve Him here."

"Should I come there?"

"No," I say, using all my strength to force that one little word from my throat. "I love you, and I always will, but I don't believe we are meant to be together. I'm sorry."

I hear the click of his receiver, and all my pent-up feelings spill out. I cry—for him, and for me. Chris is the one person I know who truly loves me and wants to marry me, and I've just severed that link. But I can't love him the way he wants me to.

After four months of deep freeze, the snow melts and green shoots blossom, as do my feelings for Matthew. This is more than friendship. *Am I in love?* I realize with a shock that I haven't felt like this about someone since I was ten and wrote my emotions into a poem for Michael, my first love. I'd begun to wonder if I was capable of feeling like that again, worried that perhaps that part of me was broken.

Whenever Matthew returns from witnessing, I feel a lightness in my chest. I wait for his hand to find mine, to feel his warmth against my own. I look forward to his breath on my neck when we can steal time alone and the sound of his laughter chasing me down the hall to my bedroom. We escape the crowded apartment to make love under the summer sun in a hidden corner of the nearly abandoned botanical gardens.

I come home from a day at the orphanage and rush to the boys' room to tell Matthew about it, but the story dies on my lips. A suitcase is lying open on his bed.

Matthew walks toward me and takes my hands. He's leaving, he says, in a voice nearly too soft to hear. He has been informed by the Area Shepherds that he must return to Moscow for punishment, due to some indiscretion at a previous Home that is only now catching up to him.

No, please God. I grab him around the waist, crushing him into me as he holds me gently. I never want to let go, but I know I must accept the inevitable. After a few minutes, I release my grip and help him fold his shirts.

As I weep into my pillow, I repeat Romans 8:28 over and over. *What good can come from this?* As my sniffles subside, I visualize a future where the pain is less sharp. The only "good" I can muster is,

At least, I will have more compassion on others experiencing heartbreak and be able to comfort them. I clutch that sliver of hope to my heart as I fall asleep.

After Matthew leaves, I'm haunted by him. Every time I walk through a door or turn into the hall, I expect he'll be there with his saucy smile. Each disappointment keeps the pain fresh, but I must force a happy face—to look sad is unloving to others and selfish.

Matthew and I write a few long love letters to each other, but two months after his departure, I receive his last correspondence. *"I met up with my old girlfriend,"* it reads. *"She has been through a lot. Turns out she loves me after all, and we have gotten back together."*

I lock myself in the bathroom, the only place I can be alone, and sit on the toilet, clutching the letter as tears stream down my face. I hear Yana banging on the door, but I shut out the noise. I shut out everything. I turn to the only help I know—God.

Huddled in my bed that night, I write in my journal, tears smudging the pen marks.

Dear Lord, take my worthless, selfish life
And end the emptiness of its strife.
Let it be melted wholly into Thee,
For only then will I be set free.

———

Free from the sorrow, free from the pain
That comes from looking for selfish gain.
Free to become as nothing to me,
Knowing that I am something to Thee.

———

I give you my whole self. Do what you want with me. I give you my marriage vows as my Husband. I promise to love, honor, obey, follow, and serve You faithfully until death fully unites us and beyond. Amen.

The idea of another winter in this place is too bleak to contemplate, so when my visa runs out at the end of the year, I don't ask to renew it.

A new missionary wave is announced: *Pioneer Mainland China for Jesus.* It is a call for Family members willing to go undercover to evangelize in China. My parents have already moved to Xiamen, the mainland China university city right across the strait from Taiwan. I submit my request for a transfer to join them. Philip and Abigail agree to pay for my plane ticket in gratitude for my teaching Emily.

When I leave Kazakhstan, I leave the name Jewel with it. It never fit me—no matter how hard I worked to be accepted, to survive, to become what they wanted me to be. I'm glad to be rid of the name, to shed a skin that has grown too tight.

It's time for a new start in a new place as the new Faith.

24

___

PRETENDING IS THE FIRST STEP TO BEING

I land in Hong Kong, and a wave of familiarity washes over me. It's good to be back.

Mom is teaching English at Xiamen University, and Dad gives businessmen informal English conversation practice and keeps an eye on Jondy and Nina when Mom is at the university. I'm going to join their undercover missionary Home as a Chinese language student at the university on a student visa. The university class fees are only $700 for the year, which we can cover by teaching English. The opportunity feels heaven sent.

I navigate using the instructions Mom sent me to take the subway from the airport to the mainland China border crossing at Shenzhen. There I hop a long-distance overnight bus to Xiamen. The orange plastic seats are really a single bed with two people squashed lengthwise into each one, a hard rectangular block at our head to represent a pillow. I'm lucky that a young Chinese woman and her six-month-old baby are in my bunk. We smile at each other tentatively. Better than being paired with the gruff man across the aisle who is puffing away in flagrant disregard for the "no smoking" sign over his head. Or his companion, who is casually spitting sunflower seed shells into the aisle.

As the bus bumps along pockmarked roads, I try to ignore my discomfort by studying the tiny Mandarin phrase book I bought in Hong Kong with the money I saved up from my toiletry allowance. I don't speak a word of Mandarin. The official language of mainland China, also known as the People's Republic of China, is a totally different dialect than the Cantonese I grew up hearing in Macau and Hong Kong. Admittedly, as a kid I didn't put much effort into mastering Cantonese beyond the witnessing phrases. Now, learning Chinese is a matter of survival.

I've barely had time to memorize the numbers one through one hundred when the bus stops for dinner at a small roadside cafeteria. The metal tables and stools glint under the harsh neon light that has my bleary eyes squinting after the dim, smoky bus. No one speaks a word of English at this remote outpost. I may not speak Mandarin yet, but I'm no fool when it comes to Chinese dining. I sit with my fellow bus passengers at a huge round table and wait for the harried waitress to turn to me. I don't point at Chinese characters on the menu at random, a rookie mistake that can result in sea slug or entrails on your plate. Instead, I take a deep breath and moo loudly.

She stares in shock, as does everyone else in the restaurant. Embarrassed but, really, who cares, I moo again, placing my index fingers as horns on my head. She giggles and nods. *"Niu rou!"*

Encouraged, I try again. "Bok, bok, bok," I say, flapping my arms for emphasis.

Ahh, the light bulb goes on. *"Ji rou!"*

My whole table is cracking up, laughing and shouting guesses. A few minutes later, I'm delighted when a lovely dish of beef and broccoli and stir-fried chicken arrive with rice. Communication sometimes means bypassing words.

After another six hours on the bus, in the early-morning light, we pull into a dirty, crowded bus station. I spot my dad, skinny as ever, bouncing on his toes, waiting for me to get off. He hoists up my two suitcases and leads me onto a city bus heading to the university. While he talks nonstop, I wonder what it'll be like to live with my parents again after three years apart and so little contact.

I'd spoken to them only once the entire year I was in Kazakhstan, a three-minute Christmas call.

I listen closely as he quickly lists off the rest of my siblings. Josh's, Aaron's, and Mary's families all live in Taiwan. Aaron married a nice Australian SGA woman (ironically her name is Jewel) while he was still in Japan; now they have four young kids. Nehi is divorced (his wife left the Family and returned to Sweden with his kids) and is somewhere in war-torn Bosnia, taking pictures of relief work for the Family and other NGOs. Caleb, the last bachelor of our family, is in Poland or perhaps Hungary. Hobo's family lives in the UK, but he never writes. Esther has emerged from four years in WS and is supposedly living somewhere in China, also teaching English.

"And guess who is living nearby?" Dad says gleefully, watching for my surprise. "Daniel and Grace's family!"

"Patrick!" I yelp. Together again after all these years!

"Yes, and Sophia. You remember Uncle Ben's daughter?"

"Typhoon 10! How could I forget!" Sophia's family had lived with us in Macau for a few years. She'd earned the nickname "Typhoon 10" at two years old. Leave her unsupervised in a room for five minutes and the contents of every drawer and shelf were in a heap on the floor.

"She's seventeen now, and Ching-Ching, Zacky and Hope's daughter, will be living with us. She arrived just a few days before you did."

Hoorah! My old childhood gang together again. I haven't seen or even heard from any of them in nearly ten years, since before I left for Thailand. *What will they look like? Sound like? Will we be friends again?*

"You know, China is opening up and allowing more foreigners in, but missionary work and witnessing are still strictly banned."

"I know, Dad," I say, glancing around nervously, figuring he doesn't expect anyone on this public bus to speak English. I had carefully hidden my Bible and Mo Letters in the bottom of my suitcases in case they were searched at customs.

A hard jerk of the bus slams my head into the seatback, and a few people standing in the aisle land on their butts. I glance through the front windshield to see an old lady crossing in the middle of the road without giving the cursing driver a glance. *Ahh, China.*

When we finally reach our stop and clamber off, Dad leads me to a hill and points to a little house perched on the side. "Up we go!" With a deep breath, I begin climbing the 150 stairs it takes to get there. A few times I pause, out of breath, *Never give in, never give in, never, never, never, never give in,* I silently quote as I pant. Mom is waiting at the door, arms open wide. Exhausted, I practically fall into them.

She looks about the same, though she's on the thinner side of her perpetual weight swings, and her face glows with energy. She hurries me inside, and Dad follows, happily dragging my heavy suitcases. We can keep only what we can carry on an airplane as we move countries, so my bags are packed without an inch of air space.

I nearly bump into Ching-Ching in the entryway, and we laugh and hug. Her face is the same, but she's filled out. Weight lifting, she confides.

She takes me on a quick tour of my parents' new home, a simple single-story Chinese house with a living room, three small bedrooms, and a typical three-by-six-foot Chinese kitchen covered in one-inch white tiles. Mom sits us down at the dining table, which nearly fills the small living room, and over a pot of jasmine tea, she and Dad outline our situation here.

"It's more open here in southern China than it is in Beijing, thank goodness," Mom says.

"Yes," my father agrees. "I haven't noticed anyone following us, but we still have to assume our phones are tapped and our mail will be steamed open and read before it arrives. So be very careful what you say and write."

"I remember, Dad."

My stomach clenches with the familiar fear of discovery.

Dad explains that while China has been slowly allowing more foreigners to enter as teachers, this leniency is new. If caught, we'd be deported, but it would be far more dangerous for our Chinese friends. They would certainly be harassed, and worse, sent to detention camps. We can't pass out posters, busk, or preach openly about Jesus.

"When we find people that we think are Sheepy, we can invite them to our home for individual Bible studies."

At these Bible studies, we need to carefully feel out each person, knowing that some of the "Sheep" may have been sent by the government to befriend and spy on us. He tells me that we need to start out by introducing simple Bible verses—none of the heavier doctrines on sex and certainly nothing about the Family. We must appear to be a normal System Christian family that has come here to study Chinese.

I turn the conversation to my parents' escapades in China these past six months. They tell me about the friends they've made, and even a few more tidbits they've heard about my siblings, who are popping out more children. Dad boasts that he has nearly twenty grandkids already. When he gets up to make a peanut butter sandwich, Mom winks knowingly and says, "Patrick has become a very handsome young man." I try to keep myself from rolling my eyes. She has never really grown up.

Mom tells me his whole family lives on the nearby island of Gulangyu, a pedestrian-only island off the coast of Xiamen. "We go there often for dinner and fellowship! Who knows what might happen between you two now that you're older?"

I shrug indifferently. Mom loves nothing better than to find something she can tease me about, so I try not to give her any ammo, but I can't ignore the flutter in my stomach. *Will I finally find out that the boy I've known since childhood is the love of my life, like Gilbert in* Anne of Green Gables?

Mom raises her eyebrows suggestively. I smile and excuse myself to go to my new bedroom, which I'm to share with Ching-Ching and Sophia. Though I'm happy to see my mom again, I'm also just a bit uneasy. Our relationship has always been rocky, especially during my younger teen years. But at nearly twenty, I'm an adult now and ready to move beyond these childhood episodes. I just hope she'll be able to treat me like a fellow adult Home member.

The next afternoon I'm sitting on my twin bed, reading a new Mama Letter, when I hear Mom yell to me from the living room, "Auntie Grace just called to say Patrick is on his way over. He should be here in thirty minutes!"

I quickly change into a nice dress, checking the mirror a dozen times, and when I give up on braiding and rebraiding my long hair, I dash out the door. There, climbing the steps, is a tall, handsome man with light brown hair. His round, freckled face has been re-placed by a strong, chiseled jaw, and through his thin shirt, I can see the lines of his body, lean and well-defined.

He speaks, and I hear the slow drawl of my brothers. The flutters of anticipation subside. "How is it that you speak exactly like my brothers?!" I ask with a laugh. Growing up with us, he'd escaped his parents' Irish lilt.

We both laugh, releasing our pent-up anxiety.

"I heard you were in town and had to see for myself," he begins, and before I know it, it's like we're back on the Farm. "Remember that time . . ." and off we go.

The goofy boy I loved still flashes through the young man who is trying to be serious. We walk the shady campus paths for an hour before he has to go. He has a few errands to run for his parents in the city, things they can't buy on the island for their large family.

"I can't believe your parents have ten kids now!" I say.

"They were trying to catch up with your family and now they've surpassed you!" he says, and we both laugh. We hug tight in good-bye as he leaves me at the bottom of the hill.

I'm panting from the long flight of stairs when I enter the tiled entrance of my new Home, where I find Mom, once again, at the door, waiting. "So how did it go?" Her eyes gleam in anticipation.

"Patrick feels like one of my brothers. No chemistry."

She looks crestfallen. I'm disappointed, too. I use one of her old French phrases. *"C'est la vie."*

At Devotions the next morning, Mom tells Ching-Ching and me, "As far as how the Home runs, we are not the leaders or Shepherds here. We expect you young adults to be responsible for yourselves. We're all on the Home Council, which means we all vote on Home decisions."

As the days pass, I start to crack through the façade of humility and submission I'd carefully built for myself in Kazakhstan. My parents aren't going to force me to share or try to break me for being opinionated. They are all too aware of their own small disobediences. I quickly recognize my parents' real desire is to be left alone to do their own thing, much like in Macau, which is fine with me.

My mom is more interested in her university job than she is in Mama Maria's latest prophecies, and while my dad still reads the Letters with us at Devotions, he's become obsessed with Hudson Taylor, the zealous British Protestant Christian who was a missionary to China from 1854 until his death in 1905. Because university classes start at 8:00 a.m., we have united Devotions only on the weekends. We generally follow the Family rules, have a schedule, go places with a buddy for safety, but the constant pressure to be the perfect disciple is lifted from my chest just a bit. For the first time since leaving the Farm five years ago, I'm able to take deep breaths, appreciating the fragrance of honeysuckle mixed with car exhaust, and my body imperceptibly relaxes.

But with my parents abdicating much of their control, a good part of the responsibility to make sure everything runs smoothly according to Family standards falls on Ching-Ching and me, which means assuming responsibility for cooking, cleaning, and caring for Jondy and Nina, who are now eight and eleven.

Out of two hundred foreign students, there are only two Americans in the entire class in Xiamen University's Mandarin language school, Ching-Ching and I (Sophia is Canadian). Most are overseas Chinese coming to learn their mother tongue, with a few Europeans sprinkled in.

It has been years since I've been in a school setting of any kind, and I've missed the excitement of learning and making progress toward a goal. I'm also curious about my System classmates, all young people my own age.

Our three morning classes are held in small classrooms furnished with dented, wooden chair-desk combos typically found in primary schools. Mr. Cheng is our character-writing teacher. He conducts our classes solely in Chinese, though our textbooks have an English translation next to the Chinese words.

Patrick, Ching-Ching, Sophia, and I lunch together in the massive cafeteria. We try to stay away from the chicken's feet, pork, and organ delicacies. Stir-fried chicken or beef with some bok choy or fried lettuce, all swimming in oil and garlic, are the way to go. Food is so cheap, with a meal costing less than the equivalent of $1, even *we* can afford to eat here every day.

Our speaking teacher, Ms. Shin, speaks perfect English in a clear, singsong voice. She is very proper with her tight hair bun, blackboard pointer, and pin-straight posture.

Today we are learning the word "love," spelled "ai" and pronounced "I," with a sharp down tone. *Ai ren* = spouse; *wo ai ni* = I love you.

Sophia tries to make a sentence—"*Zou ai.*"

Ms. Shin's stern expression shatters as she turns to the board to stifle a laugh. "Don't say that," she chokes.

When she refuses to tell us what it means, one of the other students leans over and whispers, "Make love." Sophia is our hero.

I pour my energy into my language studies and thrive in the traditional classroom environment with a teacher and classmates. In America when I was twelve, many things were so difficult—Mom's precarious emotional state, our tenuous living situation, and my own intense self-consciousness. So, it wasn't until the end of the second quarter of eighth grade that I finally felt like I was getting a grip on things and started to enjoy learning. I love the feeling of seeing myself improve every day, like I did in Macau when I was self-teaching the high school curriculum. I didn't realize I'd missed it.

After our morning classes, Ching-Ching and I return home for private Devotions, finish our homework copying Chinese characters, give Bible studies to interested Chinese students, and take turns cooking dinner and watching Nina and Jondy.

At the end of our first semester, Ms. Shin announces, "We are going to have a party for all the foreign students. It's tradition that you all perform a song or a skit. Don't forget to prepare something; you will be called onstage." Ching-Ching, Sophia, and I glance at each other and roll our eyes.

"I think they just like seeing foreigners make fools of themselves," I whisper. We've spent our childhoods performing together, so whipping up a song takes only a couple of hours of practice.

The party is at a club next to campus. When it's our turn onstage, Ching-Ching taps her guitar—"One, two, three"—and Sophia and I belt out "Bai Lai La Bamba," dancing the simple choreography. As we give our red neck scarves a final twirl over our heads under the flashing disco light, our classmates let loose a series of hoots and cheers.

Our delight with our success at the party wanes when the dean makes us perform for the entire university at every major school and cultural event. As the university's performing foreign monkeys, we're interviewed on local television and Chinese students call out our names from the dorm windows as we cross campus.

So much for being an inconspicuous Christian family.

Although we're not living off the radar quite as we'd planned, it turns out that being a minor celebrity has its perks. My Chinese classmates insist on showing me around. They take me ballroom dancing, out to restaurants, and to underground theaters (students sitting on benches in a dark room with a large TV) that show the latest American movies for 25 cents.

I feel like I'm living in a Systemite teen movie: I carry around a little purse with spending money, which I earn with actual System jobs: modeling in Chinese commercials and teaching English to Tetra Pak executives. Normally, this wouldn't be allowed, but since we must remain "undercover" here, we're authorized to earn a living that doesn't involve selling Family CDs or asking for donations. As it turns out, real work is more lucrative than canning.

As a Home, my parents, Ching-Ching, and I agree that we need to contribute only half of what we earn to the Home budget, and we can keep the rest for ourselves. I manage to keep about $100 a month, which means I can afford to go out to dinner with classmates and make choices without having to get permission for every tiny thing.

In class, Mr. Lee, my Chinese listening teacher, demonstrates how to say "Hong Kong's joyous return to the Motherland" in Chinese. The British handover of Hong Kong back to China is only a month away, on July 1, 1997. Posters and signs are plastered all over the city, and a huge electric countdown clock has been ticking off the days for months. I raise my hand one afternoon and very carefully suggest that the people of Hong Kong might not be excited to return to China.

"Of course the Hong Kong people are ecstatic! How could they not be eager to throw off their colonial oppressors and return to Mother China?" is his shocked response.

Any other viewpoint on this one topic is beyond his comprehension. I realize then that even people who consider themselves forward-thinking, modern, and cynical about their political system and history can still have indoctrination so deep they just can't see past it. I don't press the matter.

I'm aware of how precarious our situation is here, even though we feel settled and are making friends. I hear clicking on the phone line that indicates our calls are being bugged, and when we receive letters, I can see where they've been hastily reglued. I don't take it personally; the Chinese authorities monitor all foreigners.

Even under constant government surveillance, I'm enjoying a freedom and independence in China that I've never experienced before. And with the new craze of Internet cafés, I open my first Hotmail account and can communicate with people without everything having to pass through the Home Shepherds. Email solves two other problems: it's much cheaper than international phone calls, and you can keep the same address when you move, which has always been a challenge in the Family, with our constantly changing addresses and phone numbers.

Mom purchases a new laptop with her earnings and gives me her old, gray Toshiba. My first computer. It's two inches thick and weighs ten pounds, so it's not exactly portable, but I'm grateful to be able to transcribe prophecies and type letters without having to use the Home computer each time and risk someone seeing my private files.

Mom arrives home late from the dean's annual dinner for foreign teachers. She's bubbling over with excitement. "You'll never guess!" she nearly squeals. "My students got the third highest marks in the whole country on the English essay portion of the standardized test! The dean made a speech to congratulate me in front of all the teachers!"

I'm delighted at her success. She has worked hard with them and deserves it.

Like me, she is starting to see what she is capable of, that she is good at something, and, for the first time, is earning enough to support herself. Her newfound independence is sparking changes at home, too. I can see that she has basically checked out of her relationship with my dad, but I'm still not prepared when I over-hear her on the phone with her mother seeking emotional support. With VocalTec's Internet phone service she can finally make inter-national calls without the exorbitant cost.

Hoping to save their marriage, Dad starts reading John Gray. On our walks to the market, he marvels at what he's learning from *Men Are from Mars, Women Are from Venus.* He tries to follow the advice. Listen more. Buy my mother flowers every week, like she always said she wanted.

But it's too late.

"I loved your father passionately for over twenty years," Mom confides in me. "But he's never understood my need for romance, for flowers, for something pretty, no matter how often I asked. The first present he ever gave me was a black umbrella, in Paris. Then he bought me a vacuum cleaner. I used to nag him all the time, but nothing changed. I've finally given up."

I am caught in the middle, seeing both sides and feeling sorry for them both. I know I could not have stayed married to my dad as long as she has. Yet seeing him so lost and hopeful—trying his best to fix things in his bumbling, optimistic way, and losing—hurts. I'm forced to be the voice of reason and counsel between them, and step into the role of mother and father to my younger siblings.

I notice Mom is spending a lot of time with Ivan, one of the Rus-sian professors at the university. We welcome him as a potential Sheep and have him over to the house often for dinner. On these nights, I notice Mom taking more pains with her makeup and outfits, but when I chide her for flirting with him, she brushes me off. "We're just friends."

While my parents' marriage deteriorates, Patrick and Sophia start canoodling, staring into each other's eyes lovingly. I'm not surprised when they announce that they're engaged. I celebrate with them by going out for dim sum. But my happiness is tinged with self-pity; their romance reminds me of everything I don't have.

Since returning to China, I've been celibate. I've just turned twenty-one, which means there are no age limits separating me from the FGA men, but there are few Family guys in the vicinity and many more women, so for the first time in years, there's no pressure to sleep with anyone. It's a relief after Kazakhstan, but I still yearn for a romantic dinner and dancing under the stars.

For a few months now, I've been attracted to one of my Danish classmates, Johnny. But no matter how much latitude we have here, I know the Family won't tolerate a relationship with a Systemite, so I tamp down my impulses and start talking to Johnny about Jesus. He's interested in Buddhism, so we don't hang out much after that. I'm disappointed but relieved. I've avoided temptation.

As the school semester comes to a close, I receive an unexpected request. My grandma has dreams of seeing the great sights in Europe, but now that she's in her seventies, she has some mobility issues. She wants me to accompany her.

"I won't be able to go without Faith to help me," she tells my parents, working the guilt angle. Normally, the Shepherds might discourage or even forbid such a trip; too much worldly influence and no supervision to make sure I don't break any Family rules. But there are no Shepherds here.

I clasp my hands together and prepare to plead. There's no way I'm going to miss out on my chance to see the Europe I've read about in my nineteenth-century novels. Before I even begin making my argument, my parents agree. I have no idea why, but I'm not interested in second-guessing their motives.

I fly into Rome to meet Grandma. September is the perfect time of year for the two-week senior citizens' bus tour of Europe. While it's not quite the Grand Tour of my novels, I'm enchanted nonetheless. I marvel at the aqueducts of Rome still standing from the time of Jesus. I wander the ruins of Pompeii, thinking of the 1984 movie that I'd seen many times. The beautiful architecture and empty streets of Brussels and Geneva are in stark contrast to the screaming, dirty vibrancy of Asia's jostling crowds, like a stately old dame instead of a messy fast-growing toddler.

We end our trip in England. Grandma is scheduled to depart one day ahead of me, so we say our goodbyes at the airport. I'm glad to have a little time to myself before my flight back to China in the morning. I arrange to spend the night at a Family Home in London. After dinner, I help with the dishes, but as I'm sweeping the floor, two of the young Family guys tease me for being so "helpful."

"Shut it. Leave her alone," says a handsome young man with long golden curls. He looks like a Grecian god. Speaking with him, I learn he's not in the Family, but he's been friends with the guys here for years. He tells me that he often spends the night at the Home when he's in town visiting. *That's odd, I think. We normally don't have Systemites stay in our Family Homes, even if they're from out of town, but maybe that's one of the differences between the mission field and home countries, like the UK and America.*

"Is it okay if I share the guest room with you?" he asks.

I look around at the others, and they look like this is a perfectly normal request.

"I guess," I say slowly. I'm just a guest here myself—who am I to say no?

We chat and flirt as we get ready to turn in, then climb into our separate beds. But he keeps wanting to talk late into the night.

"It's late. I have to go to sleep," I finally say.

"Of course. Can you just give me a hug goodnight?"

"Sure," I say with a shrug. We're an affectionate group of people who hug all the time.

I get up and go to hug him, and he pulls me onto the bed and rolls on top of me. I think he's trying to be cute, so I laugh and let him cuddle me for a few minutes. Then I say, "Okay, now I really do need to go to bed." But he doesn't let go.

"You're not going anywhere," he says, his voice low. "I know you want this as much as I do."

"No," I say firmly, trying to wriggle out of his arms. "I don't. I do find you attractive, but I'm not going to have sex with you. It's against the rules. I don't want to get into trouble."

"No one will know."

"I'll know," I snap, growing frustrated. "I'm serious. Get off me." I shove him as hard as I can. He doesn't budge an inch.

My mind begins racing. *I'm strong. I've wrestled with my brothers my whole childhood. I can get out of this.* I push and twist my body, try to get purchase with my legs to push him off, even try to fake him out. I use every wrestling trick I know, but he is holding my wrists down and using the rest of his body to compress my legs.

I struggle to breathe, ignoring the pain radiating from my hands down through my arms. My voice comes out, scratchy but emphatic. "I am not ambiguous about this. I absolutely do not want to have sex with you. I'm not being coy or playing hard to get. This is a definite *no!*"

His teeth flash in a humorless smile, and his grip tightens. I thrash my whole body, but he doesn't budge. After what seems like hours of twisting and bucking, my whole body feels raw and bruised. I don't have the energy to keep fighting. I go limp. Exhausted, angry, and helpless, I close my mind to any other thought besides *get it over with.*

When he finally releases me, I run to the bathroom. I want to smash the mirror with my fist. I said no! I fought back with all my strength. But I still wasn't able to defend myself.

When I come back from washing up, he is sound asleep. I curl into a ball on my bed and wait for morning. I leave without saying anything to anyone.

In the hours spent flying over the dark Pacific Ocean, I ask myself, *What more could I have done to stop it? Why didn't I scream the house down?* Fear and embarrassment. Fear that I would get into trouble if I got caught in bed with a Systemite and it was reported to the Shepherds. Fear that the people in the house would take his side and not believe me. Embarrassment to scream and cause a big scene. The humiliation, the feeling that this was somehow my fault and that I would get blamed for it if I called for help, kept me fighting in silence. I was on my own. I could not trust them to take my side to protect me.

The memory sticks to my skin, accompanying me back to Xiamen, into my house, into my room, into my bed. At night, in the darkness, I write in my journal:

Alone

What is loneliness
Not touch, not sound
Not feeling, sight nor scent
But rather an absence
An absence of all the above and yet . . . even with all the above you
    can still be alone. . . .
Do you understand me? Of course you don't.
You're not me and never will be.

How could you feel what it's like in this skin?
How could I ever let you in?

I read the poem the next day. God, how embarrassing. At least no one will ever read my sad-sack journal entry. I don't believe in feeling sorry for myself. *That's what comes from growing up to be tough like my brothers*, I think wryly. *It's just physical*, I rationalize, *like getting kicked in the stomach by a horse*. Since my first raw breaking in Thailand, I've been emotionally battered enough that I'm used to pain. Ignore it and move on. I can't even speak to my mother or a friend about what happened, afraid they will report it to the Shepherds and I'll be punished. So, I bury the memory in a box and slam the lid.

As the heat of summer arrives, changes are in the breeze. Patrick and Sophia have a quiet wedding ceremony at home and move in with Patrick's parents on Gulangyu. Ching-Ching moves to Qingdao, a port city in Shandong Province, with some other Family young people. Mom plans to go traveling for the summer. I can't get a clear answer on where she's going. She's been more and more secretive; it seems we are both avoiding heart-to-heart talks these days.

After two years in China, what was once a challenge now feels stifling. I'm also ready to move on. But I don't know where I want to go. I've just turned twenty-two, and I'm still not married, an old maid, by Family standards, and I have no prospects here.

I miss hanging out with other young people my age whom I don't have to hide my identity from. So, when a group of Family teens from Taiwan comes for a visit, I'm happy to accompany them as their translator on the two-day train ride to Beijing. My Mandarin is conversationally fluent, and I can easily navigate the cities now.

In Beijing, while sightseeing at the Forbidden City, I spot a familiar face in another knot of photo-taking foreigners. It's my former Danish classmate from Xiamen University, Johnny. I can't believe I've run into him here in the millions of people in Beijing.

I jump up, waving until he spots me. He grins widely, and before I know it, he's at my side telling me he's just finished a grueling, two-month trip cycling three thousand miles up the coast of China.

When the teen group leaves, he convinces me to stay in Beijing an extra couple of days and explore the city with him. *Who would know?* Everyone at home is away traveling. There's nothing wrong with cycling the city and seeing the monuments as friends, I justify it to myself when I agree to stay.

I tingle with the thrill of being alone with him. Over the two years in China, the barriers between Systemite and friend are wearing thin with daily contact.

After two days biking through Beijing, exploring the Summer Palace and other sites, we sit together, exhausted, on the roof of the cheap Chinese hotel, where we each have our own room. We watch the bright lights of the city, listen to the honking of horns, and smell roast pork and garlic. We sit closer and closer until we're cuddling, and then he leans down. Our lips brush. I should pull away, but I don't want this to end. We gently explore each other's mouth, and my heart thuds in my chest. We make out so passionately that there's only one step more, which is when I finally get up and go to my room. I won't take that step. We promise to keep in touch, but I doubt I'll see him again. He is going back to Denmark after this, and I am going back to the Family.

My heart and mind swing back and forth. *What have I done? No one has to know. What should I do?* On the two-day train ride from Beijing to Xiamen I turn the questions over and over. For weeks after I get home, I wrestle with it. *God, please show me what to do!* I've committed one of the worst sins we can commit in the Family— sexual intimacy with a Systemite. The days of FFing are long gone, and the Mama Letters continuously remind us about the consequences of crossing the line.

Since my wayward time in Macau when I was sixteen and sneaking out of the house to be with my Portuguese boyfriend, I recommitted myself to God and to the Family. I'd liked some of the guys I'd witnessed to. I'd try to help them find peace and happiness through Jesus. Some of them took my attention to mean more than what it was, but with others, there was true affection—and attraction. But although some would write passionate letters promising the moon and stars, I'd never yielded to the temptation. I think of Johnny's lips on mine, and I curse myself for being weak.

I am a true believer. I may enjoy the more relaxed lifestyle here in China, but I still read the Bible and Letters every day. I enforce the Family's rules with my younger siblings. I pray and try to listen for divine prophecy to help guide my way.

The dangers of deceit have been ingrained in me since childhood, that if I'm disobedient or cover up a sin, God will not hear me. Over the years, God has been my only constant. He is the only one I can rely on to take care of me, to protect me and comfort me. I don't want anything separating Him and me. It's not about the Shepherds. It's about me and God.

So, I report on myself.

I type a short letter, giving the bare facts—that I'd made out with a System guy from my school—and email it to the Area Shepherds in Taiwan who supervise the few small Homes in mainland China.

The reaction is swift.

A few days later, I get a response from Taiwan. I'm to head to the main Combo home in Taipei immediately for rehabilitation. Mom's still gone for the summer, so I don't have to explain to her, which only leaves Dad. I find him in the kitchen and take a deep breath before beginning.

He's unusually understanding. "We haven't been very good examples to you recently, with everything your mom and I are going through. Perhaps we allowed too much freedom."

"No," I tell him, "this is my fault. I'm an adult, and I'm responsible for following the rules."

He gives me a hug and tells me he's proud of me for being honest. *He's the only one. Everyone else thinks I'm crazy for telling on myself.*

I am leaning against the red granite counter of the information desk in the Taipei airport, searching for Josh's white-blond, thinning head of hair. Poor guy, he's cursed with our dad's early baldness. Just as I spot my brother, I feel the counter roll under my arm. I look up in confusion to see that the three rows of large, boxy TVs suspended from the roof of the arrivals lobby are swaying from side to side.

"Hey, sis, welcome to Taiwan!" Josh smiles, delighting in my bulging eyes and hanging jaw. "You'll get used to the earthquakes."

25

THE BIG DECISION

In Taiwan, I'm put on a typical probation for three months. I'm given a closet-sized room in a two-story, thirty-person Home, instructed to reread the one hundred basic-training Mo Letters, banned from alcohol and movie nights, and assigned the worst chores. Even though I only kissed a System guy, I must take an AIDS test. The results come back negative, and I'm relieved, but I still must wait six months and then take another. Until receiving my second round of negative results, I'm not allowed to even kiss anyone.

The punishment is extreme, but I accept it willingly. I'm okay with the extra AIDS test; glad for it, even, because I did have sex with a Systemite. The rape in England rises like the smell of a dead thing. I try to ignore the memory. It's done. *No use crying over spilled milk*, I hear my Mom's voice in my head.

I never told anyone about the rape. It's hard to even call it that in the privacy of my own mind. I'm ashamed, as if it were my fault. At the same time, my conscience is clear with God. I didn't choose that, so I don't deserve punishment for it. Which is why I didn't tell on myself. It adds a layer of anxiety while I wait for the second round of blood work results, but I numb my mind by reading the same old Mo Letters over and over again.

I'm only halfway through my three-month probation when Josh shows up from Hsinchu, a city midway between Taipei and Tai-chung, with a request. Laura, who has always had difficult pregnancies, is so thin and weak after this last one, she can barely use the bathroom. They now have five children under the age of six, and instead of living with other families, they're living on their own at the moment, the pendulum of Family structure having swung from consolidation and control back to allowing a little more autonomy. Will I come help?

After obtaining permission from the Shepherds—who are only too happy that someone will volunteer for this unwanted task—I'm thrust into the role of full-time mom, cook, teacher, and cleaner for four small kids—Laura cares for her newborn. I've never had to do it all by myself before; responsibilities are usually divided up among the Home. But Laura is too frail to help, and Josh is usually gone from dawn until dusk, witnessing, provisioning, and going on garbage runs: touring trash dumps where he is likely to find good furniture, TVs, or equipment thrown away by people with more money than common sense. He can usually fix the electronics and sell them to support his family. He's never had any formal schooling, but he's always been able to take computers apart and put them back together again, build them and fix them—all self-taught.

A couple of weeks into my stay, a loud and powerful noise cuts through the black of night.

Crack!

I shoot up in bed to the sensation of the mattress jerking beneath me. In Japan, I'd been through many earthquakes, short tremors, but this is different. The entire house groans, wave after wave rocking its very foundation.

Flinging myself out of bed, I struggle to reach the doorway. The floor is undulating too much to walk. Finally, it stops, and I fly into action. I find my brother in the hallway leading to the kids' rooms, and together we grab them out of their beds, run them down three flights of stairs, and pile them into Josh's minivan.

"Stay here! Don't move!" Josh yells at the half-asleep kids, and then says to me, "I'm going to get Laura!"

He finds his wife stumbling down the stairs with their newborn and rushes her to the vehicle.

Terrified, we head for the nearest open space—a park near the river—as the largest earthquake in Taiwan's recent history strikes the tiny island. Buildings and bridges collapse, hills and lakes are created in a moment, and a hundred thousand people are left homeless. The damage is unheard of in a country that designs all its structures to withstand earthquakes.

Taichung is the worst-hit area. Phone lines are down, but we finally get word that Aaron's and Mary's families are safe and have been moved from their damaged houses to the tent cities the government is putting up for the earthquake refugees.

For the next few weeks, the aftershocks are every half hour. When the ground trembles, we freeze like rabbits staring down headlights. Waiting. When it stops, we release the breath we are unconsciously holding. *Just another small one. I'm getting used to the earth rolling under my feet*, I think in shock.

In crisis is when the Family shines. Every able-bodied, available Family member heads to the worst-hit areas to volunteer. Josh uses his van to shuttle food and water into the remote mountain villages, bringing down people who are injured and need medical attention. With the discipline and work ethic drilled into us as babies, Family members quickly form well-oiled, effective relief teams.

Over the next few months, I am impressed by how the whole country comes together, businesses donating millions of dollars of supplies and food. By Christmas, the worst of the crisis has passed, and Laura is back on her feet.

With my probation over and AIDS tests clear, I receive an invitation to move to the young adult Home in Taipei. It's a Home with five couples around my age, and only two FGA couples, one of which are the Taiwan area leaders, JB and Sweetie. This setup is supposed to give us young people, SGAs, more of an opportunity to run our own Home, rather than being in a Home where the older adults decide everything. Mama Maria recognizes our need for self-determination, within the bounds of the Family structure and rules.

At first, I'm happy to be with my peers, but my attempts to build new friendships fall flat. It's a large ten-bedroom house, but couples and families take the larger rooms, and I share a tiny room with an eighteen-year-old girl—the only other single in the home. At twenty-two years old, I am still unmarried and heading into spinsterhood by the Family's standards. I can't avoid the stigma, but I put my self-consciousness to the side and try my best to fit in. Yet no matter how much I smile, I feel a subtle yet pervasive air of jealousy and suspicion.

I soon learn that the Shepherds have instructed the married men in the house to share God's love with the single girls. The wives are supposedly fine with it, but this is blatantly untrue. As soon as one of the married men approaches me, his wife begins to ice me out. I reject his advances, but he persists, magnanimous in his willingness to share with me. This is a road I've been down before, and I don't want another breaking. Instead of resisting and rebelling, I submit, once, and then I avoid letting him catch me alone so that he can make another "request."

I make sure to schedule any sharing near my period to reduce my chance of getting pregnant. Still, there is no one I am interested in marrying and, after meeting most of the Family guys in the region, I have little hope of finding one soon.

My anxiety remains at a low-level burn while I try to put on a joyful face. The only person who seems to care that I'm suffering is John, one of the few older men who lives in the house. Married to a Japanese woman, John has a head full of white hair and kind, open eyes; everything about him seems trustworthy, steady, reliable. He often takes me along as his witnessing partner or errand buddy.

He encourages me to express myself, so I talk about how lonely I feel, about my doubts and fears, and boredom. But I keep the worst of it to myself. I look at him and the other forty- and fifty-year-old adults and see my life stretch before me in a long monotonous line. I feel like a dead tree, not learning or growing, drooping and slowly decaying. At night, I lie awake, plagued by questions. *What is the Family really doing?* We blow in and out of countries, bringing a few boxes of clothes or aid, wearing our martyrdom like a thick winter coat.

In this Home, we aren't even doing humanitarian work like I did in Kazakhstan. With the earthquake crisis mostly passed, things are back to normal, meaning we are selling CDs to raise money while showing pictures of all the good works we've done in the past. My days are the usual round robin of Devotions, cleaning, fundraising, more cleaning, with only a weekly movie and glass of wine to look forward to. For Devotions, we read variations on the same material over and over, no new ideas. I didn't think I'd miss the repetition of writing out Chinese characters, but I want to learn something, anything new.

The pointlessness hits me hard. I've always prided myself on being resilient, being able to stay positive when things are bleak, or at least being able to bounce back in a day or two. And I rarely ever cry, a few times a year at most, and I'm proud of that. *What's wrong with me?* Why do I feel like bursting into tears every day, all day long? Over and over, I feel the tears welling up in my eyes, and I ashamedly try to dash them away and buck up.

I pour my heart out in the only place I can—my journal.

Sometimes, like now, I feel so low, so worthless, like I count for nothing. Like I am not and cannot accomplish anything of note, of worth, so why live?

If I'm not doing anything worthwhile in the Family through all my struggling and trying, then why don't I just leave and live for myself. Here I feel like I'm constantly trying to please God, but I can never

make the grade spiritually, never be good enough, selfless enough.
What am I doing if I'm not making a difference?

I want to LIVE. I want to DO. I want to MOVE. I want to
SHAKE. I want to CHANGE . . .

After the tiny taste of freedom in China, I can't understand the reason I've had to sacrifice so much. Things I'd taken for granted seem almost unbearable now. I can't understand why I can't have any money or why I need permission and a buddy to walk to the 7-Eleven. I don't want to leave God's service, but I don't know how much more misery I can take. I find myself longing to be anyplace but where I am. I'd thought about it fleetingly in China, but for the first time, I seriously entertain the idea of leaving the Family.

I've heard whispers that a number of young people have left in the six years since Grandpa's passing, either to rebel against the restrictive rules and constant supervision, or to indulge in worldly behavior. Some of the FGAs blame the Internet and its worldly influence for the growing exodus.

I have no contact with the Backsliders. Once someone leaves, we don't have a forwarding address, so finding someone who has left the Family is nearly impossible. Secrecy is built into our DNA. New disciples never use their legal names; they are known only by the biblical ones they take upon joining. Even those who are born into the Family often take a different name when they get older, as I did briefly with Jewel. This makes finding people even harder. It also ensures that if someone leaves with a grudge, they will be unable to name others to the authorities. But even though I don't know how people leave or where they go, we all hear the stories about what happens to them—dark, ugly tales of how those who reject God's will end up on drugs, working as strippers, or in jail.

I don't want that to happen to me.

I reach out to the only person I know who has left the Family—

Chris. The last time we spoke I was in Kazakhstan, and I broke up with him over the phone. I'd heard he left the Family a few months after our call and moved to Taiwan, where he'd grown up. I ask a few mutual friends and discover one of them has been secretly staying in contact with him and has his phone number. Chris and I speak briefly on the phone and arrange to meet at a nearby park.

The man who shows up is not the person I remember. Chris is almost skeletal; he's lost nearly half his mass and is gaunt, drawn, and sickly thin. We walk in circles around and around the grassy grounds. Chris explains that after I left him, he became anorexic, supposedly triggered by my comments about his weight, and that he's been in and out of the hospital on health issues related to illegal drugs. He tells me he's been arrested once or twice for doing something stupid while either high or drunk. I feel responsible for this, and I resent the responsibility.

On our fifth lap around the park, the ice breaks. His sarcastic wit is as sharp as ever and we are soon laughing over our crazy times. I gently scold him to take better care of himself, but secretly I am at a loss. His life choices seem to confirm what the Shepherds have always told us, that we'll end up on drugs or in jail if we leave the Family. When it's time to say goodbye, we hug for a long time.

As I begin to pull away, he draws me closer, presses his mouth against my hair, and whispers, "No one ever understood me as well as you." My heart aches with his pain.

"Please take better care of yourself," I plead.

The next time I see Chris, he is in the hospital. One of his lungs has collapsed from drug use.

If I leave the Family, I promise myself, I will go to college; I will not do drugs or indulge in every bad thing I've been forbidden. But flashes of Chris and his fate linger. I know I am strong, that I can do what is necessary if I put my mind to it. But there is always uncertainty—undertones of Grandpa's warnings of the Devil's attacks on those who step outside God's will.

In the coming months, I wrestle with guilt. My despair won't go away no matter how many prophecies I record or how desperately I pray. My entire life I've been taught to think of college as a selfish waste of time, but recently the dream of going to college has grown from a tiny flicker into an all-consuming blaze.

Months go by, and I pray for God to change my desires and emotions. This depressed mental state is not normal for me. But I don't see a future for myself in the Family that I can stomach, and I refuse to end up bitter and angry at God and everyone else because I feel like my choices were taken away. I refuse to live life saying, *"If only I had . . ."*

Maybe this depression is a sign? Maybe *this* is God's way of telling me to leave?

I refuse to be trapped in my misery. I'd rather leave behind everything I have known my whole life—friends, family, support structure, income, *everything*—than have regrets.

I decide, finally. I. Am. Done.

I will be my own change.

Just minutes before, this had felt like an impossible leap, but once I've made my decision to leave the Family and go to college, the depression fades away.

For the first time in my life, I'm going to set my own terms.

26

———

SUFFERING IS NEVER GODLY

My decision made, I must tell the Shepherds. I stand in front of
JB and Sweetie's plain, wooden bedroom door and raise my hand
to knock. My breathing is shallow. I'm about to enact the biggest,
most impactful decision of my life. Once I say what I mean to say,
I can never take it back, even if I change my mind. I will never
be trusted in the Family again. But I'm not willing to keep slug-
ging through this unending haze of sadness. I take a deep breath,
tighten my muscles, and knock.

Uncle JB opens the door. "Hi, Faith," he says gently. "How are
you? Can I help you?"

JB always seems kind. I like him, but I don't trust him. I don't
trust any of them now. Kindness is a tool they use to get me to reveal something they can use to punish me later.

"Can we please talk?" I ask softly. "Maybe go for a walk?"

"Of course," he says, grabbing his sunglasses. He can tell it must
be serious.

JB takes me to a nearby park, and with my eyes glued to the
concrete path, we walk in silence. When I can no longer hold all
the tension building inside me, I blurt out: "I want to go to college."

With the bomb dropped, I quickly work my way through all the
reasons I've carefully crafted.

He listens silently, then directs me to sit down on a bench. He trots out the usual arguments. "You'll be failing God, leaving His will. How will you support yourself?"

I stop listening. I've made up my mind. I'm going to go to college, and that college is going to be in America. I've heard from my grandparents that American colleges are the best and provide financial aid to US citizens. As he pressures me, I tell JB I plan to return to the Family once I have my degree. But this is something that I must do. I've wrestled with the decision for months.

He tries a few more times to convince me, but there's no point. We both know he can't *make* me stay. I'm over twenty-one, and the days of physically imprisoning or forcing people in the Family are over.

Back at the Home, Sweetie tells me I won't be allowed to go out witnessing and fundraising to get money to *leave* the Family. I'll have to make do with what I have. Lowering my eyes in acceptance, I hurry to my room. I quietly close my door and dig under my mattress for the sock I've kept all these years to hold money I've earned or was gifted to me. I sort through a mixture of bills; it's a few hundred dollars in a variety of currencies. Not nearly enough for a plane ticket to the United States. I have no money. I have no way to support myself . . . Before I can let the fear consume me, I set my jaw. *Never give in. Never, never, never . . .* I will find a way.

I decide to reach out to my parents to see if they might be able to help me financially. I haven't heard from them since I left China a year ago. I don't know how they'll react to my decision to leave, but I've been an adult for a long time and this choice is my own. I am determined to go through with it, no matter what, even if my parents don't approve.

I type out a quick email to my dad to see where they are and click send. For the next day, I wait impatiently, until I finally see his name in my inbox. His email informs me that a month after I left Xiamen, my mother took Jondy, now eleven, and moved into her own apartment to be with Ivan, who she'd been secretly dating the whole time. A couple of months later, my parents traveled together to the States to visit relatives. My father saw this as an opportunity get Mom away from Ivan and put their marriage back together. But, once in America, they went their separate ways. Dad traveled to Houston to see his mother, and Mom flew to Oregon, where, for ten months, she and Jondy stayed with her aunt Virginia; Nina, already fifteen years old, stayed in a Family Home. Now, Mom's gone to Russia to marry Ivan, leaving Jondy with Dad.

The news swirls around in my mind. More than twenty years of marriage, and it's over. But they are not legally married and own nothing, so the split is relatively simple. Even though I knew they'd been having trouble, it's still a shock. Yet I also understand. In Ivan, my mom saw an educated man who could talk with her about books and her new interests. I realize that for years, she's been looking for a way out of the Family, but she only had the courage to make the leap attached to another man.

Dad seems to have moved on from the split, still living in Texas, floating around in a van with a young Mexican disciple, Maria, who is about my age, trying to raise money to go back to China.

Now that I have his phone number, I decide to call him. It will be easier to share news of my decision. To keep the peace, I tell him and everyone else—and very nearly convince myself—that my leaving the Family will be temporary, just a short stint away—a chance to go to school before coming back to continue serving the Lord. After a long diatribe on the importance of being a missionary and the waste of higher education, Dad realizes he won't budge me.

For so much of my life, I've longed for his recognition, his approval. I wanted him to praise my swimming abilities back at the reservoir, I'd imagined him rescuing us when we were sent to Thailand, and I was grateful when he showed up in Atlanta to take us back to the Farm. But with all I've learned of him, his disappointment and disapproval no longer budge me.

I email my mom, but I have little hope of hearing back in time. From what Dad has told me, she's accessing email only every few weeks.

I call my grandparents. Grandad offers to send me a couple hundred dollars, not nearly enough for the ticket and expenses to move to the US, and Grandma says she's already sending my mom money and can't afford more. I don't want to show up destitute like before. I need to find a way to make it myself.

I reach out to Dad again. I know he can't help me with money, as he hardly has any to support himself, but perhaps he knows someone who could help me. "You remember Adriano, our old Fish?" he drawls. "He is opening a new gambling club in Macau. Let me see if he might have a job for you."

"Please," I say gratefully.

The few bills in my money sock feel far too light. But I have enough in there to buy a ticket from Taiwan to Macau, which finally got its own airport!

Three days later, my two suitcases contain all my earthly possessions and I have my ticket for my flight the next morning. After dinner, I'm about to flop down on my mattress when I look up to see Uncle John leaning against the doorframe of my bedroom. He smiles a sad smile and asks if he can take me out to get an ice cream, one last time.

"Sure," I say to my old witnessing buddy and ally in this frigid little Home.

We get into his van, but on the way to the store, he passes the turnoff. Laughing, I point out the mistake and tell him he's already lost without me. He smiles but doesn't turn around. Instead, he pulls up to a rent-by-the-hour motel.

I ask what we're doing here, and he says, "I have to check on a Sheep." He explains that there's someone inside who needs our help, and he wants to talk to them before heading to the store. Can I join him?

I watch as he goes to the front desk for a key, and then I follow him down a bleak, gray hallway. *Why did he get a motel room just to meet a Sheep?* A vague dread presses on my chest, but my heart refuses to acknowledge the inconsistency of his words. I follow him as if it were any normal outing. The key scrapes in the lock. We walk inside, but there's no one there. I hear the door click behind me. Faced with a dark room and a double bed, I can't avoid the screaming question.

"Uncle John, what's going on? Where's the Sheep we are meeting?" My voice sounds high and tinny in my own ears.

"God has told me I need to share His love with you before you leave," he says.

Real panic sets in, but I try to appear as if it's just a joke or a giant misunderstanding that I can play my way out of. I tell him it really isn't necessary, that I don't want to share God's love.

But then I feel his hand take mine, and my throat closes on itself, any further words drying up as he leads me to the bed.

I've been so trained not to refuse, to obey my elders, that I don't have the words to object. All I want to do is run, but I don't have a car, a phone, or money. I have no way out. There are no other options I can think of. I'm trapped. Trapped by my own mind, which has been conditioned to never refuse an uncle.

The mattress sinks under my weight, and my feeling of helplessness howls inside.

He pushes me onto my back and takes off my clothes. I just stare at the ceiling, trying to make my mind blank as I focus all my attention on the tiny LED lights. They look like little stars, and I fly away, into them, to escape what is happening to my body.

Uncle John tells me he wants it to be good for me. I say nothing, stiff as a mannequin. I hate that he's pretending this has anything to do with me or my pleasure. I hate that he justifies this in his mind as showing me love. I'm sure he's convinced himself that if he could just have sex with me, I would feel love or enjoyment and want to stay in the Family.

But he knows I don't want this. Over the last months we've been living together, he's offered to share with me, even sending his wife once to tell me it was okay. I've declined his offers as politely as I can, thinking that as a sympathetic friend, he might not report me for refusing. But now I'm trapped.

Unable to defend myself or speak up after my first feeble refusal was ignored, I must lie there and take it. I can scream, but these rooms are soundproof. I can fight, but he's much larger than I am. Even worse, the thought crosses my mind that if I pretend to like it a little, he'll finish quicker, but I can't. I just want this to be over as fast as possible while I try to distance myself from what's happening.

A wave of nausea ripples through me as I force my focus back to the lights.

I hate him. And I hate him even more because I liked him. I trusted him. I thought he was my friend.

When he finishes with me, I remain frozen on my back. Between the physical and psychological pain, only one thing is clear: I'm never coming back.

27

ON MY OWN

It is strange being back in Macau, especially by myself. The familiar landmarks of the Hotel Lisboa and the pink and yellow colonial buildings surrounding the fountain in the Leal Senado square are comforting, while I try to navigate an upended world. It's May 2000, and the city seems smaller than I remember it. But without a buddy, I'm constantly looking over my shoulder.

Dad's old friend Adriano has hired me for the summer to teach English to the 150 new employees of his soon-to-open private gambling facility. The Legend Club is located in downtown Macau at the Landmark Plaza, just minutes from the Hong Kong Macau Ferry Terminal, to cater to all the gamblers that flood into Macau on the weekends.

Since I used all my money on airfare, I don't have the means to rent an apartment or hotel room, so Adriano introduces me to a widow who is interested in renting a bedroom in her small flat for around $100 a month. The room is tiny with a hard double bed, but she'll wait for rent until I get paid.

My first day at the Legend Club, I divide my 150 students into classes based on their jobs and English level. Their English abilities range from carrying on a simple conversation to not knowing a single word. *This is going to be challenging,* I realize, *but I can't fail.* It's my only way to make money. Or the only way I'll consider.

I spend days creating a curriculum to match each level of competency, determined to teach every single employee the words and phrases that will be immediately useful in their interactions with casino guests. With a few English workbooks, I'm creating ten different course curriculums. It's a very steep learning curve—for me, and for them.

For two months I work with the employees on vocabulary words and simple sentences, and they make good progress.

I long for the weekend, until the weekend arrives. The July heat is unbearable, and while the club is air-conditioned, the apartment is not. Early in the morning, I head to the market, but by the time I leave to make the mile-long trek home, the sun is blazing. When I get back to my apartment, my arms are burning with the weight of my groceries. Sweat is dripping down my arms and making rivulets down my legs. I drop into the nearest chair, and when I can't sit in my sweat any longer, I enter my landlady's room to borrow a fan.

She arrives home with her usual grunt of acknowledgment and walks into her room, only to burst back into the living room screaming and pointing and waving her arms. I'm scared and have no idea what is wrong. She is lecturing me on "respecting people's privacy," "other people's things," and "stealing." I'm flabbergasted until it dawns on me. *The fan.* I don't know what to say.

In the Family, we freely lend and borrow things without question, and certainly no one gets angry if you go into their room. In principle, everything is shared and ownership is frowned on. I try to calm her down, but I don't know what to do. Besides my father, I've never seen someone so angry. In the Family, yelling is abhorrent. No matter how big the infraction, we're expected to work things out with love.

While I fumble for words, she screams: "I want you out of here!" and storms out of the flat.

I walk to my room in a daze and sit on my bed, staring at my shaking hands. *System people are terrors to live with.*

When she returns a couple of hours later, I say again how sorry

I am and convince her to let me stay. But from then on, I am on tenterhooks. She doesn't want me here, and I don't want to be here. She is only renting me a room because she needs the money, but she doesn't really want anyone in her space. Thankfully, it's only a couple of more weeks until my job at the Legend Club is finished, and I'll have saved enough money to fly to America.

On a Monday toward the end of my gig, I wake up with a sore throat. The next day, it gets worse. By Thursday, I can barely teach class, and on Friday morning, I wake with a raging fever and it feels like there's ground glass in my throat when I swallow. I try to walk to the bathroom, but I'm so dizzy I can barely make it. I call in sick.

For three intensely hot days, I lay on my bed, burning with fever and fading in and out of consciousness and delirium. There is no one to call, and my landlady ignores me completely. I realize I could die here, in this bed, with no one to help me.

As always, I pray. *I know I left the Family and left Your service. But I also know that You still love me. I'm still Your child. Please heal me and raise me up.*

I try to drink sips of water, and on the fourth day, the fever goes down enough that I can drag myself out of bed and down to the street, where I stumble into a taxi and ask them to take me to the hospital. It's a last resort. I'm sure I don't have the money to go, and I have very little experience with hospitals.

The doctor tells me I have a horribly infected strep throat and prescribes some antibiotics. I recover within a week. I'm surprised at how cheap the service is; the medical system is subsidized.

I'm grateful to be better, but the experience frightens me. In the Family, someone would have brought me tea and soup and checked on me every few hours to make sure I was okay; I wouldn't have been afraid of being kicked out onto the street if I lost my job or fought with my roommate. I wouldn't have even had to *have* a job. Out here, I am truly alone in a way I've never experienced. My parents can't help. Plus, they live in different countries and keep changing addresses and phone numbers. Even if I emailed them from an Internet café, it would take days for them to respond, if at all.

Live or die. I am on my own.

I have no safety net.

Failure is not an option.

As I board the international flight to Houston, I'm grateful the summer is over, my job is finished, and I've saved enough money to make the journey to the US. My students have made impressive progress in just a few months, and I'm proud of them and of myself.

I settle into my seat and think of America, of the culture shock I experienced when I first arrived at twelve. This time, I know what I'm in for, and I have a plan. Well, a plan for how to figure out a plan. I've bought a plane-hopping ticket to visit my relatives in three states. I'm going to check out as many top colleges in those states as I can, then decide where to go to school and figure out how to get financial aid and a job. Okay, "plan" may be too grand a word, but it's enough to get me on the plane.

As the engine rumbles for lift-off, I cling to the words of my great-grandmother Virginia, words I've lived by since I left home: "Faith means stepping off the cliff into thin air and having faith that God will put the stepping-stones under your feet."

I am a different person who returns to America. I am an adult who has lived completely on my own for three months, held a full-time job, made my own money, and opened my own bank account. I've also had some disastrous sexual experiences and been sick, depressed, scared, and alone, and I survived. I'm still here.

I'd been taught that God's Family is my real family, but the minute I stepped outside the group, all ties were severed, just like when I was twelve and stranded in America with my mom, Jondy, and Nina. It wasn't the Family that came to our rescue; it was my System relatives, even those who didn't like or agree with us. When the chips are down, blood is stronger than conviction.

My first long-hop stop is Houston to see my dad and my grand-mother Eve. Houston is a hotbed of Family members and ex–Family members, and I quickly realize it's not a good environment for me. Too many people who want to hash out Family ways or immerse me in fundamentalism. Mother Eve and Steven's family have been working with the Korean churches since they left the Family, and they try to drag me to one church event after another. They all want me to accept their brand of Jesus, but I need space to figure out who I am first.

For Thanksgiving, I visit Grandad Gene and Barbara in India-napolis. My granddad, who'd promised to help me go to college if I ever decided to do so, agrees to give me $100 a month for food while I'm in school. It's not nearly as much as I'd hoped for, but I shoulder the disappointment and give him a big hug. I know he loves me; I figure he forgot that $100 doesn't go as far today as it did when he was in school. Barbara squeezes my shoulder and tells me she's proud of me, but I sense I can't impose on her nice retirement by staying long-term. I'm also not the least bit interested in spend-ing a snow-locked winter in Indiana.

I head to see my grandmother, who is living in a one-bedroom apartment in an assisted-living facility in Georgia. She was diag-nosed with Parkinson's, so she can't live alone and is mostly in a wheelchair. I'm shocked—and so grateful we got to spend time to-gether a few years ago on our trip to Europe. *Did she know about her condition then? Was that why she was so adamant about me coming with her?* I try to cheer her up by telling her my plans for the future. She's thrilled I'm going to go to college, but enthusiasm is about the only thing she can offer. There's obviously no place for me there.

My final stop is my mother's sister Madeline, who moved her family from Georgia to Monterey, California, a couple of years ago. I release a sigh of tension when I see my kindly uncle Rick waiting for me with a smile in the arrivals area at the San Francisco Airport. Being deserted by the Family at the airport in Miami has never fully left me.

After a welcoming hug, he loads my heavy suitcases into his SUV. Then he shoots me an impish grin. "How would you like to come with me to a wine tasting?" he asks.

"That sounds great!" I exclaim. "What's a wine tasting?"

He laughs. "You'll see."

What a cool way to start my life in California!

We drive to the San Francisco Marriott Hotel and head into a huge ballroom with dozens of long tables lined with bottles of wine. I've never seen anything like it. This is a far cry from the Family's regimented one glass a week of cheap box wine.

"I'm a wine distributor," Uncle Rick explains. "It's my job to go up and down the coast to events like this, tasting different varieties. Try this one first." He hands me a glass. "Swirl it in your mouth, then spit it into these silver buckets at the end of the table. Don't swallow, or you'll get real drunk real fast."

What a strange sight. All these professionals in suits, spitting into buckets. I join the fun and wash away some of the anxiety I'm starting to feel about my new potential home before the two-hour drive south to Carmel Valley.

We pull up to a beautiful, yellow, Spanish-style house with a garden. It's enchanting. Aunt Madeline is there to greet me with a big hug. Still, I'm on edge. Excited and tired but on edge. *Will they like me? Will they let me stay?*

"Erika and Erin!" I call to my twelve- and fifteen-year-old cousins. "I hardly recognized you! You've gotten so big since I last saw you!"

"You look the same," they say with a laugh.

Erika holds back shyly.

"Erika, show Faith to your room!" Madeline booms.

Rick grabs my suitcases and carries them out to the guesthouse that I'll be sharing with Erika. It's set against the main house with its own entrance and consists of one big room with two single beds and a couple of chests of drawers, and a small bathroom.

"Is this okay?" Rick looks concerned.

"This is great!" I assure him. "I'm used to sharing a room. Thank you so much for taking me in."

That night, as I climb into my single bed with the white-and-yellow quilted bedspread, I stare at a huge oil painting of a purple flower hanging on the wall. *Thank You, God, for bringing me here safely and giving me a place to lay my head.* It might not be every young woman's dream to share a room with her twelve-year-old cousin, but I know I'm lucky not to be on the streets.

When I explain to Aunt Madeline about my situation, she invites me to live with them, free of charge until I can get on my feet, as long as I help her clean the house. I'm used to cleaning, and California has an excellent university system. Bingo.

College is my single-minded goal, and I want to make sure I attend the best one I can get into. Even though it's frowned upon in the Family, I've always been competitive. *Comes with keeping up with five older brothers.* I start researching *U.S. News & World Report* college rankings and contact college admissions officers of top schools around the country. Over and over, I hear the same thing: "Well, you seem like an interesting candidate, but you have no scholastic record that we recognize."

I try to explain, telling them, "My parents were overseas missionaries, so I was homeschooled. Here are my scores from the high school exam that I took in the US. I scored in the top percentile."

The Rice University admissions counselor tells me, "Yes, but without an official high school transcript, there's no way we can compare you to other students. We don't recognize homeschool records. My suggestion is that you go to community college for a year. Make good grades, get an academic record, then try to apply."

Undefeated, I head to the local community college in Monterey.

They also don't recognize my homeschool records, but they accept the diploma.

"You'll need to take a placement exam in math and English, so we know what classes to put you in," the admissions counselor says. "Do you have SAT or ACT scores? If you get a high enough grade in one of those, you won't have to take all the remedial English and math."

Okay, I think, *I can take the test.*

I ask about tuition.

"It takes a year to qualify as a California resident, so your first-year tuition will be $3,500, as compared with $300 for residents."

The admissions officer must have seen the shock cover my face. *A whole Family Home could live on that for months!*

"You can apply for financial aid. If your family doesn't have much money, the government will give you a Pell Grant, which should just cover the tuition." She passes me the sheets of paper on applying for financial aid as well.

I head to the Monterey Public Library, a contemporary two-story structure on Pacific Street in downtown Monterey and check out the most recent ACT and SAT Kaplan study books. The books are a few years out of date, but I hope they are recent enough to help me get a good score. I have no money to take SAT prep classes or hire a tutor, strategies I see mentioned in the study books.

I sit at the dining table every day and in bed at night, working my way through the exercises. It's been six years since I looked at these subjects, so I need to brush up on everything. Staring at the trigonometry and geometry questions, I want to cry. There are whole areas of study I never had. I'll have to work around them, I finally decide, realizing the futility of trying to teach myself two new branches of math in two weeks. I tell myself the few possible questions won't count much against the overall score. Each question counts for only one point. Better to focus on the easier material I can master.

Please, God, please, please, please let my score be high enough that I don't have to take all those high school courses. Every extra class I must take means more money in tuition before I can study the courses that actually count toward college.

My SAT scores arrive in a thin envelope, and my stomach clenches as I remove the slip of paper. I scored in the 99th percentile for English! *Whew! Thank You, God!* But my lack of geometry brought my math score down to the 82nd percentile. Still, it's good enough to escape all but one remedial math class.

Now, I just have to figure out a way to support myself.

"Bartending is the best way to make money while you are going to school," my aunt declares. "Rick and I both did it in college."

My only experience with alcohol is the occasional glass of wine or beer—and my one wine tasting. "But I don't know how to mix drinks," I protest.

"It's easy," she says, waving her hand.

There's only one bar in the village, a grungy cowboy bar and diner called the Running Iron. The sour smell hits me as I push open the old wood door—a smell I will come to recognize as old beer and dirty washcloths. I squint as my eyes try to adjust to the dim light; a few neon beer signs flash lazily in the corner. *What?!* My wide-open eyes take in the brown cowboy boots and a few dusty bras hanging from the ceiling. *What a waste. I wonder if any of those boots would fit me?*

A florid-looking white man is barking out orders to the hard-bitten waitresses scurrying past. "What can I get you?" he asks me gruffly as I approach the bar.

Drawing my shoulders back to make my 115-pound, five-foot-one-and-a-half frame look more confident, I declare, "I want to bartend."

He speculatively eyes my idea of a professional, job-hunting outfit—a long A-frame black skirt that brushes the tops of my black ankle boots and a long-sleeved, high-neck mustard-color shirt topped with a black buttoned vest.

"How old are you? You look like yer about fifteen."

"I'm twenty-three," I say firmly.

"Well," he drawls, taking his time, "one of my bartenders is going to be leaving. You can shadow her for a couple weeks, learn the ropes—no pay now. But she'll train you. If you do well, you can take over her shifts when she leaves, and I'll hire you. You'll get $8.25 an hour, plus you can keep your tips. How does that sound?"

I'm elated. *Who knew it would be so easy!* "Great! Thank you!"

He smiles like he's won something. "Come back tomorrow at four p.m. and you can start training."

My first afternoon, the bartender I will be taking over from offers me some advice. "Don't ever date anyone you meet in here. All no-good dogs!" she says with venom, eyeing the men sitting on barstools, who are studiously avoiding her gaze.

"I doubt that will be a problem," I say, glancing at the barflies, who are sixty if they are a day. They show up like clockwork at 5:00 p.m. After a week, I've learned their favorite beers—Coors, Bud Light, Budweiser, Sierra Nevada. They're all delighted to have a young woman behind the bar, even if I'm not showing a bit of skin below the neck.

Guys who come to the bar love it when I chat with them and tell them stories about foreign countries, but I soon realize my stories widen the gulf between us. We have no common reference points. They know nothing about these places I've spent my life in, and I know nothing about sports, or the local high schools, or American TV shows, or music bands. I can speak four languages but not the language of American culture. Not yet.

When they ask where I'm from, I find it a hard question to answer. They could mean many things by that. Where were you born? Where do you live? Where did you grow up? Where did you come from right before this place? Or even, what is your heritage and ethnicity? I always debate whether to mention Macau or to just say, "Texas," where my dad is from.

I never mention the Family to anyone; my standard line is both truthful and vague: "I grew up on a farm in Asia. My parents were missionaries and teachers." I'm grateful that I don't have my father's last name, which is famous—no one, not even ex or current Family members, would know my last name and be able to find me. I'd be afraid they would "out" me and I'd have to give long, uncomfortable, and incomplete explanations of a life I'm no longer part of. I just want to find my new way in peace.

I'm longing to make friends, but I don't know where to start. Reading the newspaper, I see an ad for $10 dance classes. That Thursday evening, I show up at 6:00 p.m. for the Intro to Ballroom Dancing class at the local dance studio in Monterey.

As I hesitantly enter the brightly lit dance studio, I notice the group of fifteen people gathered for the dance class are mostly over fifty. *Hmm, perhaps this is not the best place to make new friends.* But the dance instructor is a confident young woman close to my age. She calls me up to demonstrate a dance move with her. We move easily and fluidly together. I may not be professionally trained, but I've been dancing in charity shows my whole life.

We laugh as she spins me, and I sense the twinkle of recognition between two sympathetic souls. This begins a beautiful friendship. She is drawn to my fierce desire to experience everything I've missed out on, to learn and grow. I love her sassy confidence, her deep acceptance of herself and others. She is a warm, loving haven where I can relax. I bring her my drive, vision, and encouragement when she is down. And we both love to dance wild and free, like no one is watching. There is no jealousy or competition between us, unlike most of the girls I've met. We can be ourselves with each other, even though I'm stumbling to figure out who I am.

But even with her, I won't talk about the Family.

Who am I without the Family? What are my desires when no one is telling me what I'm supposed to be and want? What career do I want to have?

These are very difficult questions for me. Unlike most of the people around me, I never had dreams of becoming a firefighter or an astronaut or any profession. I never had the luxury of thinking about what I would be when I grew up. My path was irrevocably set. I would be a missionary until I was martyred in the Tribulation or went up in the Rapture. There was no future to plan for. There were no skills to learn except for the limited things we needed to be able to do in the Family.

I have no idea what I might be interested in or good at. The choices are overwhelming, and I'm scared to make the wrong one and be miserable forever. I know I want to do something to help make the world better, and I need skills to do that. I think I might like to do humanitarian aid work on a much larger scale than what we did in Kazakhstan; it's the only "career" I know other than missionary. I take a career aptitude test, hoping for some guidance, but it's useless. Suggestions range from paralegal *(what's that?)*, to accountant *(snooze)*, teacher *(no thanks)*, and flight attendant *(seriously?)*. I hope I can figure this out in college.

I start classes at Monterey Peninsula College. The Pell Grant is enough to cover a lot of my tuition, but I still need to support myself and pay for insurance, books, and gas. Grandma has given me a little money to buy a cheap car, and while it's a real clunker, it gets me to school and back.

College is one written assignment after another. I loathe writing, remembering the dreadful teen Open-Heart Reports, and these research papers have minimum page counts and unfamiliar rules about content, grammar, and structure. In my homeschool curriculum, I had a few essay assignments, but my mother read them, and she wasn't that critical.

I must force myself to sit down and write each paper. The blank page, the research, creating order out of the confusion of thoughts, and, worst of all, editing. There are so many typos because I'm not trained to hunt them down.

I discover our community college has a writing center in the small library, where a couple of people are willing to help students with their papers before they submit them. I take every paper I write there, get their comments, and revise. Slowly, I improve.

The classes are not as hard as I expect; they just take hours of dedicated effort to learn the material and do assignments. I have the most fun in geology class, studying different rocks: sedimentary, metamorphic, volcanic. I keep bringing new stones to my teacher to identify, but I'm skeptical when he starts talking about the hundreds of millions of years it took to form a rock bed we see on a field trip. I've studied all the Christian arguments debunking evolutionary theory, and I'm not willing to suck down his "facts" like a sap.

"So, you're saying that this sedimentary rock would have taken many millions of years to form based on the current rate of deposition that we see in the river. Is it possible that these many meters of sediment could have been deposited quickly, say, in a massive flash flood?"

"Well, yes—I guess that's possible."

"So how can you be sure it took millions of years?"

"Hmm, well . . ."

While I'm not certain of the seven-day creation theory anymore, I don't want to accept a new theory without investigating it. Why should I just accept another teacher's beliefs as facts, when they can't prove it to me? Are those my only two options? *Why can't teachers just say, "We don't really know. This is our best working model so far, but we can see some holes, some places where the observable evidence doesn't quite fit; so, we are keeping our minds open to discover more"?*

I need to learn more to figure out what to believe.

I interrogate everything and everyone, and it's a new and liberating experience. It's a freedom: the freedom to disagree. Fortunately, my professor enjoys our debates. I suspect he's happy to have a student visibly engaged and not just taking the course to fulfill a requirement.

I'm starting to see that I was trained to not question, so I believed what the Family said, not what they did. While we were taught that men and women were equal in the Family, we were not treated the same. Why were women expected to sacrifice and sleep with men they didn't want to, and it wasn't the same for men? Why did we have to serve and service the men, all the while being told we were equal?

I'm seeing the unfairness of the expectations and messages I was raised with, that to be a good woman meant being feminine, motherly, a servant to others, and that any woman desiring a career, a different role than mother, cook, teacher, singer, or secretary, was uppity or unfeminine.

I don't know what to do with these questions or where to find answers. I don't know how to act around people my age; I have no example of healthy boundaries.

Meanwhile, I'm trying to navigate this new culture. It's different from when I was here at twelve, where, without friends, I was fairly isolated. I am an adult now, on my own, and trying to make sense of all that is being thrown my way.

I make a new friend at the bar, who introduces me to his buddies, four guys in their twenties who become like substitute brothers. As we drive around in their pickup truck, they teach me Californian slang—"phat" and "gnarly"—and we listen to their favorite American bands, including Pink Floyd, Dave Matthews, the Eagles, and I dance to the staccato beat of their hand drums around the fire as they smoke pot.

I mess up often, misreading social cues. Every time I see non-Asians, there is the cultural conditioning to lean in for a kiss on both cheeks like the Portuguese do, but most Americans just shake hands, so I try to catch myself and not to go in for a kiss.

But I'm still used to the Family's culture of affection, and I give exuberant hugs to all my friends, with unintended consequences. I don't understand why one of the guys thinks I like him just because I give him a hug, then when I hug the next, he gets confused, and so on. I try to make it clear that I'm an equal-opportunity hugger.

But some of my sarcastic cracks about men get a response of "Wow, how did you get so cynical?" Resentment I didn't know I had is starting to leak out.

Am I cynical about men? I don't want to be. With five brothers and Patrick as my best friend growing up, I've always felt I understood guys, even got on with them better than I did with women. But I can't shake the conviction that men are just out to take what they can from me.

I also can't shake the anger.

So, I put up my walls. Smiles and hugs are easy, but real intimacy seems impossible. I make it hard for men to get close to me physically. Even out here, with a few guys I went on dates with, I got pressured into sex I didn't want because, in the moment, I didn't think I could refuse. I reverted to my Family training. I was so angry with myself afterward, and with the man for pressuring me, that I almost wanted to avoid them altogether.

But despite my inner turmoil, I'm loving the freedoms that I have now. I know I can never return to the restrictive Family life. I'm going to make it out here.

I spend hours in the library reading and researching four-year colleges, trying to understand what they look for in applicants: straight-A students with leadership skills and extracurricular activities. So, I become the vice-president of the student body and focus on getting all A's.

After yet another Friday evening of campfires and four-wheeling, I realize that the friends I've made don't have the same dreams or ambitions as I do. Through the haze of smoke, they talk about leaving small-town Monterey behind, opening their own businesses, traveling. But instead of working toward those goals, they are barely dragging through their classes, waiting tables, smoking pot, and hanging out.

That won't happen to me, I think. I will attend a prestigious university, to prove to myself and everyone that I'm worth something.

I pass on the pot going around the circle. As far as I can see, marijuana makes my friends want to lay around on the couch eating chips; it clouds their senses. I want my senses crystal clear, so I won't miss out on any part of the new experiences I'm having every day. I want to feel each fully, to make up for all I have missed. I didn't leave the Family to settle. I may not be a genius or have money, but I'm going to see just how far I can go. I have ambition, even if I'm not sure why.

At the end of my first semester at community college, I've moved up from pouring beers a couple of nights a week at the Running Iron to bar manager of the popular new Italian bistro Taste Café in Pacific Grove. Soon, I can afford to move out of Aunt Madeline's home into a two-bedroom apartment I share with a friend.

I make all A's my first semester at community college and apply to five top universities, including Harvard and Stanford, and a few smaller liberal arts colleges, like Claremont. They all respond, asking me to apply again once I have my grades for a full year of school. But when the school year ends and I receive my grades—still all A's—I decide to forgo the previous five and apply to only one school, Georgetown University in Washington, D.C. I'd never heard of Georgetown while living overseas, only Harvard and Yale from movies I'd seen. But when I speak with people about college, over and over I hear "with your international background, you should go to Georgetown." I learn it is a top private Jesuit college and that its School of Foreign Service is among the most competitive in the world.

I'm invited to interview with a Georgetown alumnus who lives in Monterey.

I maintain my commitment to keep my new life separate. I didn't talk about growing up in the Family in my application, even though I thought it could help my chances. Instead, I wrote about transformative travel and my realization in Kazakhstan that bringing humanitarian aid wasn't enough; the people needed a new economic and legal system to be able to help themselves.

My interviewer is very impressed with my résumé. He can't believe that I taught myself high school with a correspondence course, and he's impressed by the years I spent doing volunteer work in Kazakhstan and Taiwan, and studying Mandarin in mainland China. He tells me that my life experiences make me a more interesting and driven candidate than many of their applicants.

Then I wait.

I tell myself not to get my hopes up as I wait for a response. My advisor tells me it's almost unheard of to get into Georgetown as a transfer student from a community college. If I don't get accepted there, I'm confident I can transfer after my sophomore year to a University of California four-year college, since they have agreements with the state community colleges. But inside I am crossing my fingers with all my might. Another semester in this sleepy little town and I'll die of boredom. My friends and I joke that Monterey is for the newly wed or the nearly dead.

When the heavy manila envelope arrives with Georgetown's crest, a thrill goes up my arms. I tear it open and almost scream, "I got in! I got in!"

Not only am I accepted to the toughest Georgetown college, the School of Foreign Service, but I've been given a tuition merit scholarship! I can't wait to tell my family!

Grandad Gene, Grandma, and Aunt Madeline are all thrilled.

I still don't have a cell phone, so I have been speaking to my parents only every few months, even though they are both in the States. Mom finally made it back from Russia. She got married to Ivan, and they're living in Connecticut with Jondy. After eight years, she's finally gotten her online bachelor's degree from Thomas Edison State University and is working on her master's degree at Wesleyan University, where she can take classes at a discount since Ivan is a visiting professor there.

Mom is just as thrilled as her parents and pretty much shrieks in my ear when I tell her. She tells me how proud she is, reminding me that all my hard work and determination paid off. Though I certainly hadn't forgotten, it makes me feel warm inside to hear her say it.

Dad is still living in Texas with Maria, now his wife, and they have a baby. When I tell him, he says, "Well, I'm just concerned about you wasting so much time when our most important job is saving souls. Don't you still want to serve God as a missionary?" I quickly hang up realizing there's no point in trying to convince him.

It's August 2002 when I say my goodbyes to everyone in Monterey and pack all my possessions into my secondhand maroon Honda, which I bought with my bartending money, a huge improvement over my first rickety car. As the morning birds sing, I sit gripping the black steering wheel, preparing myself to drive across the country, only three thousand miles between me and the next step in reaching my goal. When I left the Family two years before, I had no idea where I'd end up. Now, I know exactly where I'm supposed to be.

28

KNOWLEDGE AND TRUTH

It's hot as hell crossing the desert in the middle of summer in a car with no air conditioning. This is dry heat, instead of the humid heat I grew up with, but it still scorches, and I am no stranger to the dangers. People die of heat stroke. I remember my dad's old trick when we ran horses in the steaming tropics. So, all through Arizona, New Mexico, and Texas, I stop off at gas stations to fill little ziplock bags with ice. Back in my car, I wrap the ice in a towel and rest it on my head and the back of my neck to keep my body temperature down.

After a brutal five-day trip, I arrive at the ivy-covered halls of Georgetown University. As I walk across the well-manicured campus, past nineteenth-century Healy Hall's gray stone walls topped with spires, I feel the history in this place. The stately architecture and wood-paneled interiors remind me of the majestic buildings I visited with my grandmother in Europe. I can hardly believe I'm here. *I've made it!* My heart speeds up, and I flush all over before the next thought hits: *I'm an imposter here; I earned A's grading on a curve against community college kids.*

I continue across the lush green lawn to the large red tiles paving the ground in front of the modern Bunn Intercultural Center, a contemporary building mixed in with the old. *Why did they only take the time to create magnificent architecture two hundred years ago? Shouldn't we have gotten better over time, not worse?*

I stare at the new students and their parents as they scurry to and from dorm rooms and campus offices and feel overwhelmed and a little envious. I know nothing about this elite world. And I am on my own. *How can I possibly compete?* I take a deep breath, raise my chin, and head to the admissions office to get my dorm assignment and figure out my classes.

For a sophomore transfer to Georgetown, I luck out. Somehow, through a glitch in the housing lottery, I'm assigned to one of the coveted campus houses: a cute little three-story building with a bedroom at the top, a living room in the middle at street level, and a basement kitchen. My roommate is a Palestinian woman who takes me to one campus party by way of introduction and then moves in with her girlfriend off-campus. Within a week, I have the whole house to myself. I'm twenty-five and living alone for the first time in my life.

I'm six or seven years older than most of my classmates, but I look eighteen. I'm constantly getting my ID checked twice by bartenders. After telling a couple of students my real age and seeing them pull back in shock, I just pretend to be the same age as everyone else in my classes. Let people assume what they will. I want to fit in, not create more distance. I'm already on the outside looking in.

I may look and sound like one of "them"—my accent is almost American—but I'm told that I speak differently.

"When you talk, it's strange," says one of the seniors who lives next door. "Like you're reading from a book. It's so . . . correct."

There's something strange about how I talk? How can I change that when I can't hear myself?

I gravitate toward students who seem to be having an equally difficult time relating to conversations about sports and high school achievements. I often mispronounce big words because I've never heard them spoken, only read them in books. References to most music stars, bands, TV shows, sports, and popular products earn a blank stare. My substitute brothers in Monterey could take my pop culture education only so far.

For my first Halloween party, I dress up as Rebecca from the novel *Ivanhoe*, with a long deep red dress and a black net veil covering my face. *This will be an easy one to guess*, I think, smiling to myself. Nope. Not a single classmate has any idea who I am, even when I tell them. I'm flabbergasted. *Surely, they read Walter Scott in school?* I'm a century out of step.

Eventually, I make friends with a couple of geeky girls, Olga, a brusque Russian student who came to America for high school and stayed to attend university, and Bridget, a shy, big-boned Irish Catholic girl from Boston. One gift of growing up as I did is that I can see past social constructs to who people really are. I don't feel as out of step with other foreigners and nerds, who are even more socially awkward than I am. With this small circle of newfound friends, I begin to experience a little of my missed teenhood—going to parties and dating, sharing study tips. But we are all serious students. I'm not here for a good time.

My tuition scholarship covers the cost of my dorm room and the required health insurance with federal loans. But it does not extend to food and daily essentials. The monthly $100 dollar stipend from Grandad helps me stock frozen dinners, noodle packets, and apples. I get even thinner, but I don't have any pocket money for anything that isn't essential to live. I take a twenty-hour-a-week work-study job that sucks up my afternoons, combined with a full class load in far more demanding courses than community college; I must work smarter, not longer.

At Georgetown, I begin to see America without my programmed filters. I'd grown up learning that America was the evil Babylon, the Whore, but now I see all these idealistic kids who genuinely want to make the world better. These are the people who plan to go into government, with high ideals about liberty, freedom, and justice. But I also see they have no idea about real life outside of America.

Despite the restrictions in the Family, we had firsthand experiences of how the rest of the world lives that most Americans never experience. We were not separated from what went on in the countries we lived in. We ate the cheapest local food, wore local clothes, and lived in local neighborhoods, not expat enclaves. We learned the local customs and languages so we did not offend people and could better reach them with the message of Jesus. We learned about their governments and politics to navigate life safely. We were on the ground, bringing humanitarian aid to the poor and disenfranchised. And we saw the friction created when foreign aid workers tried to implement their programs based on Western culture.

We were out almost daily talking about the problems and struggles of real people: government leaders, beggars, and even mafia bosses. I saw everyone has pain, and everyone wants happiness, love, and good things for their families.

Even the professors seem to be ignorant of the real world as they discuss shuttering the sweatshops in Asia. I know that in many of these countries, if you close the factory sweatshops, the young girls will be forced into prostitution. I've seen the young prostitutes on the streets of Thailand, where the Family has ministries to witness to rescued child sex slaves. *Don't be proud of closing Nike's sweatshops,* I want to tell the International Business professor. *It's better to create incentives for the sweatshops to implement humane conditions.*

But even though they are commenting on policy from their US-centric bubble, their hearts are in the right place. I have not seen this kind of idealism and desire to help the world in the young people of other countries I've lived in. *This is part of what makes America great, why so many people will do anything to come here,* I realize, and I'm grateful to be among them.

To graduate from Georgetown's School of Foreign Service, every student must master a foreign language, and I choose Mandarin. I'm also catching up on requirements in history, and taking political philosophy, which is the only class I actually loathe. I start out eagerly reading the writings of each philosopher, only to be told the following week why that philosopher got it wrong—Plato, Hobbes, Locke, Hume, Rousseau, Kant, Smith. *Why are they teaching us about all these guys who got it wrong? Why don't they jump to the end and educate us about the ones who got it right?* This is a stretch for a mind trained from birth to think in absolutes, where the authority figure gave me the "right" answer. It takes a while to appreciate the ability to analyze and attack each theory.

But the real shock comes in a required class called "The Problem of God." Growing up, I'd always been taught that the Bible was the inspired and perfectly accurate Word of God, literally true in every aspect. Now, I read that multiple councils of churchmen and politicians, who historians admit were more interested in political power than spirituality, decided which writings were the "inspired Word of God" and should be included in the official version of the Bible, and which books, including any written by women, should not.

Grandpa said that God protected His Word so it could come down to us unchanged throughout the last few thousand years. But that didn't fit with what I knew of human nature and reality. So supposedly another group of men in power, priests, were able to translate the Bible perfectly from multiple languages into English, without getting a single word implication wrong? What about the guys who translated the Aramaic into Greek before the English translation?! Even the English translations of the Bible are different! Grandpa claimed the King James Bible was the most accurate, translated by hundreds of priests in 1604 for the new political Church of England. *But how do we know they got that one right?*

Was there never a time when King James might have put his oar in or made a suggestion about how a tricky phrase should be interpreted? Did the misogynist culture or the will of the church in the Middle Ages never affect interpretation?

I also learn that the Bible was written long after the actual events occurred, sometimes hundreds of years, and the stories were initially passed on orally. I've played the game Telephone; I know how much a story can change in just one pass around the circle. My logical mind is at war with my deepest, most foundational beliefs—I feel the internal stress of these contradictions ripping me apart. The familiar comfort of certainty is suddenly gone. *What is true?* I wonder desperately. *How can I know?*

I do my best to ignore my uncertainty. To compartmentalize it. I can't afford to have a spiritual crisis. I have another paper to write, another class to finish. Community college was a vacation cruise compared to the workload at Georgetown. I shelve these questions about my beliefs to think about later.

To keep up with the challenging classes, I pull many long nights in the library and spend a lot of extra time rereading the course materials carefully. My commitment and razor-focus pay off. That first semester, I receive all but one A–, the one B+ coming from political philosophy—I guess the professor didn't like the *Star Trek* reference in my final paper, or perhaps it's because I wrote the final exam paper all night long, bookended by final exams in two other classes. I didn't realize I could move an exam if I have more than two in forty-eight hours.

My routine continues through my sophomore year and into the next. Halfway through my junior year, one of my deans calls me into her office to tell me I have a shot at graduating summa cum laude. I just have to pull off straight A's for the next year and a half. My jaw drops. I never thought I'd be able to compete with kids who'd gone to top-tier high schools and had years of formal education. As soon as I see what's possible, I double down and work even harder. I attend every class, taking detailed notes. When it's time for a test or a paper, instead of spending sleepless nights in the library reviewing all the reading, I regurgitate what the professor talked about in class, which, it turns out, is exactly what they want to hear, just like in my brief grade-school experience. They give you the answers, you learn them, and then they grade you on how well you can recite them with a slightly different flavor.

I have precious little time for fun, and there are times I resent how much harder I must work than many of my peers. I see them driving new cars their parents bought for them and I wish I had that support. But I quickly catch myself. I have something they don't. I know why I'm here, and I appreciate this opportunity in a way they can't understand. I'm going to college not because it is expected of me but because I fought for it. I realize that my parents gave me an important gift. I don't have a prep school education or even a cafeteria card, but I can work my butt off. If I could sweep the village streets until I had blisters on my hands when I was eight years old, I can certainly work long into the night rewriting an assignment until I get it right. Those blisters, too, have worked out to be for my own good.

Studying by myself at my dented metal office desk each morning as a young teen in Macau developed self-discipline. I might not be smarter or have their advantages, but I know I can outwork them, and I will. It's going that last step, when you are already exhausted, that makes the difference. "Stubborn bull," my mom called me; I preferred "determined."

Like many things in life, it just depends on the context.

My only real distraction is Rob, a military man who is attending law school while working for the Justice Department. I meet him one night on my way to a formal dinner for the Institute for the Study of Diplomacy. Though our initial conversation is brief, he is so impressed that I can speak with him in both Mandarin and Russian that he tracks down my email address on the campus system. After he makes several attempts, I finally agree to a date at the

Sequoia, a fancy restaurant on the Potomac River. During the meal, I learn he is a bit of a prodigy, with a résumé of impressive accomplishments at a young age. Though only in his twenties, Rob has already written a book. He speaks with authority on a wide range of topics and has a job, a red Corvette, and his own apartment. We couldn't be more different, but we also discover unexpected similarities. We both had outsized responsibilities as children, grew up with horses, had missionary experience, and understand the value of hard work. He's cute—not exactly my type physically, but intellectually, I've found my match.

After a month and a half of dedicated pursuit on his part, and decorous evasion on mine, we begin to sleep together, but every time we have intercourse, I experience intense pain. When I flinch, Rob doesn't push through, like I'm used to guys doing; he stops and asks what's wrong. I tell him it's fine, that I always have pain during intercourse, but Rob refuses to accept this rationalization. This isn't okay, he tells me. This isn't normal.

With his patience and care, I begin to understand my body. Slowly, I feel myself responding in new ways. He shows me the wonderful world of cunnilingus, which Grandpa had decried as dirty. I learn my body needs this to lubricate properly, so I don't experience pain. Eventually, sex becomes truly enjoyable.

Rob becomes my companion, friend, and lover, but still I'm holding back. About six months into our relationship, he begins asking more pointed, persistent questions about my background. His parents, Seventh-Day Adventists, want more information about the woman he's dating. I hate to lie directly; most people are satisfied with my canned response of "My parents were nondenominational Christian missionaries and volunteer workers." But from things I've let slip, he knows there's more. He's my boyfriend. I'm closer to him than anyone I've met since leaving the Family. *Perhaps I can trust him with the truth and reveal the secret I've kept for the last three years.*

After I finally tell him, Rob looks up the Children of God and finds a thick government file, complete with various conspiracy theories I've never even heard of. As an employee of the Justice Department, he is freaked out. He has a temper, and he loses it, yelling at me, accusing me of compromising his security clearance. He wonders if he needs to contact the government to report himself and me. I'm crying, trying to calm him down, but he won't stop yelling. I assure him I'm not in the Family anymore. I left three years ago. I have no designs on infiltrating the government for the Family, or any other conspiracy theory. The more he shouts, the more I shut down. The end of the relationship seems imminent, and I crumple up on my bed, scared and angry.

The next time we speak, I'm prepared for Rob to say goodbye, but he does something entirely unexpected: he pulls me closer to him. Part bully, part confidant, he pushes and pulls, dragging things out of me like the military-trained interrogator he is. I'd been taught to keep anything about the Family's nonconformist beliefs and sexual practices secret on pain of death. I was taught that if I talked, the Antichrist forces would kill me or the government would throw me in jail. Even though I now know this is not true, speaking still feels like a betrayal. My ingrained childhood training and fear are hard to overcome. But Rob pulls the stories out of me, slowly, one at a time. I begin small, revealing my childhood encounters with Uncle T and Uncle Steven, and then I go deeper, into Benji and Uncle John. I cry, which is horribly embarrassing, and compensate with jokes, trying to make light of it all.

Rob is furious on my behalf. Seeing how upset my stories make him helps me understand just how bad it was. I knew there were things that happened to me that gave me a terrible feeling in my gut, but I thought the problem was with me, that I wasn't yielded enough to God or sacrificial enough. He tells me that it wasn't my fault, that I don't need to carry that shame.

Rob is pushing me to see things through a new lens. Seventh-Day

Adventists believe that you must keep the Ten Commandments to be saved, as well as believe in Jesus. This doesn't make sense to me; no one is perfect.

I speak with conviction as I show Rob verse after verse about the Law of Love and the end of the Ten Commandments. He counters with other verses about the endurance of the law of Moses. My mind spins. *Perhaps what Jesus meant when He said "the end of law" meant the end of the hundreds of Old Testament Jewish laws, but not the Ten Commandments that were given to Moses on the mountain?* I didn't know.

To see if this theory could be right, I use the summer break before my senior year to research every verse that talks about "the law" in the Bible. Did the original biblical verses use a different Hebrew or Greek word for "law" when referring to the Ten Commandments than to the extended Torah law by the Pharisees? How could I tell if one law had passed away and another endured? There were so many contradictions. I spend days with an online Bible CD, searching terms and translations. I also look at all the verses that the Family used to justify the Law of Love. When I reread the various translations complete with the historical context, I must admit they mean something completely different. *But then what did I experience in the Family?*

Rob explains that being told to have sex with men I didn't want to was not love; it was rape. In criminal law, you don't have to physically hold someone down for it to be rape. Compelling someone to have sex when they don't want to through coercion and fear of punishment is also rape.

I think back to the Family. I was never afraid that a Family guy would rape me by force. He would be excommunicated. All sex was supposed to be consensual and loving. But of course, no man in the Family would need to use force, because a woman would be obligated to agree to have sex if he asked her. And even without physical force, it was incredibly painful to have to "willingly" have sex with a man, because I was afraid of punishment.

But—was I ever coerced? The Shepherds never said, "Have sex when you are asked, or you'll be punished." The pressure was more subtle, like what I experienced in Kazakhstan. If I was unwilling to sacrifice my body and have sex with someone I disliked, it was a "symptom" of my lack of dedication to Jesus and my unyieldedness. Technically, I was never punished for not having sex; I was punished for being unyielded when I refused sex. *So, wasn't that the same thing?*

I think back to that horrible night with Uncle John and realize the word "rape" never crossed my mind. Now I recognize it for what it was. Even though he didn't hold me down, he was still psychologically forcing me to have sex when I didn't want to, after I'd declined, so it was rape. Even if I had to pretend to be willing, it was rape. Even if I was frozen and unable to think of a way to escape, it was rape. I didn't shout, "No!" and fight back with force, because like many women, I was conditioned from birth to be submissive, obedient, and pleasing.

My eyes are finally open, and I can see that the coercion I experienced was a violation of my body and mind, all excused by the lie of obeying "God's will." The Law of Love was an excuse for a great deal of abuse.

I feel like I'm falling into a black hole and watching everything I thought I knew turn into wispy nothingness. When I left the Family, it wasn't because I believed the Family was wrong; it was because I longed for independence and my mind thirsted for knowledge like water in a sun-parched desert.

Now, I'm trying to make sense of a world view flipped on its head and reprocess my memories through a new perspective.

I turn to Rob for advice. He tells me I can find the answers I'm looking for with the Seventh-Day Adventists. His family are strict practitioners, and he, too, is a true believer. I listen as he explains the tenets, but the more he lectures me, the more I notice a familiar militant attitude, though very different from the Family in many ways: his doctrine prohibits jewelry and makeup as well as the consumption of meat and alcohol—not to mention no sex before marriage.

He tells me he'd like to introduce me to his parents, as a good example of a healthy, loving, long-term relationship. Yet despite his devotion, Rob explains that he's strayed from the path, and so out of respect or intimidation, he asks me to lie to his parents about everything we are doing—eating meat, drinking alcohol, and having sex before marriage, none of which I consider morally wrong.

At first, I go along with him, hiding when his parents show up, running around the house to conceal wine bottles and hotdog buns. But while part of me has been trained to be compliant, another part of me is learning to rebel. I don't want to fall into another trap. I love Rob, but isn't he just one more person trying to impose his beliefs? I didn't fight for independence to go back into hiding or ask permission from someone else. I'm in a struggle between my mind and my heart. But I'm starting to listen to my inner voice, to question things that don't feel right, to fight back.

I slowly realize that I've made the classic move of dating someone like my father: a teacher, preacher, youth prodigy, hard worker, someone who is dynamic, good with people, grew up with horses, confident, and controlling with a trigger temper. Even the pain is familiar and comfortable. As I grow more confident, Rob can't seem to release the role of teacher. The very security and intellectual authority that attracted me to him starts to feel like rough ropes on raw skin. Neither fear nor love is incentive enough to stay bound. Eventually, I end our romantic relationship, choosing to remain friends.

29

NEVER GIVE UP

I travel back to Monterey for Christmas break. Just six months after I left for Georgetown, Aunt Madeline moved Grandma into a nursing home there. Mom, Ivan, and Jondy also moved there for my mother's new job and to be near Grandma in her declining years, so it's a little epicenter of family that makes visiting easier. My sister Nina is not with them. She has chosen to remain in the Family and moved into a Home in Portland, Oregon. My mom says that at sixteen, she's old enough to make her own decisions.

Since I've come back to the US, I've made a point of getting to know my blood relatives. I need roots, and I want to make up for missing out on those years. I spend Thanksgivings with Grandad and Barbara and Christmases in Monterey at Aunt Madeline's house.

Over a glass of wine, I tell my mom that I've studied the scriptures in their original context, and I no longer believe Grandpa's teachings that "God's only law is love" means that we were supposed to give men sex or that Flirty Fishing was condoned by the Bible. I watch for a reaction, but her expression does not change.

"Yes. Well, that was the revelation, the new wine," she replies. "Strong meat is for adults, and milk is for babes."

It's a classic Family line meaning that the interpretations of the Bible that are easy to accept are like milk for babies, and the shocking new revelations are only for adults who are strong enough not to doubt God's word.

I describe what I've learned, the reality of what happened to me in the Family, that submitting to sex when I didn't want to was rape. She grows visibly uncomfortable, wide-eyed and fidgety. She may have left the Family nearly five years before, but she is not ready to let go of the dream that "Love is everything. Anything done in love is clean and good with God."

"The message was right; it was just executed poorly," she argues.

Closing my eyes, I take a deep breath and smother the scream inside me. Once I've mastered myself, I clearly and calmly share my reasoning. The longer I speak, the more my anger changes to pity. I think, *If I lived my entire adult life and gave everything for something that turned out to be a lie, would I want to face it? Or would it be easier to live in the illusion as long as I could?*

I don't attack her or even ask for an apology.

I explain my reasoning and leave it at that.

When I return to Georgetown for my senior year, I decide to live with six other students on the Jewish dorm floor. On my trip to Monterey, I learned that my mother's family has Jewish ancestors going back to Rabbi Koppel in Poland in 1789. My great-great-grandfather Louis Smadbeck was written about in a book called *Jews of the West* for inventing a copper smelting technique to help the Arizona miners. I want to get in touch with my ancestral roots and begin attending Shabbat and observe Yom Kippur services. But once again, I'm an outsider. I know all the Bible stories, but none of the heritage songs and traditions.

And I still wrestle with unresolved questions from my own religious upbringing. After all my research and conversations with Mom and Rob, I'm still on my own, reeling with information and yet at a loss for answers. *What was real, and what was a lie?*

Even after all I'm discovering, my mind resists taking that last step. I can't disavow Grandpa. *Okay,* I rationalize. *So maybe Grandpa got it wrong. Lots of people and churches have misinterpreted the Bible from the beginning of Christianity. It doesn't make them bad people, just incorrect.*

Since leaving the Family, I have purposely avoided communicating with current and ex-members, aside from my blood relatives. I don't go on the ex-member website or join online groups or even try to find old friends. I don't want to be trapped into religious arguments or sucked into a whirlpool of anger and bitterness. I just want to make something good of my life, and it takes all my energy to focus on the positive and move forward. The occasional contact I have with my older siblings who are still in the Family allows some news to filter through.

I'd heard a whisper that Davidito—the prince, the model disciple touted by Grandpa as one of the final prophets of the End Time, who, as described in the Book of Revelation, would call down fire on the Antichrist—had left the Family. But I'm not prepared for the email I receive from Aaron on January 16, 2005: "Check the news, Faith. It's about Davidito."

I do a quick search online and read that twenty-nine-year-old Davidito has fatally stabbed his former nanny before turning a gun on himself.

I can't believe it. The Family has always boasted about how we had the best young people in the world—well-adjusted, mature, happy, and dedicated. "A good tree cannot bear bad fruit, and a bad tree cannot bear good fruit" Matthew 7:18. The violence seems too horrific to be true.

But the story is all over the news. According to the article in the *New York Times*, Davidito had invited his former nanny to dinner in Tucson, Arizona. After the meal, he asked her back to his apartment, where he stabbed her to death. He then drove his Chevy to the small desert town of Blythe, California, where he shot himself with a semiautomatic handgun, but not before making a video about it and calling his wife to explain what he had done.

To keep the Family from putting their own spin on events, he had released the video of himself loading the weapons and discussing why his mother, Mama Maria, had to be stopped. I would later learn that Davidito had apparently extended the dinner invitation to her, but she'd sent the nanny instead. He considered them all guilty, so he went ahead with the attack he'd planned.

It is unfathomable to me how anyone could do such a thing, much less Davidito, whose child-rearing years had been chronicled in *The Story of Davidito* and hundreds of *Komics* we'd all read growing up. *How could this happen?*

In an open letter to the Family, he accuses his mother and nannies of years of molestation. "Something has to be done about these child molesters," he writes. "Because only then can we feel some semblance of justice." Reading his words feels like a punch to my chest.

My entire life, I'd been trained to dismiss and excuse the things that people said and wrote about Grandpa as the bitter lies of Backsliders. And I'm horrified to realize I'd still been doing it. But when I read Davidito's description of his life in Grandpa's home, in his own words, I hear the ring of truth. His stories are impossible to deny, and I can feel the smoke screen of holiness clearing.

If the Family and Grandpa were right, this should not have been possible. I know what the Family will say as clearly as if someone were reading me the explanatory Mo Letter: "This shows the terrible things that can happen when someone leaves the Family and rebels against God. Goes to show that no one is safe, so don't let the Devil cause you to doubt for even a minute." But that sounds like so much hot air now.

For the first time, I'm able to consciously acknowledge that my grandfather was evil and perverted. *How traumatized must Davidito have felt to think this was his only option?* I can't agree with the murder, but I mourn for the sad, trapped young man I'd tried to cheer up in a Moscow apartment a lifetime ago. I feel deeply sorry for

Davidito, both for the little boy who was so traumatized by years of abuse and for the young man who believed the only way out of his ongoing nightmare was death. If only someone had been able to show him another way forward.

In light of this new and disturbing perspective, other life stories begin rearranging themselves in my mind with new meanings. I think back on my own early sexual experiences. *Were they child abuse?* According to society's definition, certainly. But whose standard for morality is correct? Grandpa pointed to countries where the age of consent is twelve as justification for his views, but having lived the experiences, I couldn't agree.

How did I feel when it happened to me? I examine my own experiences. I didn't feel traumatized by my mother's openness about sex, just embarrassed, though now, I certainly question whether it was age-appropriate. I can logically see that sex is a natural function of life and teaching children to accept it as such, without shame about their bodies, must be correct. But I recognize the sick feeling I had any time an adult touched me in a sexual way, when they pushed into my space, anytime I was pressured, *at any age*, to engage in sex, as trauma. I never felt that with the innocent sex games I played with Patrick at naptime when we were five. Why? Where is the line?

I think about my peers. All the girls I know who are my age and who were subjected to adult-child contact in the Family reported that they felt traumatized, while most of my brothers claimed they enjoyed their early sexual experiences. Do boys have such a different relationship with sex than girls? Is it the simple biological facts of intercourse that make a difference—penetrating or being penetrated? What about when there's no penetration? I know boys raped by men experience the same trauma, but I've also met men who feel enormous shame from an adult woman engaging them in sexual acts at a young age. What is the thread that creates trauma? I realize trying to come up with a standard based on individual experiences is too vague.

But if we cannot find an accurate answer, how can we prevent more abuse?

Twenty-three years of indoctrination doesn't disappear in an instant. In the few years since I'd left the Family, I had been unconsciously building an entirely new frame of reference for behavior, morality, and reality—a new mental model of the world. Davidito's closing act allows me to finally put it all together, to understand that so much of what I was taught were lies. That my childhood was taken from me, that I was violated. The tightness in my chest travels down my arms; I want to punch something. Hard. I can't understand how my parents could have done this to me when they both experienced another way growing up.

Hadn't they been raised in a world where sexual relations with children were viewed with horror and aberration? How could they be complicit in this?

But my anger is tempered by my recognition that lies aren't always intentional, and that you don't have to be conscious that you're doing something wrong to *be* wrong. A person can fully believe in the justice and Godliness of their cause and be horrifically, violently wrong. Abusers can believe they are acting out of "love."

The guise of love and freedom and nature is a beautiful smoke screen that often masks violations and manipulation.

I have a new understanding of the world and a void in my stomach. *How can I trust anyone, even myself, ever again?*

I was taught that the System was the matrix and we, the Family, lived the reality; but the Family was just another matrix with its own myths.

My world has turned upside down, but it hasn't stopped. Final exams are racing toward me, and I refuse to let the trauma of my past destroy my future. This is everything I've been working toward for five years. I've gotten straight A's in every class for the last year and a half. One more hurdle left to see if I'll make summa cum laude.

I spend the remaining weeks of the schoolyear vacillating between feeling angry, exhilarated, and overwhelmed, culminating in a busy week of final exams. When the grades are due to be posted, I race to my room and sit glued to my computer, clicking refresh, refresh, refresh.

I check the online campus system one more time and see that yes, my final grades are up! I receive all A's—and one A– in Management of Multinational Enterprises. My heart drops, but my disappointment is instantly replaced by determination. I've worked so hard to make summa cum laude. I'm *not* going to be defeated now.

I march to my professor's office and knock on his door. When he answers, I don't waste any time and lay it out: he gave me an A–, but I deserve an A.

We've discussed his marks before. He likes to take off half points for misusing hyphenated words and refuses to change those marks despite my providing spelling evidence to the contrary.

With a sigh my professor tells me, "Kids come to me about this all the time and I've never changed a grade for a student, but you're welcome to try to prove me wrong only regarding substantive content, not grammar."

I turn on my heel and head straight to my room. That night, I dig out every single one of my old papers and exams. I hunt through every debatable mark he's ever given me, and then I find a citation in the assigned reading to support my work. Like Churchill, *I'm not giving in.*

I return to the professor's office with the evidence. Now that I've found my voice, I refuse to silently accept injustice. I show him each place he marked me wrong where what I wrote on the exam was in the textbook. His skepticism melts into reluctant admiration, as, point after point, he concedes that I'm correct. As he tallies the minor grade changes, he looks up in surprise. "Well, I'd never believe it, but you're right. You did get an A."

I walk out of his office exultant. I did it! I'm graduating summa cum laude.

Grandad and Barbara fly in from Indiana and Mom flies in from California to attend my college graduation. It fills my heart to celebrate this momentous occasion with them. I've felt so alone through the struggles of this journey. I'm glad they will be here to share in my victory.

I'm most surprised that my father shows up. Our few phone calls had always ended with him advising me to give up this "waste of time and money" and go back to be being a missionary. His presence means more to me than I'll admit, even to myself. My dad still lives in Houston. He now has four children with Maria—at last count, I have thirteen siblings from him—and works with Chinese churches, often living off the kindness of others, and sometimes doing construction work. He has been cut off from the Family financially—never given an explanation, he just simply stopped receiving his monthly stipend.

In the rush of all the college ceremonies I'm required to attend, it's hard to find any quiet time to catch up with him and the rest of my family, and I don't really try. My revelations are still too raw, and my thoughts are too confused for me to debate them with my parents. I will deal with them later, when I can understand them better.

I'm being honored with multiple academic awards, including the medal for exceptional achievement in my major, which my dean tells me they don't give out every year, only when the committee determines a student is worthy.

As my father attends the various award ceremonies, he recognizes for the first time that I've done something big. He puffs up, proud as a peacock, boasting about me to everyone. It's nice to hear, but I don't need his affirmation anymore. I knew what I was fighting for.

30

THE TRUTH WILL SET YOU FREE

I don't have much time to enjoy my victory. After graduation, I pack everything I own into a U-Haul and head back across the country to Berkeley, California, where I have been accepted to UC Berkeley School of Law. There are no scholarships, but at least I can get loans.

I'm not particularly excited to go to law school. It's a practical decision motivated by self-protection, not discovering what I truly love. My greatest fear as a teen was becoming a single mother, destitute and unable to care for myself and my baby. I'd thought that college would ensure that that could never happen, but midway through my senior year, I'd realized too late that college didn't translate directly into a job with a good income. Worse, after four years, I still didn't know what profession suited me. All I knew is that I didn't want to be a teacher. *Been there; done that.* So, master's degrees were out. An MBA seemed to be more about networking than learning, and it still didn't guarantee a job at the end. That didn't seem very secure to me.

After reading countless career books and looking at advanced-degree programs, I decide on law school. A lawyer is a profession with a skill set, like a plumber. With a law degree, I could always hang out a shingle and make a living, no matter where I ended up. My choice is about survival, not passion.

I'm delighted with the camaraderie of my classmates. I decide that I will still study hard, but I won't stress over every grade like I did as an undergraduate. I'm going to enjoy myself more, say yes to drinks, and balance schoolwork with fun. I'm going to get a little younger.

My enlightenment begins in a contracts class, in which I come to appreciate how the law runs every area of our lives, regulating everything from garage ticket stubs to home ownership to marriage.

The teacher pounds into us the five elements of an enforceable contract or agreement.

1. Offer with a clear object—the parties must understand the terms of the deal.
2. Acceptance.
3. Exchange of value. Both sides must provide value or it's a gift, not a deal.
4. Mental ability—children and people with mental incapacity cannot contract because they must be able to appreciate the consequences of their agreement.
5. No undue pressure—using pressure to force someone to do something is blackmail.

What I thought would bore me is fascinating because it's all practical; it's how the world runs. *How do regular people live without knowing how this works? They'd get screwed every day.*

The law revolutionizes the way I see the world. More than learning the law itself, I'm learning to think like a lawyer, the principles of critical and analytical thinking—how to pick apart arguments, base them in facts, and spin facts to suit a theory. It all helps me to understand what leaders, groups, and societies do to build an ideology and defend a point of view.

I turn thirty in law school, but most people don't know. I feel, act, and look like I'm in my early twenties, like most of my peers. And just like in college, I never mention the Family. The strange thing is, the more I pretend to belong, the more I feel like I might actually belong. My classmates and I are experiencing all these new things together for the first time, and in some areas I'm far more mature, in others more innocent. We all stress over our grades, debate the ethics of judicial decisions, and compete for summer law firm internships. Although Berkeley Law School has even lower acceptance rates than Harvard Law, we don't have the cutthroat competitiveness of the East Coast schools. We form study pods, share notes, and go for beers after finals. I don't have the traditional school backpack mentality or shoulder strength, so I start a new trend of using wheely bags for heavy law textbooks. Everyone laughs at me the first semester, but by the next semester it's caught on.

I dig into classes on the development of the legal system in China, and I organize the first law school delegation to the National People's Congress. But my favorite activity is during my last semester of law school, which I spend as a Hansard Fellow and intern at the British Parliament in London, writing a paper comparing the political systems of China, the United Kingdom, and the United States through the lens of their supreme courts and rule of law. It's fascinating to see how the position of the high court among the branches of government affects the entire political ethos.

The time passes in a beautiful blur, exceptional in its normality. I can make enough money as a law firm intern in the summers to live on during the school year if I'm very careful, so I don't have the added burden of work with a full class load. My body, always strung so tight, can relax just the tiniest bit. Georgetown may have sharpened my mind, but Berkeley rounds me out as a person.

After I graduate, I start my first professional job as a lawyer at Skadden, Arps in Los Angeles, one of the top international law firms. When my first paycheck arrives, I see just how far I've come from canning in parking lots. The starting salary of $175,000 is more money than my dad made in ten years.

I'm earning good money, and though the work is intense and

stressful, the freedom of not scrimping, of being able to afford my own apartment, a decent car, and non–thrift store clothes is exhilarating. It gives me a new sense of independence and value—and an ability to stand up for myself. I'm doing international mergers-and-acquisitions (M&A) worth billions of dollars, including the sale of Skype in 2009, valued at $2.75 billion.

After a couple of years in the Los Angeles office, I'm sent to Hong Kong, where my knowledge of the Chinese language and culture can be put to good use. But despite enjoying a great salary and first-class flights and fine dining, something is missing. I want to do work that's meaningful, to build something of my own, not just push papers for multinational companies.

At the end of 2012, I move from Skadden, Arps Hong Kong to a smaller California firm, where I head their corporate law practice, and then, in 2018, I open my own corporate law practice as outside general counsel for select clients.

I love solving problems and helping my clients achieve their goals, but I also have a nagging feeling that I haven't yet achieved my own goal. There's something bigger that I still need to do, but the answers are buried deep in my mind, under layers of dust, blocked off with caution tape.

When I left Skadden, I begin my personal quest in earnest. I voraciously read self-help books and attended seminars—to understand, to heal, to separate the truth from the lies in what I was taught in the Family and in the world around me.

I read Alice Miller's *The Drama of the Gifted Child*, and immediately recognized myself and many people I knew by the characteristics we develop as coping mechanisms from abuse. But mostly, her insights help me understand what can happen with parents who physically beat, or even sexually abuse, their children. The book describes how people who think of themselves as "good" can dole out violent spankings or other forms of child abuse without empathy. According to Miller, when some people experience abuse as children, they cut off their own self-empathy, so they cannot feel empathy for the person they are abusing in return.

Imagine being in the body of a small baby smacked for the first time—the fear, shock, horror, anger, and violation of her whole be-ing. In a baby, all those negative emotions must be sublimated and cut off because that child must love the perpetrator of violence in order to stay alive. That person is their sole source of survival. The only hope is to break the cycle through reconnection to that small inner child as an adult.

Gasping, I realize that despite my outward success, I'm still using the same coping mechanism I used as a child. I'm still sublimating and cutting off my emotions—but it's no longer because I need my abuser. My survival instinct has driven me to snuff out my feelings, to be dependent on no one, to be invulnerable.

I feel the walls I've constructed around myself begin to shake, as if someone's removed a small but foundational block from be-neath my feet. Since leaving the Family, I've seen vulnerability as a weakness. Hadn't my life experiences demonstrated over and over that whenever I'm vulnerable, I end up abused and raped? When I yield and let down my barriers, hasn't someone always used it to manipulate and hurt me? To protect myself, I've built a fortress. I've become financially and emotionally independent. I've thrown up shields of positivity and logic. I've looked forward, not back.

But has this helped? I've continued to be pressured into things I don't want, including sex. I either keep men out or let them walk all over me. Longing for connection and then reacting to feeling taken advantage of, I close off my heart until I can be more callous than the person I'm with. Vulnerability no longer feels like a choice, but an inability.

Realization slices through me. *How can I have the love I desire with all my being if I cannot be vulnerable, if I cannot let people in and give them the power to hurt me again?*

I must deal with my wounds.

I have three tools to start with. One is knowing that no one is coming to help. No matter what anyone has done to me in the past, I am the only one who can do anything about it now. I alone am responsible for my happiness and success and healing.

The second is the conviction that I don't have to be broken, that healing is possible, and I am going to figure out how. I believe we are not here to suffer; we are here to grow—to find a way to heal and be happy and whole, despite the pain we encounter.

The third is the knowledge that I am not helpless; I can always act. I do not have all power, but neither am I powerless. I always have the power to change what I'm experiencing in any moment by focusing my attention on something good, and I can always choose to do so.

With these tools, I journey on the long road to healing. It's the beginning of a new kind of openness to love and pain and fear and fulfillment. My tools don't protect me from getting hurt, but they show me I always have a way to get better.

It takes my parents more than a decade after leaving the Family before they are willing and able to admit they were wrong and apologize to me for the abuses I suffered in the Family. My parents were always horrified by any accusation of child abuse in the news media. They saw themselves as loving, Godly parents doing everything in their power to raise Godly children. But I see it's how they defined child abuse that makes all the difference.

My dad apologizes to me and his other older kids for the harsh spankings and punishments we received when we were younger. Some forgive him, some don't.

He is a product of his upbringing, and there are many ways he still struggles from that. He never finished high school, had a formal paycheck, or held a job, and he can't break the cycle of poverty mindset. He and Maria divorced after six years, so he's a senior citizen with no income, living in a camper and raising four small children on social security. But his positive attitude of faith in God's ability to provide never falters. He has gone back to the church and is very still entrenched in the Bible and Jesus, but from a more traditional perspective. With the benefit of hindsight, his youngest children experience a more mellow, loving father than the one we grew up with.

My mom similarly comes around. For years after we returned to the US, she and I spoke only every couple of months. She needed space to really examine her life and be able to recognize that her long-cherished beliefs were wrong and damaging to her kids. Davidito's murder/suicide shook her up and helped her to reexamine things. The woman he killed had been her friend in her early days with the Family in Europe.

In time, she apologizes to me and my siblings. "I just want you to know that I'm so sorry for what happened to you. I'm sorry for what happened in the Family. I can see now that a lot of that was really wrong," she says.

Despite everything, I applaud her for creating a new life for herself after she left the Family in her fifties, which few older-generation Family members did. She went back to school and earned a master's degree and got a stable job as a language course editor, which she held for twenty years, socking away every cent she could into her 401(k) to provide for herself in retirement. When she was deciding to leave Dad and the Family for Ivan, her mother told her, "After I divorced your father, every time I took on something new and accomplished it, it gave me the strength to take the next step. It will be the same with you." My grandmother's words have proven true for both of us.

My mother is smart and loves to learn and is willing to change. She has an excitement about life and new things and new challenges, no matter her age. This openness to learn has allowed us to grow together in the last few years. I'm able to share therapeutic processes with her that have helped me, and she uses them to heal. We have honest talks about what happened in the Family and our new perspectives. So, it's never too late.

Esther was the most dedicated disciple of all and never really left the Family. For thousands like her, the Family just disintegrated around them. In 2010, Mama Maria ended the communal living mandate, effectively disbanding Family Homes, leaving thousands of people nearing retirement destitute with no way to support themselves in their old age. For forty years, disciples were taught to never think about the future, but "be like the flowers and birds, who don't sow or reap," or save for retirement; they just expected that God would take care of them. Many former Family members in their seventies are left to live off meager social security benefits in mobile homes. While some of the young people born into the Family have managed to go back to school, many continue to struggle to overcome feelings of inferiority caused by their early lack of education.

Over the years, more of my siblings and their families settle in Texas. Most don't decide to leave the Family; they just drift into greater independence. They are all doing their best to make their way in a world they were ill-prepared for. They have successes and failures and struggle with health issues, divorce, and financial setbacks and advances like most people.

As I discovered, there are stages of unraveling a strong indoctrination, and that can be the hardest journey. Some of my siblings still maintain Family beliefs, while others reverted to more fundamentalist church beliefs and laugh at the Family's extreme doctrines. A few are on the journey of true questioning—the hardest path of all—where one is willing to recognize that everything they believe might be a lie.

The only way to logically determine what, if anything, is actually true is to be open to the possibility that none of it is. If it's true, you don't have to protect it—questioning it deeply only reveals more and strengthens it.

My parents tried harder than most to be good parents and good people, but this is the danger when you believe something false: you will act in ways that harm and violate others, even if you intend to do good. This is why we must actively check our most cherished beliefs against logic, against an accurate standard.

Our beliefs are mental chains that have been forged over generations. It is uncomfortable for us to question and test them with logic and discover that the conclusions that seemed unbreakable are made of clay, not iron, that crumbles with the slightest tap of the hammer of logic. I have not finished my quest for truth—it is continuous and joyous. Old ideas crumble as new truths are revealed through rigorous questioning.

I feel like I started life as an old lady. I was robbed of my teen hood, and by the time I was seventeen, I thought I knew everything about everything. But in the words of Albert Einstein, "The more I learn, the more I realize how much I don't know." Now the world has become a massive amusement park filled with unlimited knowledge and experience. With endless opportunities, I keep getting younger.

And most importantly, even though I still deal with the repercussions, I'm truly grateful for every single experience. Without them, I wouldn't have had the understanding I needed to create the framework that answers the questions that plagued me for years.

All things did work together for my good, but not automatically. I had to choose to create good from it and turn my traumas into strength.

I Own Me

I place my silver high-heeled pump on the makeshift black wooden step leading out onto the TEDx stage and pause to draw in a deep, calming breath. *You can do this,* my forty-one-year-old-self repeats silently. I ignore the little girl inside my head screaming, *Don't do it! You've been keeping this secret for almost two decades. Walk out on that stage and tell your story, and you can never take it back. They will attack you!*

I take another deep breath and imagine giving my scared inner child a big hug. *We'll be fine.* I don't want to tell the story I'm going to open with. I hate talking about being abused. I don't want anyone pitying me or thinking, *There's that weird cult kid. Poor thing, she must be so messed up.*

But to show the importance of what I've discovered, I have to tell this story, as painful as it is. In the nearly twenty years since I've left the Family, I've kept my past a secret from all but a handful of people and done everything I could to succeed and fit into society. I've wanted people to see the person I'd made of myself: the classy, strong, and happy woman I've become—not a victim of a past I could not choose or change.

During that time, I've pondered what went wrong. My family created a whole new society in their quest to be the perfect Christian disciples. *How could incredibly idealistic, fairly smart people engage in and submit to these terrible abuses? How could people claiming to hear from God and dedicating their entire lives to serving humanity inflict such harm on their children?*

I knew my grandfather made the typical mistakes of the guru.

He believed his own press that he was the divinely anointed prophet of God for the End Time. If he was the mouthpiece of God, then his ideas and inclinations were justified as Godly or at least excusable. He surrounded himself with sycophants and yes-people, most notably his second wife, Maria, who encouraged his most outlandish ideas and depravity. He cut himself off from anyone, including his children, who might have challenged his new doctrines.

Rooted in the patriarchal, religious model of control, he was not content to just give his message. He used sophisticated methods, employed by communist revolutions, like self-criticism and public approval or reprimand, to manipulate his followers' daily lives for "their own good." This way, he perpetrated his evil on thousands of his followers, among them countless children, as God's revealed truth.

He accentuated the us vs. them mentality to isolate his followers from outside influence, conditioning them to distrust outsiders as liars and evil so Family members would dismiss inconsistent viewpoints. He made sure people could not acquire enough resources, so they remained dependent economically on the group.

He normalized practices and beliefs that were viewed as aberrant by traditional society (though still widely practiced, like child abuse), by flooding people with images and content that gradually made it less shocking, then accepted, over time. He used the elite mentality to get his followers to isolate themselves into a controlled environment where those practices and beliefs could flourish, unchecked by mainstream disapproval.

I might add that he was not as creative as I once gave him credit for. He drew from the beliefs and attitudes prevalent in his time and gave them his own flair—beliefs that I still find in segments of society today, everything from the subjugation of women, polygamy, the End Time, corporeal punishment, and free sex.

Sifting through these ideas helped me understand a lot about how my grandfather was able to have such power over people, but I still needed to get to the core—the seed of corruption that twisted good intention into abuse.

Particularly because as I talk with my "normal" friends, I start to see how prevalent sexual abuse against women and children is in all levels of society. It is a secret no one wants to look at, or, perhaps, are too afraid to see. Even my mother, one of my sisters, and I had all been the victims of forcible rape in "normal" society.

In May 2018, I finally discovered it.

My life experiences and legal education come together in my personal eureka moment.

I pull out a piece of blank paper and a pen and draw the first circle.

"Aware," I write in the center—I am an aware, conscious being.

I draw a second circle around the first.

"Body," I label it. I own my body. This is my most fundamental right.

I, as an aware, conscious being, spirit, whatever you prefer to call it, have a property right in my own body. To use a legal term, my body is my property. Some people bristle at applying the word "property" to the human body because they feel that it demeans the nature of the body; but for me, this designation brings immediate clarity.

From my legal background, I understand that the term "property" doesn't apply only to inanimate objects or land; it is *anything that has value*, tangible or intangible. But more importantly, I understand the implications of property ownership far better than I do my relationship to my own body.

I also see the unique position the body holds in the category of "property." Unlike other types of "property," such as inanimate

objects, we can never give up our fundamental right of ownership in our body so long as we are alive. It is an inalienable right,
meaning we cannot be separated from it, it cannot be taken from
us, and we cannot give it away.

Without this right of ownership of our own bodies, there would
be no moral wrong in slavery, rape, or murder. This is the principle
those famous freedom fighters were trying to articulate when they
proclaimed that we have the "right to Life, Liberty, and the pursuit
of Happiness." They said to King George III, "You don't own me! I
own me!" They messed up by not applying it to all humans.

With my background, this revelation has a very specific implication. I wasn't being unloving or selfish or a tease when I withheld
my body from men. Men had no excuse for groping me or pressuring me. I wasn't a "bitch" for telling them to keep their hands
to themselves. Dressing sexy didn't excuse a man who is being
grabby; and flirting wasn't an excuse for rape. Just like leaving my
wallet on a table or painting my car red isn't an excuse for stealing
it. Theft is theft. My body is mine fully and I have no obligation to
make it available to anyone if I don't freely choose to, without people pressuring me through guilt or God. Full stop.

In the Family, I was told, "You don't own yourself. You belong to
God" (1 Corinthians 6:20). But what the leaders meant was, "Your
body is our property, and you need to do with it whatever we tell
you." This lie is harder to detect because it sounds so noble when
shrouded in scripture.

This illuminates for me the big mistake of many Family members and people who follow charismatic leaders. People who buy
into the lie that they do not own themselves, can justify, or at least
excuse themselves for, committing all kinds of violations against
humanity, including child abuse, religious wars, or the millions
slaughtered under communist regimes. Because when a person
turns over ownership and control, they also turn over their sense of
moral responsibility to the leader. After all, "If I'm following God's

will (or the government's), then any pain caused is God's (or the government's) fault, not mine. I'm just doing what I'm told." But just as we cannot give up our property right in our own body, neither can we abdicate moral responsibility for our actions. People shy away from this principle because accountability is scary.

Our susceptibility to cults comes from our desire to have a source, an authority, to tell us what to do and what is true. This is how we are trained by the school system that specializes in telling us the "right answers" and giving us an A for regurgitating them, instead of teaching us to use a logical process to figure out what must be true for ourselves.

But, as I discovered, accepting absolute responsibility is power. Only I have the ability to make my decisions, control my thoughts, dictate my emotions, and succeed or fail. It's too easy to slide into the quicksand of blame. How many times have I seen friends and family say, "I can't get better until you do X," or "I can't move on until you say Y"? How many have let this hold them back from healing and happiness? Never again will I wait for someone else to hand me my power. I'm able to move forward only when I acknowledge that what I do is up to me.

I draw a third circle around the smaller two, labeling it "Creations."

If I own my body, I also own everything my body and mind creates: my services, inventions, art, products, and even my reputation.

One of the cornerstone beliefs of the Family was that everything belonged to the group, communist style—our money, possessions, art and songs, hard work and service. Not only were we supposed to do everything for free, we didn't own our work in the first place because we didn't own our bodies.

As I draw a fourth circle, I think, *What comes next?* After I create something, I have the right to exchange it for something else I want. I label it "The Deal."

I think back to my contracts law class, remembering the five governing principles of a valid agreement. I realize that just as "undue pressure" in the creation of a contract makes the contract unenforceable because the other party did not *willingly* accept the terms of the deal, when we use manipulation like guilt, lies, and fear of punishment to pressure someone to do what we want, that amounts to theft, or worse.

The Family and other cults use a twisted interpretation of religious texts, lies, and psychological punishment to get us to do what they want. My grandfather, like many leaders, was not content with just sharing his message; he had to control how people lived it. This is the line where even a good philosophy can become a violation. Many of Grandpa's messages were taught, and still are taught, in society and churches. He made a lot of good points, which is how he got so many people to follow him. But he wanted to control every part of his followers' lives. How did a practice ostensibly conceived to lovingly and sacrificially care for the needs of others, sharing, become rape? It all came from the same model of power: coercion for control. He proclaimed freedom from the law but was steeped in a patriarchal model of top-down control that demanded obedience.

I also realize that power is the key to sexual abuse. Anytime there is sexual trauma and abuse, there is a power disparity—either real or perceived. Where one party in the interaction is in a position of power, whether physically stronger or higher in a hierarchy or even a social position or age, there is a possibility, not a certainty, of abuse, and the situation must be handled with extra care. This was why I didn't have any trauma associated with sex play with my childhood peers.

But in any kind of sexual relations between adults and children, the power disparity is inescapable. A child is biologically programmed at an unconscious level to please adults who represent power and survival. This means children cannot give meaningful consent, and any "consent" involves undue pressure. They also don't have the emotional maturity to understand the nature of the act—which violates the fourth principle of mental ability. Which is why even if they engage "willingly" at the time, they experience emotional trauma, sometimes delayed, when they realize what was done to them, what was taken from them.

But it doesn't have to be something as serious as sexual abuse. *How often is my daily life overrun with things other people guilt me into doing?*

I realize if I fully own something, I don't owe it to anyone else unless I make a free agreement to provide it in exchange for something else I value—not manipulated through guilt, fear, or lies. What freedom! I begin to pay attention to any feelings of pressure or obligation as a red flag, and I ask myself, *Why am I doing this? What would I choose without any guilt?*

I flip the paper over, and on the back side I draw the same set of circles for the law.

Violations of the body: Slavery, murder, rape, and assault.

Violations of our creations: theft, slander (violating reputation), copyright or patent infringement (stealing ideas).

Violations of the deal: blackmail, fraud, and breach of contract.

I realize I need to add one additional circle: "Impact or Effect."

Violations of Effect explains how much responsibility you bear for things that you contribute to but are not fully within your control; for instance, a mob boss telling his henchman to assassinate someone, even though he didn't pull the trigger himself; or my grandfather telling his followers to molest children even though he didn't physically touch each child himself.

I'm blown away to discover that everything that we consider the moral law fits into one of these circles. These principles are not the law. They came before the law, and the law was written to codify them. Unfortunately, the judges, lawyers, and legislators often lose sight of the fundamentals and modify the law to please the people in power. How often are these core principles obscured by people who use our confusion about these rights for their own benefit?

I stare at what I've drawn, and I realize I've crystalized our fundamental moral philosophy, the DNA of our legal system, morality, and human rights into a single simple diagram that I can teach to a curious eight-year-old.

As cool as that is, the real power is what happens in my own life.

It is like turning on the light in a dark room. I can clearly see all the obstacles I'd been bruising my shins and bloodying my toes on. Now, I can chart a clear path to my goal: personal freedom without violating others.

With a secure foundation to stand on, I can begin to let go of the false walls of invulnerability. I know I can choose what I allow in my space. It's not all-or-nothing. I can slowly experience healthy boundaries. Letting go of the fear still takes work, but now I know where I'm going—I have a map. And the more I dig into these seemingly simple principles, the more gems of insight I discover.

I realize that one of the reasons my grandfather was able to get so off track in some areas was that he had no ethical benchmark, no yardstick to measure his "revelations from God" against. No immutable standard that he could not twist through scriptural interpretation.

When good and bad, freedom and control, abuse and love are all mixed together without an objective standard, it can be incredibly hard to separate the lies from the truth. Even ideas that are beautiful, like "Love God and love your neighbor as you love yourself," become abusive when twisted through misinterpretation to benefit oneself and are imposed through manipulation and force. This is why we must actively check our most cherished beliefs against logic, against an accurate standard. Violations of the three primary property rights cause harm.

As I research the statistics of abuse against children and women, both sexual and physical, I realize it's not just cults—it's a world culture—one that will not end until we are each absolutely clear on accurate boundaries, the code of conduct to make sure your "freedoms" don't violate others.

These three rights are a lens to clarify every decision. Am I applying coercion or pressure in order to get someone to do what I want? Am I violating their right to make a free decision over what they do with their own time, money, and body?

These are the distinctions we must clarify to ensure that in our desire to build a better world, we do not create greater harm. The way to live free and harm none.

This is why I'm willing to share my most painful and shameful experiences onstage. So that others can find freedom through claiming their own right to their body. So that people can have a clear standard with which to measure themselves and their leaders by asking, *Does this teaching, or the implementation of it, violate the principles of self-ownership?* I know everything I've been through will be worth it if I can embed in the minds of my listeners this understanding of property rights in one's own self, body, creations, and deals.

I may be second-guessing my outfit of cherry-colored jumpsuit and white cape jacket, but not my decision to tell my truth. I momentarily squint at the bright stage lights as I walk to the large red circle on the stage floor, feeling the weight of the audience's stares.

For this I'm willing to risk it all: My professional reputation—*What will my clients or potential employers think?* My social media anonymity—*Isn't going public making myself a target for attack?* My dating persona of a nice, successful, relatively normal young woman—*How will I date? Won't this freak guys out?* My carefully constructed outer shell was about to be shattered by the wrecking ball of truth—*Who will be left standing?*

It doesn't matter. I'm doing this for those who have been op-
pressed, manipulated, and abused and need the words to stand up
for themselves. For the vision of a violation-free world for our children, where we each claim our rights and rise free together.

I'm ready.

I hear my voice ring out across the room, *"I own me!"*

GLOSSARY

BREAKING—If a person persisted in disobedience to the Family rules or leaders or had a bad attitude—proud, independent, vain, selfish, unhappy—or other character flaws (all called NWOs, meaning Needs Work On), they underwent a public announcement of their sins, often at Devotions, then complied with a punishment, written confession, and prayer designed to humiliate them and make them desperate to change.

BURN AFTER READING—Internal publications by the Family that were required, under threat of excommunication, to be destroyed after reading them. Often, these publications were advisories containing policy changes or notifications of things that might cause issues with law enforcement. A typical publication was a page or two long, though some were as long as thirty pages.

DEVOTIONS—Every day, for two hours after breakfast, everyone gathered to sing inspirational songs, pray, and read the latest Mo Letters.

DISCIPLES—Members of the Family.

DROP OUT—"Dropping out" and "forsaking all" meant giving all personal possessions and wealth to the Family and leaving the world behind to join the Family as a full-time disciple, devoting one's life to being an unpaid missionary.

END TIME—The time in which we were living, just before the Rapture or the Second Coming of Jesus, in which the Antichrist will arise and persecute all who do not worship him.

END-TIME ARMY—Family members were God's elite, disciplined army. Our mission was to save as many souls as possible before the Rapture.

EXCOMMUNICATION—Being kicked out of a Family commune and cut off, unable to see or talk to any Family members (even your own children), for committing an excommunicable offense.

FISH—A Systemite man (very occasionally a woman) being Flirty Fished.

FLIRTY FISHING (FFING)—Family women flirted and had sex with System men to show them God's love, acting as "bait" to entice men to come to Jesus, give donations to the Family Homes, and occasionally join. FFing ended abruptly in the mid-1980s with the prevalence of AIDS, but the principle remained: using sexy and flirtatious women to attract recruits.

GET OUT—The mandated daily hour of outdoor exercise.

GOATS—People in the System who were not receptive to the Family or questioned too much.

HOME—Full-time Family members must live communally in Homes and obey the Home Rules laid out in publications. A Home could have been as small as ten people (e.g., a large family and a few unrelated adults or teens), or as large as two hundred people living on a large property with multiple buildings. Homes with over fifty people were called Combos and were relatively rare.

JESUS BABY—A baby born to a woman as the result of FFing, considered God's blessing.

KIDZ TRUE KOMICS—Comic books for kids that retold the Mo Letters in a cartoon format, designed to teach everything from washing hands before a meal, to sex and Flirty Fishing, to how to pray.

MO LETTERS—Grandpa's writings, many of which came in the form of newsletters and were sent to Family members around the globe, provided direction and instruction. These letters were believed to be the inspired Word of God, and members were conditioned to never doubt anything Grandpa wrote.

PROBATION—Severe punishment that usually lasted three to six months. Family members on probation could not engage in sex or in the few privileges (e.g., watching a weekly movie) allowed to a disciple. They also had to reread the Basic Training Letters, the one hundred letters a recruit must read.

PROVISIONING—Asking businesses to contribute food and goods to support the volunteer work that Family Homes were doing. All Homes lived off provisioned food and goods.

SHARING—"Sharing God's love" through sex with a Family member who was not your spouse.

SELAH—A high-security secret. The term was based on a biblical term, which means "to think or ponder on."

SHEEP—People in the System who were receptive to the Family's religious message.

SHEPHERDS—A term for Family leadership. While the adults in a Home could vote on minor decisions as a Home Council, Home Shepherds, often a married couple, could overrule it. They were responsible for guiding and disciplining the members and reporting to the upper-level leadership. There were also Area, Country, and Regional Shepherds, who monitored Homes on a larger scale.

(THE) SYSTEM—The world and society outside the Family.

SYSTEMITES—Anyone who was part of the outside society, the System, rather than in the Family.

TITHING—Ten percent of all the money Family Homes made or any money received by a disciple (e.g., monetary gifts, inheritances) had to be sent to World Services as a tithe to support Grandpa's Home, the higher-level leadership, and the publications.

TRF SUPPORTERS—A later designation of Family members who tithed and still wanted to receive Mo Letters but didn't follow every revelation and requirement for full discipleship. They were considered a lower level of Family member, but in reality, they were ostracized from fellowshipping with Family Homes. When someone was TRF'd, no Home would associate with them for fear their lack of dedication would contaminate the body of Christ.

WITNESSING—Proselytizing. Being a witness for Christ meant communicating to people about Jesus. It took many forms, including talking one on one, singing songs about Jesus, passing out religious pamphlets, Bible Studies, and skits. **LITNESSING** was a form of witnessing, in which a disciple passed out Lit (religious literature) and typically asked for donations.

WS (WORLD SERVICES)—The administrative centers of the Family. The people in WS edited, compiled, and printed the Mo Letters, collected tithes, and monitored worldwide activity. They lived in secret Homes, or *Selah Homes*, to avoid the authorities.

ACKNOWLEDGMENTS

I want to express my gratitude to my brilliant agent, Becky Sweren, who went above and beyond to get this book to publication; to Liz Stein, my HarperCollins editor, for believing in and supporting me and doing the hard cuts; and Lisa Pulitzer, for her efforts researching, fact checking, and editing. And to my readers, you make all this worthwhile.